MW00328886

POLITICAL CORRUPTION

The Underside
of Civic Morality

Robert Alan Sparling

PENN

UNIVERSITY OF PENNSYLVANIA PRESS

PHILADELPHIA

Haney Foundation Series

A volume in the Haney Foundation Series,
established in 1961 with the generous support of Dr. John Louis Haney

Published by
University of Pennsylvania Press
Philadelphia, Pennsylvania 19104-4112
www.upenn.edu/pennpress

Printed in the United States of America
on acid-free paper
1 3 5 7 9 10 8 6 4 2

Library of Congress Cataloging-in-Publication Data
ISBN 978-0-8122-5087-9

CONTENTS

Contents

What Is Political Corruption?

The study of political corruption has been beset with definitional disputes for some time now. While people periodically speak of corruption as if it had a fixed, unchanging meaning, scholars attempting to define the term with precision repeatedly stumble on the variety of significations it can have. The exact behaviors that are considered corrupt vary depending on historical, geographic, or cultural contexts. The purchase of offices was a regular practice in the ancien régime; today it is frowned upon (or at the very least rebranded as a "public-private partnership"). Paying for a public service such as the service of a judge was once considered perfectly acceptable, but today we would balk at such user fees. Purchasing votes used to be widespread practice; now it can only be done through tax breaks and "pork" projects. Clashes between competing conceptions of corruption are not hard to find; they are particularly striking if one juxtaposes the mores of gift and market societies. And it is not merely between societies that such differences manifest themselves—the dimensions of corruption are contested within societies themselves, with people exhibiting radically opposed views of what behaviors or attitudes constitute a breach of civic integrity.[1] Nor is it an uncontested matter whether the term "corruption" refers to behavior, character, mores, beliefs; or whether the thing corrupted refers to a "system" (as in "systemic corruption") or to the behavior or character of an individual or a group.

There are, to be sure, important commonalities that one can discern across history and geography. In many states where the conspicuous prevalence of bribery, nepotism, and clientelism might lead one to suspect that different attitudes toward these behaviors obtained, one finds that the populations nonetheless widely term these behaviors corrupt and express views quite consistent with those in countries where people rarely encounter bribery;[2] in many different historical periods with strikingly different conceptions of political office, we encounter lamentations about corruption that appear perfectly intelligible to our late modern understanding. But though such commonalities should warn us against cultural or historical relativism, we must nonetheless remain attuned to the great difficulty of establishing a fixed, universal definition of corruption. Is it bribery of officials, nepotism, partisanship? Is it the decline in civic virtue or the loss of social rootedness? Is it the decline in piety? Is it the attendance to private interests over the public good (however defined)? Is it "duplicitous exclusion," as Mark Warren would define the democratic conception of corruption? Is it the opposite of "impartiality," as Oskar Kurer, Bo Rothstein, and Jan Teorell have proposed? Does corruption merely speak to breaches of existing laws or norms, or can there be entirely legal behaviors and relationships that are nonetheless corrupt? And how are such matters to be determined?[3]

There is currently a small but growing literature of a philosophical nature on the subject of corruption's precise definition. Warren's work has attempted to define corruption in terms of the norms of democratic theory; Seumas Miller has sought a wide definition of "institutional corruption" capturing the great variety of abuses that come under that name. Others such as Lawrence Lessig and Zephyr Teachout have sought a definition anchored in the republican tradition of the American founding. Others yet have attempted to define the concept as a breach of impartiality, drawing on liberal political theorists such as Brian Barry. Without entering into a detailed examination of these important contributions here (we will visit some of them in the course of our study), let us merely note that in spite of these laudable efforts, the philosophical study of corruption's meaning remains relatively marginal in both the field of corruption studies and in political theory. In a recent survey of this debate, Mark Philp and Elizabeth Dávid-Barrett lament that "the absence of significant reflection in political theory on the nature, forms, and sources of corruption is a serious failing of the subdiscipline."[4]

While there are some notable exceptions,[5] Philp and Dávid-Barrett's lamentation is correct: discussion of corruption within political theory has tended to be sporadic. The relative absence of sustained reflection on the concept should be somewhat surprising, for not only is corruption a prevalent worry in our public culture today (for reasons I need not elaborate), but, if J. G. A. Pocock is to be believed, it was "from 1688 to 1776 (and after), the central question in Anglophone political theory."[6] If this is the case (and, while we will have cause to revise many of Pocock's arguments, we may agree with his general claim about the centrality of corruption discourse in the "Atlantic" tradition), then the absence of corruption as a central matter of concern for political theorists today should give us pause. How could a concept so central to both contemporary public discourse and to our political-philosophical tradition have such little space in political theory today?

If political theorists have in the main not been focused upon the question, the more practically minded students of corruption have tended to downplay the philosophical problems entailed by the term. A great deal of literature begins by recognizing definitional difficulties, but attempts to settle these questions quickly in order to fix on a definition that can serve as a tool for social-scientific advancement and legislative action. Arvind Jain, for instance, writes, "Although it is difficult to agree on a precise definition, there is consensus that corruption refers to acts in which the power of public office is used for personal gain in a manner that contravenes the rules of the game."[7] There is much to be said for this formulation, but I fear that there is no such consensus about it. An active community is studying "institutional corruption," which addresses precisely those types of corruption that do not contravene the "rules of the game" but rather are a product of poor rules.[8] The root of Jain's definition is the phrase used most often by international organizations such as the World Bank: "Corruption is the abuse of public office for private gain."[9] This definition has the virtue of being expansive. Of course, the definition is somewhat limited in focusing solely on governmental office (Transparency International prefers the more neutral "entrusted power"), in focusing only on behavior, and in tending toward thinking in terms of individual breaches of norms rather than structural pathologies. More important, the definition raises more questions than it answers, for how are we to understand all of these terms? The difficulty is not that "abuse," "public office," and "private gain" cannot be defined; the difficulty is that such definitions are replete with presuppositions that can become straitjackets. The way in which such terms are defined is always overladen with political and normative assumptions. Susan Rose-Ackerman, one of the most prominent economists to study corruption, begins a handbook on the subject by noting (with some regret) that there is a tendency in her field to eschew moral reflection: "Writing on corruption often stakes out a moral high ground, but economists are reluctant to sermonize on right or wrong."[10] No doubt some discussion of corruption slips into sermonizing—that is a danger in all moral discourse—but there is, in the social-scientific wariness of moral categories, a greater danger of slipping into moral inarticulacy. From the perspective of economics, there is doubtless much to be gained by eschewing moral discussion in favor of measuring things like illicit transfers of wealth. But whatever progress this bracketing of moral matters permits the economists to make (and it is not negligible), it can be harmful if it is allowed to substitute for the task of ethical and political philosophy, for it closes off avenues of discussion and, indeed, eliminates from consideration entire traditions of thought (among which are traditions in which the very normative assumptions of modern economics would themselves be considered corrupting). The discourse of political corruption bears a heavy normative load, notwithstanding the persistence of scientific attempts to keep "values" from contaminating facts.

I wish neither to condemn the social scientists' desire to delimit their realm of inquiry nor to castigate practically minded reformers seeking a toolkit suitable to their task, but rather to indicate that political theory must proceed in a different manner. And the concept of corruption in particular merits sustained normative reflection, for it is of much greater significance than is often recognized. The concept of political corruption is fundamentally an expression of political morality; to denounce corruption is to affirm some vision of integrity, wholeness, or political health. In an important 1997 article, Mark Philp made the straightforward observation that "one line definitions of political corruption are inherently misleading because they obscure the extent to which the concept is rooted in ways of thinking about politics—that is, of there being some 'naturally sound condition' (variously described) from which corrupt acts deviate."[11] While there is a small but important body of work dedicated to the question,[12] a great deal of inquiry on the subject has tended to neglect Philp's basic insight and to proceed by attempting to settle definitional questions at the outset.[13] Such a procedure is fully sensible if one has a practical penchant: if, say, one wants to pursue cross-national comparisons of corruption levels, or one wishes to evaluate the effectiveness of different policies, one cannot be satisfied with shifting and contested definitions. The difficulty, of course, is that the definitions such scholars settle upon tend to assume and reinforce a given set of normative presuppositions. In spite of the empirical sophistication of the literature on the subject, there continues to be a degree of philosophical neglect pervading thought on corruption that would surprise us if the concept in question were liberty, representation, justice, rights, power, autonomy, or any of the myriad terms that are the heart and soul of political discourse.[14]

Perhaps this derives from the fact that serious inquiry on the meaning of corruption opens up a vast field of contested political questions. For corruption is a negative concept, one structured by its opposite, the positive conception of healthy political relationships. To inquire into the term is to question our own politico-moral ideals. Corruption discourse often has the effect (and possibly even the purpose) of displacing politics because it attempts to police relations between citizens and their institutions while taking as given the very contours of a healthy polity. To explore the nature of corruption is to open up to questioning those very contours.

This book explores how a political metaphor of sickness, dissolution, and dirtiness orders the political imaginary. Judith Shklar once observed that philosophers have tended to focus much more on virtue than vice;[15] similarly, corruption has tended to be overshadowed by its opposite. But just as freedom must be understood in light of our understanding of servitude, just as the virtues cannot be conceived without their corresponding vices, so too must political integrity be understood by its opposite. The manner in which corruption is conceived structures political life, for the way in which we divide the corrupt from the pure defines our relationship to the public realm, to the law and to each other. The lack of focus on the study of corruption in political theory may be a further symptom of what Charles Taylor has called the "ethics of inarticulacy," the avoidance of substantive discussion about the basis for our moral claims. But if the concept has such importance, then we cannot begin with definitions, or even begin by delimiting the scope of the inquiry. The urge to stipulate an acceptable definition at the outset is sensible and practical, but it is anti-philosophical, foreclosing questions about the nature of the good regime and the good life. Equally important, the urge to stipulate a definition a priori is *antipolitical*, for it circumvents debate over substantive questions via definitional fiat. Consider the following concrete question: is a personal campaign donation of three thousand dollars to a candidate for public office an example of political corruption? Of course, there is a simple legal answer to this question—in jurisdiction X it is acceptable, in Y it is not. But behind the decision to set such limits—and behind the various challenges to such laws—are important underlying assumptions about the manner in which private interest relates to the public, the nature of political integrity and the acceptable methods of political participation, the manner in which individual interests are to be aggregated in a representative democracy, the type of dependence such a donation entails, the nature of influence and incentives, the place of gifts and reciprocity in the public realm . . . the list could go on at some length, but the point to emphasize is simply that to think about this question entails thinking about a set of anterior questions that are the heart of the tradition of political philosophy.

The subject of this study, then, is not the ins and outs of bribery, nepotism, conflict of interest, state capture, and so forth, material on which there is a growing and excellent empirical literature, but rather the *discourse* of political corruption. We will explore its contours in several important moments in modern political philosophy from the Renaissance to the early twentieth century. Corruption discourse, this work insists, is fundamentally political morality. What is more—and here I offer a more controversial claim—it is political teleology, for it hangs on the presupposition that there is a type of healthy regime and officeholder. Herein lies the paradox of the concept's use today: corruption discourse suggests a falling away from purity, health, or integrity, yet it flourishes today in a context that is inarticulate about its moral ideals and wary of teleological thought. This adoption of a morally laden vocabulary by those who have a professional aversion to political morality should give us pause. Corruption is the reverse of legitimacy and integrity; it is the dark shadow behind a conception of how societies ought to be ordered and what norms ought to govern public and private life. Shedding light on our assumptions about corruption is an important dimension of our search for self-understanding.

I have said that the discourse of political corruption is teleological. By this I do not mean that it entails a historical teleology (though it might), but rather that it entails something akin to the Aristotelian view that there is such a thing as a manner of living politically that is most conducive to human flourishing. There is much to be said about the degree of ethical monism the concept entails, but it is insignificant speech to make use of this concept in the absence of a thick conception of political wholeness. A metaphor referring to dissolution, disease, and dirt, "political corruption" opposes conceptions of wholeness, health, and cleanliness. The paradox of corruption discourse today is that it thrives in an age that conceives of itself as thoroughly cured from that strange mental aberration of final causes and thick descriptions of the good. I wish to suggest that when the language of corruption is employed by avowedly anti-teleological writers, they are engaged in a terminological contradiction and are unwittingly involved in the propagation of an image of the natural or healthy society. Indeed, such writers are fully as hubristic as any propagators of classical accounts of the good, for they seek to propagate their imaginary universally, but their aims are hidden (willfully or not) under such deceptively nonpolitical sounding banners as "reform," "good governance," "quality of government," and "transparency."

My purpose in this book is to examine the manner in which the concept has been deployed by some of occidental modernity's more thoughtful philosophical expositors. I indicate a variety of ways in which the language of political corruption has been invoked in modernity and suggest that all of these different ways of understanding political pathology live on in contemporary discourse, rubbing up against one another uncomfortably. The book proposes neither a complete history of the concept (which would be unwieldy),[16] nor an exhaustive survey of modern political theorists' views on the subject, but rather an exploration of seven important and distinct modes in which the concept has been deployed since the Renaissance: leadership ethics, republicanism, the politics of transparency, nostalgic denigrations of the bureaucratic state, liberal moderation, revolutionary purism, and the ethics of bureaucratic office. The presentation, while chronological, is purposely not a linear history of how the concept has developed from one form to another in a straightforward evolution toward a univocal "modern" definition. Each mode of understanding corruption has its distinctive contours and suggests distinctive types of cure. The modes overlap in important ways, but more often than not they clash. And the contest between them is both philosophical—in that they presume underlying normative principles and conceptions of human flourishing—and political—in that they entail different modes of ordering the public thing.

This work examines continuities and discontinuities of the language of corruption in political thought from the Renaissance to the twentieth century. It both situates arguments in their historical contexts and argues for their continuing relevance in contemporary political thought. In so doing, it will equally offend the universalist and the strict historicist. The study is premised on the observations that the concept of corruption has had numerous meanings historically but that important family resemblances exist between deployments of the term, and the discourse of political corruption has a structure and function that is stable and enduring. The visions of corruption that I shall examine are not mere historical artifacts.

We ought, in general, to be wary of both the universalism that runs rough-shod over historical particularity and the historicism that treats political ideas as historical fatalities. To engage with the textual tradition is to inhabit the intermediary space between history and eternity. The visions of corruption and its cure on offer here all conform to certain moral intuitions we encounter in contemporary thought, just as they all inspire important ambivalences. I wish to bring to light these ambivalences and to render clearer the moral and political presuppositions of these different manners of conceiving of corruption.

Through a series of chronologically ordered philosophical snapshots, then, we will explore the concept's use in seven historical moments in which anxieties about corruption were running high. The discussion within these pages has a certain relation to J. G. A. Pocock's *The Machiavellian Moment*, which did so much to uncover the centrality of corruption in republican discourse, particularly in the sixteenth and eighteenth centuries. But this book takes distance from Pocock's account, disaggregating some of the uses of corruption that Pocock takes to be part of a continuous republican political language. There are different forms of republican corruption talk, and there are some protagonists in the Pocockean story that I argue should not be placed in the republican tradition at all.[17] On a methodological level, there is something in the grandeur of the historical narrative Pocock pursued that I have not attempted. This book is historical in the sense of attending to the contexts in which the authors expressed themselves, but—in distinction to Pocock's avowed philosophical abstemiousness—it is philosophical in its normative aim. My primary goal is not to offer a grand narrative of a political language's development and adaptations as it moves through different historical contexts. This work canvasses, rather, a number of important modes in which the term has been—and continues to be—deployed in occidental modernity. It does not provide an account of the concept's *evolution*. The reader should not infer that the final position we examine—corruption as the sullying of pure Weberian bureaucracy—is a culminating point of a continuous story of the concept's growth and transformation. Like the other conceptions of corruption canvassed here, Weber's vision of corruption has a distinct history in the development of the modern administrative state, but my purpose is not primarily to narrate that history; it is rather to delineate the contours of this mode of thinking of corruption, and place it in conversation with other competing conceptions that are derived from our intellectual tradition and that continue to live on today.

If there may appear to be a slightly uneven weighting of the historical periods selected for examination, with the sixteenth and eighteenth centuries bearing the brunt of the weight and the early twentieth century bringing up the rear, I wish to insist that this is not a judgment on the relative historical importance of these periods; it is rather based on the paradigmatic nature of the instantiations of corruption discourse that I wish to examine. Had the work's intention been to provide a thoroughgoing history of corruption and reform, it would have delved into a number of different modern periods. In the Anglosphere alone, one would need to give much greater attention to the seventeenth century (a period in which the mores of a patronage economy ran up against widespread worries about bribery and a debasement of mores).[18] The great civil service reforms in nineteenth- and early twentieth-century Britain and America would have equally been essential movements to examine; and historians of corruption would naturally also want to study of the twists and turns of corruption and reform through the twentieth century.[19]

The texts examined in this work represent enduring and philosophically compelling manners of thinking about corruption and its cures. In each case, we will be engaged in a transhistorical conversation linking these authors both with present concerns and with classical political philosophy that spoke of corruption and integrity in terms of wider ethical and political ends. The word "corruption" is powerful; like a curse, it leaps readily from the mouths of the aggrieved. But being precise about the term is less easy to do for it demands a fuller account of political health and integrity than is generally on offer. Modern political thought is haunted by the ghost of classical regime analysis, a form of inquiry that refused to consider city and soul in distinction from each other and refused to see civic integrity in terms divorced from an account of the good. An overarching argument of this book is that modern thought on corruption would do well to embrace the ambitious goals that classical political philosophy set for itself.

CHAPTER 1

Corruption Discourse
and the Ubiquity of Distinctions

Let us begin with some doggerel from the eighteenth century:

Through all the Employments of Life
Each Neighbour abuses his Brother;
Whore and Rogue they call Husband and Wife:
All Professions be-rogue one another:
The Priest calls the Lawyer a Cheat,
The Lawyer be-knaves the Divine:
And the Statesman, because he's so great,
Thinks his Trade as honest as mine.[1]

So sings Peachum, the embodiment of corruption in John Gay's *Beggar's Opera* (1728). Both thief catcher and fencer of stolen goods, Peachum casts doubt on the very distinction between just and unjust. In *The Origins of Totalitarianism*, Hannah Arendt reflects on the reception of Bertolt Brecht's *Threepenny Opera* (1928), a work that brought Peachum's argument to a generation already prone to seeing things his way. Arendt suggests that the play's declaration that morality is but a thin veneer under which lies the reality of dogs eating dogs was widely applauded by audiences who thought the message of "erst kommt das Fressen, dann kommt die Moral" (first comes eating,[2] then comes morality) had pierced through a prevalent hypocrisy: "the irony was somewhat lost when respectable businessmen in the audience considered this a deep insight into the ways of the world and when the mob welcomed it as an artistic sanction of gangsterism."[3] The

Threepenny Opera, like Gay's *Beggar's Opera*, is an unrelenting denunciation of a corruption that has permeated society. But the effect of this thoroughgoing attack on pretentions is to leave the audience in a universe where all is permitted. Gay's play remained a satire of Hogarthian dimensions—and satire, like corruption discourse, depends upon moral boundaries. Brecht's version seems beyond satire and is thus profoundly destabilizing: it appears to undermine the very moral categories that make moral denunciation possible. Brechtian stagecraft—producing a sense of alienation in the audience—reinforces this. Indeed, it can have the effect not of inspiring the sociopolitical reflection that he sought but rather of awakening a sense of the absurd, a vertiginous nausea born of the erasure of moral distinctions that had previously structured one's worldview. As Arendt suggests, some gangsters might well have left the theater with a self-satisfied air, confirmed in the moral rectitude of gangsterism; an alternate effect of the play—at least on those on whom the irony has not been entirely lost—is to cast the viewer into a sense of helplessness, where the laughter derives not from a simple superiority that one has seen through bourgeois pretense but from a kind of despair at not knowing which way is up.

If corruption is as generalized as portrayed in these plays, it seems difficult to see what political project might possibly be capable of facing it. Might the term "corruption" itself not be mere obfuscation? Brecht's humor is so bleak, one despairs for a political remedy, and his subsequent communism seems more like a *salto mortale* than a solution.[4] In the *Threepenny Opera*, fundamental distinctions disappear; the police and the crooks are two sides of the same coin, and the possibility of nonpredation seems remote. The audience emerges from the theater wondering if, in the famous exchange between Alexander the Great and the pirate (in which the pirate claims that the difference between them is merely one of scale),[5] the pirate was not expressing something true of all rule. Without Brecht's overt call for socialism, his drama can feel like an ode to Callicles. The very term "corruption" and the entire moral vocabulary surrounding it come across as ideological mystification, and we sing along with the chorus, "verfolgt das Unrecht nicht zu sehr" (do not persecute injustice too much).

There are good reasons for taking a Brechtian attitude toward corruption discourse itself. For corruption discourse (as we shall see in Chapter 2) often sounds a note of individual moralism in instances of systemic oppression. As such, it can serve as a mask, a pretense that the most egregious examples of abuse are mere individual moral failings. Such moralizing discourse can serve to reinforce domination. In numerous authoritarian societies accusations of corruption are useful means for inter-elite competition; red hot fury at the convicted deflects from the more systemic nature of exploitation. Moralizing tones can also take on global dimensions, as accusations of systemic corruption are employed to discipline countries caught in global power structures that are already exploitative. There is something highly suspect, after all, in the accusation that the relative poverty of Greece, Portugal, Spain, or Italy in the European Union is due primarily to "corruption." Students of post-Soviet transition can equally appreciate the skeptical attitude toward corruption discourse.[6] The same can be said of postcolonial societies. It does seem dodgy that local elites who extract massive riches in poorer societies are termed corrupt, while in the wealthy world elites who extract massive resources from the poor world are considered job creators. (Transparency International's "corruption perceptions index," while an interesting tool in many respects, can have the unintended effect of reinforcing neocolonial stereotypes: the color-coded map emerges every year with a bright yellow West and blood red in the global South.) Suspicions are further nourished by the fact that the very rise of anticorruption efforts in the period following the Cold War is replete with ideological overtones (liberalism's mopping-up effort, as it were). The war against corruption can appear galling in an age in which we witness state and regulatory capture to such an extent that wealthy countries' governments create vast structures (national and international tax havens, regulatory loopholes, structures of economic dependence) permitting behavior that is perfectly legal, but of dubious legitimacy given that its very purpose is to subvert democratic will and legal protections.

But an attitude of suspicion toward the discourse of corruption can never be the end of the story, for the term is often wielded by those below, who are much less subject to false consciousness than would-be vanguards assume. The discourse of corruption remains a live, emancipatory language capable of attacking the illegitimate exercise of power even when such power is cloaked in legality. Corruption discourse can serve to mask exploitation or to condemn it. It can buttress systems of domination or undermine them. It may be employed by Socratic figures denouncing feverish cities; it may be employed to feed hemlock to those very figures. But whether it be turned to radical critique or complacent defense of the reigning order, the discourse of corruption is an inescapable element of life wherever there is the regular exercise of entrusted power. And corruption discourse is always about policing lines—first and foremost between kings and pirates.

We must, then, begin our study of this discourse by insisting upon two related distinctions. The first is the fundamental moral distinction between legitimate rule and predation. This distinction, for all its apparent common sense, must be defended against those who would see it as moralizing at best and ideological obfuscation at worst. The second is the separations between realms of activity, and between, loosely speaking, that which is "public" and that which is not. I say "loosely speaking," for the distinction between public and private as we widely conceive of it is not at all universal, and the manner of dividing these things is, indeed, a central question of political philosophy itself.[7] In Sparta and Rome no less than in ancien régime France the personal was political. The feudal king's "state" was his condition, his legal standing. But this does not mean that distinctions between public and private have no place in those regimes.

There is a universal tendency to think about institutions, people, and practices that serve the good of the group as being special, bound by norms regarding the group's good and capable of being perverted. Marcel Mauss speaks of a Haida chief who failed to give a lavish potlatch as having a "rotten face."[8] Nothing in classical Haida culture approaches the public-private distinction of late modernity, but there is a clear communal disapprobation of a breach of norms pertaining to this important community role—ought we to be surprised to learn that the Haida deployed a metaphor indicating decay? Bo Rothstein, exasperated by cultural relativists, has put his finger on the universal core of corruption discourse: "My argument departs from the idea that it is difficult to envision a society without some public goods. The point is that when these public goods are handled or converted into private goods this is generally understood as corruption independently of the culture."[9] As evident as this might appear, it is an important point. Rothstein correctly notes that something we might term "public goods" can be located in every collectivity, and the core of corruption is injustice. Unfortunately, he subsequently overreaches by making the unconvincing suggestion that the distinction between public and private and the conception of corruption as the opposite of impartiality are more or less universal. "Public" functions do entail a special relationship between rulers and the ruled: but how these lines are drawn and what the relationship is between the mores of the public and nonpublic worlds are essential elements of how the term "corruption" declines in a given political language. The way in which corruption is conceived in a feudal monarchy will differ from the manner in which it is understood in capitalist modernity, and it will differ from the manner it is conceived in a republic like Sparta, where the basic acts of eating, mating, and exercising are civic duties that are matters of public concern every bit as much as the activities of a judge. Norms, too, will shift. Rothstein cites social-scientific evidence that throughout the world people seek *impartiality* from public officeholders. This might be a widespread desideratum, but if it is, it merely indicates the cultural success of a certain imaginary favoring the types of separation characteristic of the modern "Weberian" state. To mention just one notable exception to this rule, consider the thought of Ibn Khaldun (1332–1406), the great admirer of social solidarity of Bedouin tribes. For Ibn Khaldun, corruption derived from the diminution of "group feeling" ('*asabiyyah*), a concept that looks very much like the antonym of impartiality. This group feeling is the most important source of strength and vitality of a community. While he thought impartiality was always good in some instances (in the office of a judge, for example), he did not celebrate it as the soul of integrity—on the contrary, impartiality becomes more important in large, corrupt urban settings which have less group feeling, and thus require centralized authority and strict law to replace lost mores.[10] Where and when partiality is a good are questions of a political and philosophical nature that have admitted of radically different answers throughout the history of political institutions and political philosophy.

Discovering what is steady and what is shifting in corruption discourse entails saying something about the ubiquity of the distinction between the legitimate and illegitimate behaviors and dispositions of those entrusted with authority. This, in turn, entails saying something about the split between what we commonly term "public" and "private." The definition of corruption that is dominant today (used by the World Bank, among others)—the abuse of public office for private gain—has been criticized for being excessively focused on individual behaviors and for being insufficiently attentive to classical republican concerns about a general depredation of mores or civic decline. Some have even wanted to insist upon a strict separation between these two sorts of discourses. But in fact they are difficult to disentangle, and the World Bank's definition can be made to fit almost any conception of corruption, so long as one interprets the terms properly. Aristotle's distinction between legitimate and deviant forms of government turns on the distinction between rule in the interests of the

ruled and in the interests of the ruler (*Politics* 1279a). There is clearly a
public good—the interests of the ruled—that can be undermined by the
holders of office abusing that office for private gain.[11] When, in classical
republican discourse, wealth and luxury are termed corrosive and corrupting, the reason is that they are thought to lead to an oligarchic disposition
in which the city is treated as a means for private domination: this is a
betrayal of the public good. Alien as this view is from the understanding of
the economists at the World Bank (who offer no moral disapprobation of
luxury and think, rather, in terms of individual officeholders breaching
rules for private gain), the two conceptions are visions of the public good
being undermined or usurped for nonpublic (or anti-public) ends.

Public, Private, and the "State": Continuities and Discontinuities

So far, I have suggested that there are family resemblances between varieties
of corruption discourse and that it is important to retain the moral core of
the concept entailing some conception of a public good subject to abuse.
But, of course, the devil is in the details, and we need to attend to how the
notion of public office and the mores required for its legitimate exercise are
constructed in any given context. In our zeal to avoid anachronism, however, we ought to make certain that we do not fall into reified historical
categories. Interpreters have tended to founder on the Scylla of false universalism or the Charybdis of historicism. In brief, I am suggesting that worries
about corruption are indeed perennial, though the manner in which the
concept is deployed varies radically. And this variety, I am arguing, is not
merely the stuff of historical contingency.

To see the commonalities among the varieties of corruption talk—to
understand why contrasting conceptions of political corruption belong to
the same family—one must take care not to overstate the strangeness of
ancient ideas or the radical novelty of modern ones. Much hangs on the
degree to which the distinction between public and private governing the
modern state is an unprecedented phenomenon. Quentin Skinner has given
an intricate story about the emergence of the "impersonal" state. It has
much to recommend it, but I wish to suggest a nuance. For while the word
"state," *status*, originally described a *condition*, rather than some independent, objective Weberian entity claiming a monopoly on legitimate use of

violence, the notion of a polity as an object of analysis independent from its ruler and its members (and, indeed, bearing proto-Weberian marks of exercising legitimate violence for the control of its territory) certainly existed in classical antiquity. That is, while the *politeia* was its citizens, it could also be thought about in an abstract manner, as a legal order or an institution.

According to Skinner, the key aspect of the modern state is that it is impersonal in the sense of being distinct from both rulers and the ruled. Now, I do not challenge the claim that modern states are novel in many ways, as is the *manner* in which we tend to divide public from private, and we will have cause to revisit the conception of "impersonality" that is at the heart of some late modern visions of integrity, but there is something misleading about Skinner's presentation that can have the unfortunate effect of blinding us to a universal dimension of corruption discourse. The notion that there exists some entity, institution, or moral person analytically separable from the actual flesh-and-blood rulers and ruled is quite prevalent throughout Western history, even in instances in which it appears to be absent. Consider one example that Skinner cites as a clear case of the absence of this distinction: "A writer like [Jacques-Bénigne] Bossuet, for example, deliberately sets out to obliterate the distinction between the office and the person of the king. . . . He insists that the figure of the ruler 'embodies in himself the whole of the state': *tout l'état est en lui.*"[12] But Bossuet did exactly the opposite. The complete phrase from his *Politics Drawn from the Very Words of the Holy Scripture* is the following: "The prince, insofar as he is a prince [*en tant que prince*], is not regarded as a particular man: he is a public person; all the state is in him [*c'est un personnage public; tout l'État est en lui*], the will of all the people is contained in his will."[13] Bossuet goes on to speak of the prince as one imitating the divine form of God. The qualification in the first sentence is the key to the doctrine: "en tant que prince." For the prince, *en tant qu'homme*, is clearly *not* the embodiment of the public will. This is the classic "two bodies" doctrine so famously explored by Ernst Kantorowicz: there is a quasi-divine, incorruptible element of majesty that is its public aspect, and there is the natural person of the king. The two are united, but this is what makes political morality so important, for it is the duty of the corruptible person to attempt to imitate the incorruptible God. "The prince dies," writes Bossuet, "but the authority is immortal and the state always subsists."[14] A writer like Bossuet deliberately *emphasizes* the distinction between the office and the person of the king. The whole point of this type of argument is to remind mortal, corruptible kings that their majesty is derived from its public character and requires of them an integrity fitting of a God: they are to model themselves on an incorruptible, eternal form because that is their vocation as kings. We will have cause to examine the virtues of monarchs in the next chapter, but let us merely note that the discourse of corruption in this setting relies upon the possibility of the public person being led away from eternal duty by a false conception of self-interest or by irrational passions. This is why law is so very important, for it rises above the corruptible world of becoming: "Interest and passion corrupt men. The law is without interests and without passions."[15] The private person of the prince must attempt to overcome all variability and to comport himself in the image of the unchanging and incorruptible being that his public person—his office—requires him to imitate.

Bossuet's argument is a modern, absolutist manifestation of a view that has deep roots in eras that predate the emergence of the modern state. The medieval king has both a public and a private aspect. Consider John of Salisbury (ca. 1115–1176), who claimed that the king "does not . . . truly own that which he possesses in the name of someone else, nor are the goods of the fisc, which are conceded to the public, his own private property. Nor is this a surprise, since he is not his own person but that of his subjects."[16] So in the era of the highly "personalized" polity, the notion of a distinction between public and nonpublic is fundamental.

What of the ancient *polis*? It is common—and correct, as far as it goes—to insist that unlike the modern state, which is an impersonal entity that stands above its citizens, the *polis* was its citizens, and hence that it is incorrect to employ the word "state" as a translation of this ancient term. But, as Mogens Herman Hansen points out, "It is true that the modern state is often seen as an abstract public power, but we must not forget that it is also often identified with the body politic. It is also true that the Greek *polis* is usually identified with its citizens, but we must not forget that it is also often seen as an impersonal abstract power above both rulers and ruled. When both modifications are added, the alleged contrast between polis and state in this particular respect becomes so attenuated that it virtually disappears."[17] I do not have space here to enter into Hansen's argument, nor do I want to make too great a revisionist splash by entirely overturning the position that the modern state (and its claim to sovereignty) is a historically novel phenomenon. I simply wish to insist that it is incorrect to assert that the notion of a public thing conceptually separable from the person of the ruler(s) and the person of the ruled is a phenomenon peculiar to the modern "state" form.[18]

I make this point—with admittedly scattershot examples—because there is an important—and importantly misleading—argument that one often encounters in connection with the distinction between modern and premodern notions of corruption. "The Greek term *diaphthora* and the Latin [*sic*] term *corruzione*, in spite of their usual translation as 'corruption,' refer to an understanding of corruption that is quite foreign to our modern one. Political corruption is an exclusively modern phenomenon made possible only after the rise of the public/private split and the concept of interests."[19] The author of this sentence, Peter Bratsis, has offered one of the more interesting recent treatments of the concept of corruption, and I will touch on it below, but I take issue with his argument for a number of reasons. Bratsis correctly wishes to overturn the ahistorical treatment of the concept that assumes late modern manners of dividing private and public are universally valid. But while it is certainly true that radical differences exist between deployments of the term "corruption"—this book highlights those differences—it also important not to treat the Greek, Latin, or Italian terms as *essentially* distinct from contemporary concerns.[20] So-called older conceptions of corruption live on: the fact that, say, the U.S. Supreme Court only recognizes corruption in the form of illicit quid pro quo exchanges does not alter the fact that plenty of American citizens see the concept in ways similar to the civic republican rhetoricians of their country's founding.[21] Part of my purpose in this book is to indicate that competing conceptions of corruption are constitutive elements of constitutional debate itself—whether we think about corruption in Machiavellian, Bolingbrokean, or Montesquieuan terms will have radical implications for our conception of the healthy regime.

This claim has historiographical as well as political significance—when readers inspired by the work of J. G. A. Pocock see the term "corruption" employed in the eighteenth century, they tend to leap to the conclusion that the term is indicative of a civic republican mind-set. But in the eighteenth century, as now, competing conceptions rubbed up against one another in public discourse.[22] The differences in conceptions of corruption are not historical fatalities but live political issues, even if some modes fit less comfortably with modern conditions. And apparently modern conceptions of corruption are rather old. The currently widespread view of corruption as individuals abusing entrusted office for private gain (a conception whose paradigmatic instance is the bribe) is to be found again and again in ancient, medieval, and early modern sources.[23] Even in historical instances in which the term "corruption" is deployed to mean a widespread decadence, a degradation of mores, and a loss of civic spirit, we find the concept also evokes straightforward images of official functions being abused for illegitimate private gain.

In examining examples of behavior considered corrupt in previous ages, we see mixtures of the familiar and the strange. Consider, for example, the paradigmatic case of corruption, the bribing of a judge. There is a conviction as ancient as the Old Testament that the public role of judging ought to be kept pure from pecuniary considerations: "And thou shalt take no gift: for the gift blindeth the wise, and perverteth the words of the righteous" (Exodus 23:8). Naturally it is not gift giving as such that is being denounced here; it is a particular practice, *shohadh* or *shachad* (the term is translated in more recent Bibles as "bribe"), that is being denounced.[24] This is the type of gift that undermines the very activity of a judge or a witness: truth perceiving and truth telling. In this, Rome is in concord with Jerusalem. Cicero derided the judge who sells his office or who employs it for the sake of friends at the expense of truth. (This, despite Cicero's own skill at bribery.)[25] The judge, after all, has two aspects, one that accords with his individual appetites and one that accords with his public role. To allow his appetites or the norms of reciprocity to enter into his judicial deliberations is to forfeit the character of a judge. The view that moneymaking ought not to conflict with the duties of office is behind the idea that Plato's *Kallipolis* should eliminate private wealth for guardians, thereby eliminating the duality of a person's mixed roles of moneymaker and officeholder. The Platonic doctrine of the well-ordered soul internalizes the separation of functions, placing the rational element in control of the spirited and the appetitive. The complexities of this teaching aside, there is a widespread and rather well founded opinion that if a judge sells her opinion to the highest bidder there isn't really much point in having a judge at all—moneymaking and judging are different activities. But though one can find near-universal approbation of this norm, it is nonetheless not universally true that gifts to judges are impermissible. Early modern judges accepted gifts regularly. Francis Bacon was famously convicted for corruption not because he had received gifts but because the gifts were deemed bribes, corrupting of his judgment.[26] In many U.S. jurisdictions today, campaign contributions to elected judges from potential litigants remain permissible. In ancient Israel judges who refused *shachad* did receive gifts. Indeed, to appear before a king or judge in ancient Israel without a present was to fail to honor his authority. In the same way, after all, God (in whose image judges are modeled) receives gifts (sacrifices), but his judgment is not thereby perverted.[27]

Animadversions against the receiving of inappropriate benefits are fully present in ages in which patronage economies are in place. Consider an example from the eighteenth century. Lord Chesterfield may have been accused by Samuel Johnson of having "morals of a whore and the manners of a dancing master," but he was rather stern in his advice to his son:

> If you should ever fill a great station at Court, take care above all things to keep your hands clean and pure from the infamous vice of corruption. . . . Accept no present whatever; let your character in that respect be transparent and without the least speck, for as avarice is the vilest and dirtiest vice in private, corruption is so in public life. I call corruption the taking of a sixpence more than the just and known salary of your employment. . . . Use what power and credit you may have at Court in the service of merit rather than of kindred, and not to get pensions and reversions for yourself or your family, for I call that also, what it really is, scandalous pollution, though of late it has been so frequent that it has almost lost its name.[28]

Apart from the moralistic attack on avarice (which late capitalist society no longer considers a vice), Chesterfield's definition of corruption would be perfectly understood by any administrator today. But Chesterfield likely did not experience cognitive dissonance in soliciting and obtaining a pension for his mistress and a place on the Board of the Admiralty for his brother,[29] not to speak of the fact that his illegitimate son to whom his famous letters were addressed had his diplomatic career entirely due to his father's influence. The point is not that Chesterfield was a hypocrite (which he doubtless was), but rather that he saw no clash between the patronage economy in which he participated and the high-minded deprecation of self-enrichment at public expense. I merely wish to indicate by this example, first, that the conception of corruption at work in Chesterfield's letters is extremely familiar in spite of his inhabiting an age in which patronage was not necessarily viewed as corrupt, and, second, that there is always something tricky about the relationship between self-interest and public duty.

The Policing of Lines and the Crafting of Character

There is, then, a degree of continuity between radically different eras on the abuse of public functions, but the manner in which this worry manifests itself can differ radically based on mores and constitutions. Human beings have lived in myriad political forms, and their modes of imagining collective health and sickness have varied radically, but there are certain continuities in the discourse of political corruption: it always entails a conception of a public good and of public office (be this treated in a narrow manner of government employees or a wide manner of citizen responsibilities toward the public thing), and it always entails some illegitimate disposition that is anti-publicly oriented. Political corruption is an abuse of the public thing, but the key is how abuse and the public thing are understood.

Thus it is imprecise to insist that the distinction between public and private is not universal. What one ought to say is that the way in which public roles are conceived and the extent of the "public" are not universally agreed-upon matters. Early modern England, for example, was shot through with offices and roles that were clearly of a "public" nature even though the officeholders—from street cleaners to church wardens—were not in any way "government" employees, or dependents on the crown.[30] There are always complex interweavings of roles and duties, and if it is anachronistic to take certain contemporary formulations of the public-private distinction as universal, it is equally dubious to neglect the universality of a notion of a common good or duties toward the collectivity. The way in which duty is articulated is naturally shifting and controversial, but giving an account of the "public" thing and the duties and roles surrounding it is at the core of political theory.

Corruption worries are often heightened in moments in which lines are blurred or overridden. These lines themselves can at times appear arbitrary. We have noted instances in which judges were expected to receive gifts but were forbidden to receive bribes. A matter, it would seem, for casuistry (that undervalued art). In the gray area between the world of reciprocity (in which is located the gift) and the world of impartiality (in which is located the public function of a judge), the danger of cross-contamination is high. A World Bank publication from 2000 writes of the problem facing postcommunist transition countries: "The boundaries between state and economy remain murky. The fusion of the state and the economy that characterized the communist system has been replaced in most of the countries by a new order, but one in which the separation of private and public interests has not been adequately defined."[31] No doubt postcommunist Russia is a place in which our pirate's lament would be well received. But boundaries are difficult to establish clearly in many contexts. When is the petitioning of one's government civic engagement, when is it "lobbying," and when is it state capture? The answer one gives depends on the way in which one conceives of the relationship between public and private interests. The boundary is necessary for the concept of corruption to work; the definition of corruption is about boundaries.

But whence come these distinctions? Peter Bratsis consults the anthropologists. Drawing on Mary Douglas's famous discussion of "matter out of place" in *Purity and Danger*, Bratsis suggests that modern corruption discourse follows similar patterns to the various divisions between pure and impure that Douglas cataloged.[32] Bratsis notes the disingenuous moralizing tone of some corruption discourse, and he argues that the very concepts at stake in the anticorruption movement—in particular, the concept of the state and the distinction between private and public—are wrongly treated as eternal, objective entities; they are, rather, the product of ideology, tied to particular symbolic systems and reinforced by daily practices. Bratsis thinks the state form and the division between private and public are products of modernity and of the emergence of the commodity form, which habituates us to reinforce distinctions between the "king's two bodies" (he refers to Kantorowicz), between the abstract and the concrete. Bratsis tries to make sense of what appear to be arbitrary distinctions between realms of public and private where some forms of exchange are permitted and others not (campaign donations are permitted, private gifts are not; "pork" politics is permitted, clientelism is not; and so on), and he suggests that these things can be interpreted with the same methods with which Douglas interprets the apparently arbitrary distinctions between clean and unclean foods in Leviticus. For Bratsis, modern corruption discourse is not the same thing as classical discourse, which was about decay of government, but is more about the contamination between realms (a distinction about which I have already expressed some reservations). He thinks this leads to a fetishization of the public-private distinction that hinders serious political reflection: "The real problem is not that something is out of place; it is that there is no political process through which we can posit what we think the good society is."[33]

This argument is very fruitful: Bratsis has correctly drawn our attention to the manner in which corruption discourse reinforces distinctions between spheres, and he rightly argues that in much contemporary corruption talk, the most important political questions are foreclosed by a discourse that assumes a set of distinctions the political theorist should want to question. When we fail to interrogate the function of corruption discourse we essentially abandon the real work of politics. He writes, powerfully, "Illusions of purity and the desire for order have replaced real politics; that is the problem."[34] But I can only offer two cheers to this assertion, since it fails to integrate fully Mary Douglas's chief insight about the importance of the purity/impurity dichotomy. Unlike Douglas, who saw the ubiquity of symbolic systems and who wished to explain—rather than explain away—the need for notions of wholeness, Bratsis sees his role as lifting the veil and revealing the public-private divide for the bourgeois scam that it is (the subtext is that it is *as absurd* as the rules in Leviticus). His language is of "illusion," "fetishism," "revealing," "unmasking": this is the noble tradition of ideology critique. Bratsis is entirely correct in his call to political philosophy, and he is extremely perceptive in his treatment of the ideological implications of given manifestations of the public-private distinction, but he overshoots the mark when he says that the "real problem is not that something is out of place." Corruption discourse cannot be *overcome* by politics; on the contrary, politics—"grand politics," if you will—is always about establishing the lines demarcating which places things should occupy.

Douglas writes, "Pollution dangers strike when form has been attacked."[35] This is certainly something that is at play in claims of political corruption. For corruption discourse—whether classical or modern—depends upon lines. At the most basic these can be the lines between the insider and the outsider—it is, indeed, one of the more sinister aspects of corruption discourse that the stranger has often been an object of pollution anxieties.[36] Other lines separate spheres of activity. Corruption worries wax when the frontier demarcating professional roles from personal interests have been muddied. Another way of saying this is to go Michael Walzer one further and say that all politics (and not merely liberalism) is the art of separation.[37] Or, to put it yet another way, it may be that the definition of justice to which Socrates and his young friends finally arrive in the *Republic* is not as alien as we might think.

There are lines demarcating fields, spheres, and even parts of the soul, and behaviour lauded in one place is condemned in another. A relatively recent, contrarian book celebrating the benefits of corruption insists that because corruption is a form of reciprocity and exchange, it is actually morally superior to the sterile, rule-abiding morality of the self-righteous. Gaspard Koenig writes that corruption is the glue that holds societies together.[38] His argument, while loosely based on Mandeville, is premised not merely on the tension between virtue and utility, but also on the existence of gray areas between the duties of friendship and reciprocity and the duties of office. Koenig plays up this grayness in an attempt to make the distinctions appear meaningless (so that to oppose bribes becomes equated with opposing reciprocity more generally). Peachum would agree. But pirates are not kings, and difficult distinctions are the stuff of political philosophy (just as unconscious distinctions are the stuff of ideology). The difficulty of establishing the precise nature of the lines we draw is no argument against lines themselves. The drawing of these lines is—or ought to be—a central preoccupation of political theory. The notion of a separation between that which serves the public good and that which does not is not an illusion of bourgeois modernity, but is a universal element of political life. What is shifting and unsteady is the manner in which the public good is conceived and the manner in which roles are divided. We have noted that in Sparta every aspect of the citizen's life was part of his or her civic office—the notion of corruption certainly did not separate the household sphere from the "public," but it denoted a falling away from the public virtues due to a contamination by nonpublic—that is, noncivic—desires (such as the desire for wealth). Members of a community that places weight on formal legal legitimacy would deem corrupt many social practices based on kinship ties and the gift economy; the reverse is equally true. Gandhi castigated English legalism as thoroughly corrupting classical Indian society.[39] The civic republican conceives of a professional standing army as a sign of thorough corruption; the Weberian sees such amateurism as itself impure (as we will see in Chapter 8). One system's corruption is another system's purity, but clashes between competing conceptions of corruption and purity ought not to be taken as signs of irreducible pluralism: they are rather invitation to political philosophy. (We will return to this tension between the universal and relative nature of the concept when we explore its employment in the work of Montesquieu.) Where the anthropologist might study the symbolic construction of the state and its boundaries in a given cultural or national context, the political philosopher is concerned with regime forms, the conscious articulation of where such boundaries should lie.[40] Overcoming oppressive symbolic systems is, indeed, the duty of ideology critique. But we must never think that we can escape the bounds of symbolic systems, nor can we escape the need for a notion of a public good that has boundaries. A central task of the political philosopher is to render lucid that which is inchoate in political concepts, and corruption is a concept that is particularly opaque because it does not announce itself as a central, ordering concept of just rule, yet it functions as such.

In this chapter, then, I have defended the moral language of corruption and purity against the suggestion that it is moralism or ideological mystification. I have also suggested that the diverse manners in which the term has been employed should not blind us to the common thread: the discourse of political corruption polices the bounds between the use and abuse of public roles. And I have argued that reflecting upon this ought to be a central goal of political philosophy. I have also suggested that attunement to historical context should not serve as a pretext for reifying historical categories. There is no single, straightforward "modern" conception of corruption; there are, rather, numerous, very different manners in which the term has been employed throughout the history of political thought. Nor is modern thought about corruption and purity entirely at odds with classical concerns. However, one thing distinguishes all of the modern philosophers that we will explore from their ancient counterparts: it is the difficulty in recapturing the type of teleological political philosophy that helped classical political thinkers make sense of the distinction between good and deviant regimes and of the relationship between the healthy city and the healthy character. We will see this emerge in a number of the tensions and ambivalences of modern political philosophy's impure quest for purity.

Chapter Synopsis

The next chapter begins by examining the subject of ethical leadership, exploring the classic tool for the prevention of corruption in monarchical regimes, the so-called mirror-of-princes tract. It examines one of the most important Renaissance versions of the genre, Erasmus's *Education of a Christian Prince* (1516). I argue that those who denounce mirrors of princes as moralism are not entirely incorrect to do so, but that the reason is not that the cultivation of ethical character is an unworthy or quixotic pursuit. Rather, it is because mirror-of-princes tracts, due to the limitations imposed by the genre itself, cannot truly reap the harvest of the classical tradition of political philosophy to which they appeal. In brief, the soulcraft of ancient political theory is unthinkable without the statecraft that its most powerful thinkers thought its necessary condition. Erasmus's text reveals this spectacularly, for it contains an important tension between lofty expectations for humanistic moral education and a clear argument that such education is highly unlikely to overcome the moral corruption caused by monarchical regimes themselves.

Chapter 3 turns from the character of princes to the first of two chapters on the character of republican citizens, exploring the foundational modern republican theory of corruption found in Niccolò Machiavelli. Here can be found the clearest expression of corruption discourse's uprooting from its classical roots. Machiavelli, the chapter argues, is baffling because he makes use of the teleological language of purity and corruption without anything approaching a classical conception of the fully realized political life. I propose that a number of important tensions in Machiavelli's republicanism can be understood in light of this paradox, and I argue that Machiavellian purity entails a balance of malignities and a republicanism of distrust.

The fourth chapter offers a competing conception of republican purity, a republicanism of trust, conceived as a radical mutual transparency. The subject of the chapter is Étienne de La Boétie's *Discourse of Voluntary Servitude*, a tour de force of humanist political writing that, like the work of Erasmus, refers back, somewhat misleadingly, to a unified body of classical wisdom and, in particular, to a classical republican distinction between corruption and liberty. The chapter reflects upon the difficult notion of "transparency," a term that today has come to be widely treated as the antonym of corruption. The chapter argues, by means of an interpretation of La Boétie's rich and enigmatic text, that there are two manners in which we can understand transparency, one entailing radical distrust and the other entailing radical trust, or what the ancients termed "political friendship." La Boétie offers a philosophy of radical trust, but it is, indeed, much more extreme than classical Aristotelian *philia politikē*. The chapter highlights both the inspiring nature of this ideal and the worrisome presuppositions it entails concerning the civic education required for fraternal transparency.

In Chapter 5 we turn to a deployment of corruption discourse that bears certain resemblances both to mirrors of princes and to Machiavellian republicanism, but is indeed a highly distinct, traditionalist invocation of the concept. The subject of the chapter is Henry St. John, 1st Viscount

Bolingbroke, an extremely influential opposition writer in early eighteenth-century England who argued that the English constitution was vitiated with a systemic corruption that was subjecting a formally free state to de facto arbitrary government. He offered a vision of corruption as *dependence*, and he castigated the new centralized bureaucratic military state as a font of corrupting dependencies whereby the public good was systematically usurped by financial interests. It is precisely the characteristics of the modern state itself that Bolingbroke feared were introducing an avenue for the abuse of the public good. The chapter argues for the cogency and continuing relevance of this argument, but it equally suggests that independence is an ideologically promiscuous ideal, and that the pure constitutional condition to which Bolingbroke appealed entailed not a generalized independency but a differently ordered set of dependencies that he thought had been undermined with the rise of the central state. I suggest that Bolingbroke's modern analogues be understood as engaging in a similar nostalgic project.

Chapter 6 examines the first modern political philosopher to make corruption not merely a central theme but a philosophical term of art in his examination of regimes: Charles-Louis de Secondat, baron de Montesquieu. In Montesquieu's thought, we see an account of corruption that frames it both in relative terms (the nature of corruption depends on the regime) and in absolute terms (there is a form of utter corruption that is the political *summum malum*). Offering skepticism about ideals of purity, Montesquieu provides, in his celebration of the English constitution, a supremely ambivalent model of the free modern state in which corruption is checked by the corrupt. Neither charmed nor awed by the free English character, Montesquieu offered a qualified admiration for a regime that promised to navigate modernity without sinning against that thin but important normative standard, human nature.

Chapter 7 turns from Montesquieuan moderation to its opposite, radical republican purism. Here we compare two contemporaneous republicans seeking to achieve radical purity, Maximilien Robespierre and Immanuel Kant. The pairing of the incorruptible and the intellectually immaculate, surprising as it might be, is not without precedent and is born of a desire to explore the implications of pursuing radical purity as a political ideal. Liberal political thought has, not without justification, been captivated by the terrifying image of Robespierre, the radical purist whose incorruptibility itself is perceived to be the source of his monstrosity. Against such an interpretive stance, this chapter defends the idea of political purism, but argues that it is only in its Kantian form—a form that is much more philosophically pure than any imagining of Robespierre—that purism can avoid the enormities committed by the "incorruptible."

Chapter 8 brings us to what is one of the most recognizable aspects of good governance models today: Weberian bureaucracy. Weber's ideal type—which has often functioned as an administrative ideal *tout court*—is ultimately premised on the ethical and psychological distinctiveness of bureaucratic office from other realms of social existence. The chapter argues, by means of an exploration of Weber's use of the language of corruption, that administrative integrity is predicated on the maintenance of these distinctions between realms of human endeavor. This is a model of good governance that has widely been termed antipolitical, but I argue that this is a misreading. For Weber, bureaucratic purity was only possible when there was a strong and separate realm of political deliberation and decision. The chapter reflects on the ethical ambivalence of the Weberian model and the separations it entails. The Weberian view of an uncorrupted polity is, I suggest, under attack today, and we would do well to reflect on the price that would be paid were it to disappear.

The book concludes by returning to the question of the political importance of corruption discourse and the distinctions between ethical spheres that it entails. It considers the ambivalence of the competing ideals discussed in this book, and it makes a larger plea for articulacy about our moral-political ideals. Each of the conceptions of corruption canvassed here entails some vision of the public thing being abused; each places weight on the question of officeholders' character and the structure of the constitution. Each represents a vision that lives on in contemporary thought. And each offers important insights for our current predicament. None, however, is without its moral flaws and tensions—we will conclude with a wider call for the type of ambitious political philosophy that can rethink political health today in a world skeptical of such demanding moral categories.

CHAPTER 2

The Character of Rulers

Corruption and Integrity in Erasmus's
Education of a Christian Prince

The massive mirror-of-princes literature that dominated political thought in the medieval and early modern periods (not merely in Latin Christendom, but also in the Byzantine, Arab, and Persian worlds) was animated by an idea that is somewhat alien to our ears today: that the integrity of a political community is entirely dependent upon the moral character of its ruler. Most modern thought has been skeptical of the possibilities of finding integrity where there is unchecked power. We are much more the heirs of Montesquieu than of Seneca, and we tend to read mirrors of princes as impotent moralizing engaged in by those with no other intellectual resources to confront abuse. Sheldon Wolin says of Seneca's *De clementia* (On clemency), perhaps the dominant Roman model for Western mirror-of-princes tracts, "we find that absolutism has paralyzed the ability of philosophy to do more than offer comfort."[1] The liberal project has generally been content to accept Kant's city of devils, placing character formation on the back burner, or indeed classing it among perfectionist taboos (a point, admittedly, contested by liberal virtue ethicists). In general, much modern thought eschews moral pedagogy, preferring to think of structures and incentives rather than ethical transformation. Certainly most corruption reform proposals in the social sciences take human motivation to be a largely fixed and unchanging thing, influenced by external rewards and punishments. Hence the constant attempt to "incentivize" (monstrous neologism!) ethical behavior. Soulcraft is out of style.[2]

But not all contemporary anticorruption discourse is content to organize devils such that they can get along. The proliferation of studies in "leadership ethics" suggests that the reigning principles of the mirrors of princes continue to have a subterranean influence. In popular discourse, it emerges aboveground. In the wake of the last great financial meltdown, a common trope in popular political discourse was that excessive greed had infected the financial systems and corrupted the political system and the regulatory controls. That is, along with arguments about systemic failures, one commonly heard political leaders giving vent to fiery moral condemnation. Now, proposals for reform were generally based on structural changes that placed disincentives on corrupt behavior (back to cities of devils). But the references to morality and character were not mere populist flourishes—or if they were populist flourishes, their popularity was a result of a widespread feeling that public office is a trust and that those who seek to undermine that trust have committed a grave moral violation. And we see this feeling reflected even in the writings of theorists whose entire raison d'être is to structure incentives to influence rational self-interested actors—consider Susan Rose-Ackerman, who, while generally focused on incentives, stressed the importance of "moral constraints upon self-seeking behavior."[3] This is not merely a popular intuition: there is a reasonable view held by some in the anticorruption community that one cannot construct a model of constant surveillance and accountability that will undermine the possibility of malfeasance—at the end of the day, government integrity requires some sort of moral foundation.[4]

Allow me to elaborate. One widely cited definition of corruption in the social sciences is the formula given by Robert Klitgaard: $C = M + D - A$. That is, "corruption" equals "monopoly" power plus "discretion" by officials minus "accountability."[5] Doubtless this expresses some sensible rule of thumb, but its deficiencies leap off the page. Beyond the rhetorical gesture of the mathematical formula, all of the terms—and in particular "accountability"—require elucidation. The claim itself—that oversight and accountability reduce corrupt acts—could be subjected to empirical study. But regardless of the empirical validity of the claim, it is worthwhile noting that this formula implies that there is no such thing as moral responsibility. We are assured that in the absence of surveillance and threat, there is no virtue. (Kantians would scoff that if one is virtuous merely because one is accountable, one hasn't the least conception of virtue.) If Klitgaard's formula is correct, there is not merely no such thing as a good monarch but no such thing as an honest human being. For we all find ourselves in situations where we have power and discretion and are sufficiently able to avoid accountability. Under the formula, there is therefore corruption even if we conduct ourselves well. Conversely, the formula implies that if we lived in some dystopia in which no one had discretion (or responsibility) and all government offices were surrounded by cameras and ubiquitous distrust, we would be entirely uncorrupt. I do not argue for eliminating accountability; I merely suggest that where there is government, or indeed any form of governance, there are always elements of discretion and monopoly power (when praised, it is called leadership or responsibility), and not every moment is—or should be—governed by some mechanism that ensures accountability. To think that accountability is the only cause of integrity in government is akin to thinking that fear of the law is the only reason one doesn't steal purses and push their owners in front of buses. Surely one of the main desires in anticorruption efforts is to make people who do hold powers act in the public interest even—and especially—in instances where they are not observed. All of which is to restate something obvious: moral agency must remain an important category in the analysis of corruption, even if moral responsibility remains a difficult matter to legislate into existence.

One widespread response to the problem of corruption in high places, then, is moral education. While often derided as a naive, ineffective, and unreflective response to social ills, moral pedagogy is nonetheless alive and well today in the form of "ethics training." And if the attempt to inculcate virtue in leaders strikes many as risible, it is an endeavor with an ancient pedigree. The mirror-of-princes tract is the classical philosophical response to the problem of unaccountability. It has become standard practice to disregard these works as empty sermonizing, interesting for what they tell us about each age's political ideology, but of dubious philosophical utility. I will suggest here that that judgment is not incorrect, though for reasons that are not fully understood by the genre's detractors. The mirror-of-princes tract is not blameworthy because it focuses on moral education; it is blameworthy because it does so without regard to the nature of the city in which the soul is crafted. The mirror-of-princes tract, despite its several-thousand-year lifespan, is the most justly derided technology of virtue because it is, by definition, inattentive to the question of regime. It propagates classical virtues, but it generally does not—due to the limitations of the genre itself—consider the links, of fundamental importance to classical political philosophy, between city and soul, regime and moral character. It is because of this that the mirror-of-princes writers and, I suggest, their modern children, the professional ethicists, appear to be the purveyors of snake oil.

In this chapter we will focus on one of the most influential early modern mirrors, Erasmus's *Education of a Christian Prince*, a text, I argue, that contains two levels of argumentation, one in keeping with the established mirror-of-princes tradition and another making reference to a classical tradition of political philosophy in which the most important question is that of the best regime. Erasmus, in keeping with the humanist project of renewing a conversation with the classical past, locates himself in an undifferentiated classical philosophical tradition that includes such authorities as standard mirror-of-princes authors (Isocrates, Xenophon, and Seneca) and the giants of ancient political philosophy and regime analysis, Aristotle and Plato. He positions his text as the reliable guide to this unified classical voice. But the tradition's philosophical unity is illusory; indeed, there is a powerful tension between the classical mirrors of princes, which, because of their pedagogical purpose, forgo examination of the effects of regimes on souls, and the classical tradition of regime analysis in which the crafting of city and soul are treated as inseparable projects. This tension emerges if one attends carefully to Erasmus's argument. I suggest, indeed, that Erasmus was aware of the tension, and was exploiting it in a typical example of the "dissimulation" that he often thought the necessary expedient of the scholar in a world filled with tyrants.[6] Erasmus's *Education of a Christian Prince* is a text with two dimensions: one is a quixotic quest for the cultivation of right opinion in its target, the young prince; the other is a more profound argument about the very limitations of this style of treatise itself. That is, Erasmus was both fully committed to the importance of soulcraft and skeptical about the possibility of achieving it in strict monarchical conditions. We will conclude with some thoughts about the implications of this observation for leadership ethics in every era.

Erasmus and Mirrors of Princes

The character of rulers is naturally a matter of ancient and universal concern; we could cite the Bible, we could cite Xenophon, or Confucius, Al-Farabi, Al-Ghazali, Augustine, Christine de Pizan, Giles of Rome, John of Salisbury, Petrarch, Fénelon, or any number of important writers, and the infinite industry of literary historians never stops digging up neglected examples of the genre. (Anyone familiar with *Havelok the Dane*?)[7] But while the late medieval genre of the *speculum principis* is so profuse as to defy enumeration,[8] its classical sources are well known: Isocrates (whose "To Nicocles" Erasmus translated into Latin and placed before his *Institutio*), Xenophon, Seneca . . . one might expand or refine this list as desired, but the general pattern is constant—a model of princely excellence is offered as a pattern to be imitated. Such *specula* literature is not confined to the education of princes, and it is essentially tied to a functionally differentiated society. Mirrors of prelates, wives, husbands, ladies, soldiers, Christians, courtiers abound—mirrors that serve as moral guides, others that serve as satires. They exist to provide models of behavior and character appropriate to certain stations in society. Scripture equally serves this function—the books of Kings (and indeed, the scriptures generally) are among other things an unequaled example of the genre, despite the radical difference between the scriptural emphasis on piety and the classical emphasis on virtue.[9] But to understand humanist versions of this genre it is essential to understand their intertextuality—they must be read in conversation with the sources they cite. For if humanism means anything, it is about a conversation with classical and sacred textual authority.

Today, one tends to read mirrors of princes in relation to Machiavelli's *Prince*, generally treated as the decisive refutation of this moralistic genre (though periodically claimed to be its continuation).[10] Certainly, if one seeks a text that appears the polar opposite of *The Prince*, it is difficult to beat Erasmus's *Education of a Christian Prince*, written only a short time after the Florentine treatise (and certainly in ignorance of the other work). Erasmus's virtuous king is a pacifist, a Christian, one who seeks to be loved rather than feared, one who is not rash, who shows clemency, whose kingdom ultimately exists for spiritual good, not for the goods of this world . . . we might continue at some length. Most strikingly, Erasmus insists that there is no essential difference between the morality of princes and subjects or between the morality of Christians and pagan philosophers. But though the comparison to Machiavelli can be fruitful, I suggest that we are better served to study Erasmus's text in terms of the literary models to which it consciously points.

This genre of writing is above all a pedagogical tool; its purpose is avowedly perlocutionary. Since princes are not generally philosophers—and young princes even less so—the genre tends to entail allusions to philosophical sources rather than outright philosophical argument. At the same

time, the genre tends to present this exhortatory activity as itself philosophical. Erasmus took up, in a decidedly un-Platonic way, the *Republic*'s suggestion that princes should be philosophers. He also declared that "being a
philosopher is in practice the same as being a Christian" (15). Of course, to
suggest otherwise would be to expose a breach between faith and reason,
and it would be a breach that this type of brief text would not be in a
position to mend. It is likely that Erasmus thought philosophy and Christianity perfectly reconcilable, but, as we will note below, he did not actually
think the same could be said about philosophy and rule. And what is presented as philosophy in this text is, rather, didactic moral precepts under
the authority of authors that Erasmus thinks princes have no time to read.[11]
Indeed, the text is philosophically frustrating, for Erasmus loads argument
upon argument, with some claims having radically different underpinnings
than others. "Even when everyone applauds you, you should be your own
severest critic," he says, cultivating the princely conscience and calling for
disdain of praise or blame. The very next line begins, "Your life is open to
view: you cannot hide," suggesting that praise and blame of others are an
appropriate basis for self-evaluation (52). In a manner consistent with other
texts of this sort (and even with Machiavelli), Erasmus holds out historical
glory—fame through the ages—as the reward for following his advice (33).[12]
Yet virtue is its own reward, he repeatedly insists, both in this life and the
next. His periodic insistence on the utility of virtue in this life does not
prevent him from also avowing that the Christian prince is, most of all, a
fool (20)—that is, his single-minded devotion to duty and God is something that will look foolish in the world's eyes (a Pauline theme developed
brilliantly in the *Praise of Folly*). On this last point, we might, in passing,
qualify the oft-made charge that Erasmus was an "idealist" (that is, that he,
unlike Machiavelli, had his head in the clouds).[13] He was not blind to the
possibility that Christian morality might clash with political utility; despite
at times claiming otherwise, he canvassed this possibility, urging the Christian prince to *abdicate* rather than permit himself to yield to the necessity
of committing injustices (19), a suggestion that might have struck his royal
reader as somewhat impertinent.[14] But once again, the text does clarify the
relationship between the cardinal virtues and utility. Honesty is the best
policy, except when it isn't, in which case one evokes a stoic Christianity.
The "philosophical" element of Erasmus's job is to convince the ruler that
virtue and interest need not conflict—pursuing the public good is the road
to glory, and virtue is its own reward. But the young prince will not be

brought round to this position through a serious (and dangerous) process of elenchus and dialectic. The method described by Erasmus never rises above the type of conditioning that Plato's *Republic* suggests for the pre-philosophical stages of education: from a Platonic perspective, the Erasmian prince attains right opinion, not knowledge.

The mode, then, is exhortatory and didactic, and the fundamental claim of the text—which is itself a justification for the text—is that such didacticism can foster virtue in the leader. But does Erasmus consistently present moral admonition as useful? There is a very odd passage in the *Christian Prince* where Erasmus quotes at length the advice of Pollux, a Greek pedagogue of imperial Roman princes: "Praise a king in these terms: father, mild, calm, lenient, far-sighted, fair-minded, humane, magnanimous, frank, disdainful of wealth, not at the mercy of his emotions, self-controlled, in command of his pleasures, rational . . ." (the list of virtues continues for a full page [35]). Few could object to the virtues extolled by Pollux, and Erasmus goes on to say that if a pagan could paint such a picture of virtue, think to what heights a Christian should be expected to rise. But it is surely odd to cite, without any comment, Pollux, the teacher of Commodus, widely described as the perfect image of the tyrant (a judgment Erasmus shared).[15]

What are we to make of this strange silence on the failure of Pollux's education to make a virtuous man out of Commodus? Surely placing the moral teacher of Commodus so prominently here cannot be innocent, and it has the effect of reminding the learned reader of the generally ineffective nature of this type of moral education. It is natural to ask whether the great models of the genre had any useful effects upon the leaders for whom they were written. Seneca's *De clementia* instructed Nero. In Erasmus's day, Sir Thomas Elyot's *Boke Named the Governour* taught Henry VIII (not always celebrated for his virtue); Guillaume Budé's *Livre de l'institution du prince* (Book of the education of the prince) sought to instruct Francis I (who waged endless war against Charles V); and Erasmus himself, in the *Christian Prince,* sought to teach the young Charles, Archduke of Burgundy and king of Aragon (soon to become Holy Roman Emperor Charles V), and elsewhere he tried his hand at making virtuous princes of Henry and Francis. Charles, of course, spent his life happily ignoring Erasmus's irenic message and waging war against Francis I, and he cannot be said to have ignored the finer details of corruption, bribing his way to imperial election. Throughout the history of the mirror-of-princes genre of writing one would be hard-pressed to find an example of a ruler seriously improved by it.

But to ascribe to Erasmus naïveté would be erroneous. The text begins, after all, with what amounts to a lamentation that modern monarchies tend to be hereditary, a form he terms, citing Aristotle, "barbarous," privileging entirely absurd criteria such as nobility of ancestry (3). Given, however, that these are the corrupted conditions in which modern monarchies find themselves, "the main hope of getting a good prince hangs on his proper education" (3). That is, the text was not breathless enthusiasm for the educator's power, but rather, as Richard Hardin writes, "a desperate remedy"[16] to a constitutional condition Aristotle had decried as perverse. The text, then, contains at its outset an implicit critique of the very conditions that make it necessary.

The Good Prince as the Bulwark Against Corruption

Erasmus, then, sets himself the task of making existing princes virtuous: the prince "must be the least corruptible of men" (90). The country's fate is almost entirely dependent on the success or failure of this educational project, and "no one . . . brings such appalling disaster upon the affairs of mortal men as he who corrupts the prince's heart with wrongful opinions or desires, just as a man might put deadly poison in the public spring from which all men draw water" (2).[17] The metaphor of corruption as poison or sickness and the prince as the well of all things good or bad in the state is repeated throughout the text: "the corruption of an evil prince spreads more quickly and widely than the contagion of any plague. Conversely, there is no other quicker and more effective way of improving public morals than for the prince to live a blameless life" (21, see also 23). This invocation of princely exemplarity is perhaps surprising—after all, is it not the job of the clergy to invoke Christ as the exemplar? Erasmus might have a professional duty to think so, but he is well aware that eyes are much more drawn to earthly power than to spiritual purity—hence his project of urging princes to imitate Christ (though how a prince is to manage this is never explained). Public virtue springs from the prince, just as public corruption equally is occasioned by the imitation of princely vice (16–17), and the prince's virtue springs from a solid education.[18]

Erasmus deploys the term "corruption" in a manner consistent with the imprecise but influential definition we have seen, "the abuse of public office for private gain." He spends much of his effort insisting that the prince must always look to "public advantage" over any "private" concerns (6, 7, 19, 25, 52). He derides those "who feather their own nests at their country's expense" (53), and he warns the prince that if he engages in nepotism or the sale of offices, he ought not to be surprised to see his magistrates engaged in the same behavior (92–93). He celebrates the image of judges who are depicted not only as blind, but without hands so that they cannot accept bribes (49). Erasmus's teaching is straightforward: "follow what is right, do violence to no one, extort from no one, sell no public office, and [be] corrupted by no bribes" (19).

If corruption is employed by Erasmus in a manner that seems quite familiar to us, it is equally used in a wider moral sense that is less common in public discourse today (though I have noted that it is never entirely absent). Corruption entails moral decay—particularly the loss of self-command—that affects leaders and occasions a general loss of popular virtue. The prince must be a perfect Christian, a condition that, in Erasmus's view, combines classical virtues with Christian love. But if this language of self-command is little heard today, a number of his political proposals would not be out of place in contemporary anticorruption manuals. Once the educational magic has been worked on the prince, he may turn his attention to reducing corruption by example, education, structural reforms (reducing inducement to corruption) and deterrents ("there should be more severe punishment . . . for a corrupt official than for a common criminal" [85]). Public offices should not be venal or wasteful, and luxurious offices should be reduced; tax farmers, usurers, monks, and even—or, rather, especially—soldiers are a drain on the state and the seeds of decadence.[19] In a manner reminiscent of public choice theorists who argue that government regulation invites corruption, Erasmus insisted that there should be few laws and that they should be simple and not open to complicated interpretation (90). Similarly, he questioned the utility of treaties, bits of paper, he thought, whose very use was itself a sign of their users' dishonesty and a mere invitation to lawyerly quibbling (94). But note: Erasmus's argument was not that laws would create opportunities for rational actors to seek rents; rather, he thought that such laws permitted immoral actors to make gains and prevented moral actors from assuming responsibility. This is a subtle but important distinction. It is not that people are naturally selfish value seekers. Legalism undermines our capacity to take responsibility for our actions. He laid emphasis primarily on virtue over law—indeed, as is standard in anti-legalist arguments, law itself is often depicted by Erasmus as an enemy of virtue. Everything comes down to crafting—in prince and society—self-command. This permeates society. There is a German expression popular among anticorruption reformers: "Der Fisch stinkt vom Kopf her" (a fish rots from head on down).[20] The people learn from the prince's good or bad example, but their virtue is also conditioned by the legal structures in which they are organized. But as to the fish's head, the only thing available to the humanist is moral pedagogy found in the conversation with classical authorities.

Mastery, Paternity, and Kingship in the Classical Traditions

But which authorities? Naturally, if the point is to cultivate a *Christian* prince, one might think scripture the best source. But the Bible is much less in evidence in the *Christian Prince* than classical models. The very first sentence of the text appeals, in the same breath, to two authorities, Aristotle and Xenophon. I would like to suggest that these two authors represent two competing classical traditions of thought, one entailing political philosophy and regime analysis and the other the tradition of moral exemplarity. In *The Education of a Christian Prince*, Erasmus runs them all together as philosophical authorities, though elsewhere he makes clear that, for instance, there is a difference in kind between the philosophy of Aristotle and the precepts of Isocrates.[21] I suggest that the clearest tension between these two sets of influences concerns the key Aristotelian distinction between monarchy and tyranny.

Erasmus was indebted to Aristotle's basic distinction between good and corrupt regimes: the corrupt forms entail rule in the interests of the rulers at the expense of the ruled (25–26). But Aristotle had done more than suggest that these two regimes were merely characterized by different attitudes on the part of the rulers: a fundamental claim of the *Politics* was that rule over a polis differs essentially from rule over the family or over slaves (*Politics* 1252a), a distinction ignored in "barbarous" countries. Erasmus's question "What is a king but a father of very many people?" (34) might find some Aristotelian support in the claim that the father rules over his children in a manner equivalent to monarchical rule (*Politics* 1259b11), but there is an important difference between Aristotle's claim of analogy and Erasmus's insistence that they are activities that differ only in degree. If Erasmus treats monarchical rule as not essentially different from paternal rule, does he think it differs from mastery? Erasmus cites Xenophon's claim that it is divine to rule over free men and base to rule over slaves (38).[22] But it is worthwhile noting that the text on whose authority Erasmus is relying here—Xenophon's *Oeconomicus*—is not a mirror of princes, but a mirror of the householder outlining the correct method for ruling over slaves.[23] Xenophon's argument is that one can get the best service out of slaves by treating them well and making them obey willingly. That is, the purpose is to make them, by means of carrots rather than sticks, complicit in their own subjection. The *Oeconomicus* does exactly what *The Education of Cyrus* does—it treats ruling and mastery as activities that have similar requirements. Aristotle had also spoken about willing obedience as an element of kingship, but he had insisted that no free man could willingly be ruled in a manner ungoverned by law (*Politics* 1295a15–25). By citing this passage from Xenophon uncritically, Erasmus implicitly accepts the Xenophontean erasure of the distinction between kingly and despotic rule, between king and tyrant, for Erasmus appears to accept Xenophon's claim that the rule of a *despotes*, or master, can be rendered acceptable to free people. In keeping with his pacifism, Erasmus will later denigrate Cyrus as a rapacious prince (62), but he will never suggest that there is any difference between masterly and political rule other than that of the ruler's virtue and comportment.

Aristotle (infamously) wrote that the master-slave relationship need not be abusive. In instances where the slave lacks the capacity to reason, his interests are served by obedience to the rational master—their interests are one. (In this sense, "despotic" need not necessarily mean "tyrannical" for Aristotle.) Erasmus appeals to this Aristotelian claim (44–45) to argue that a prince must equally see his interests as of a piece with those of his subjects. Now, Erasmus is not saying that the two relationships are identical—rather, his argument is that if even slavery, the hallmark of an exploitative relationship, can be made to entail some mutual benefit, should not the prince recognize the degree to which he too must have concern for his subjects? Nonetheless, for someone versed in Aristotelian political thought, the analogy is unnerving, suggesting (contra *Politics* 1252a) that subjects are to princes what Aristotelian natural slaves are to their masters.

Erasmus does not think subjects less rational than princes—on the contrary, he places weight on their rational nature, urging princes to give rational justifications of their laws to their subjects (though he would deny subjects the permission to "voice ill-considered opinions of the prince's laws").[24] But immediately following this argument for rational justification, he turns again to Xenophon's *Oeconomicus*: "Xenophon shrewdly demonstrated that all creatures can be made to obey by two things in particular: inducements, such as food, if they are of the lower sort, or caresses, if they are nobler, like the horse; or blows, if they are stubborn, like the ass. But since man is the noblest of all creatures, it is only fitting that he should be induced to observe the law by rewards, rather than coerced by threats and punishments" (81). When one reads "Since man is the noblest of all creatures" directly after hearing about the importance of rational justification, one expects an Aristotelian claim about human possession of *logos*. The turn back to animal inducements is somewhat of a letdown. While it is certainly humane to recommend sparing the rod, it is striking once again to see the ruler's art reduced to the art of rearing animals. Erasmus suggests that some small minority of subjects will obey willingly—that is, according to their own judgment (81), but the majority will require carrots and some others will need sticks. (He devotes significant space to advice on how these should be administered.)

Certainly, Erasmus argues that rulers must not treat the ruled as masters treat slaves, but the example to which he points is that of Augustus, who "thought it offensive to be called 'master'" (40). Erasmus avoids, one suspects more carefully than neglectfully, indicating the true reason Augustus felt the need to hide from the Roman populace the fact that he had finally and irrevocably altered the republican constitution. In contrast to Aristotle —but fully in keeping with Seneca's *De clementia*—Erasmus's entire tract suggests that the distinction between *dominus* and *rex* is merely one of temperament and character. Indeed he cites Seneca's claim that the distinction between tyrant and king is not one of title or regime, but of deeds (25).[25] Erasmus can well employ republican phraseology, "he who turns free citizens into slaves will have devalued his empire," but he retains the Xenophontean or Senecan position that it is possible to have free "citizens" under the absolute rule of an emperor.

This erasure of Aristotelian regime distinctions is equally evident in Erasmus's treatment of the necessary things a king must do to retain public love. In a surprising moment of realpolitik, Erasmus, counseling princes on how to avoid being hated or subjected to contempt, suggests that princes should delegate unpopular tasks and personally do popular ones (70). This

is a less violent version of the policy Machiavelli illustrated with his story of
Remiro d'Orco, and it is striking not only that Erasmus offers such ignoble
counsel, but that he refers his reader to Aristotle for this advice: Aristotle
gives this counsel in the passage of *Politics* book 5 where he discusses the
measures a *tyrant* can take to preserve his rule (*Politics* 1314–1315).[26] Indeed,
many of Aristotle's recommendations to tyrants can be found in the *Christian Prince*; but what for Erasmus would make the tyrant into a prince for
Aristotle merely turn a "wicked" person into one who is "half wicked only"
(*Politics* 1315b8).

Of regime forms, Erasmus writes, "it is pretty well agreed among the
philosophers that the most healthy form is monarchy" (37), and he cites
Aristotle to support this claim. But though this was a widespread interpretation of Aristotle, it is important to note that kingship was a highly
problematic institution for Aristotle. When it was under the law, it was
acceptable, but true kingship, kingship above law, was tyrannical unless
the king was so exceptional as to be semidivine, "for men of pre-eminent
excellence there is no law—they are themselves a law" (*Politics* 1284a13). But
here Aristotle thought such greatness dangerous; thus he expressed sympathy for the institution of ostracism, even if it entailed the absurd injustice
of excluding the great. Erasmus takes as given the king's supremacy over
law—the king is "the embodiment of law" (79)[27]—and he places his emphasis on merely warning kings not to interpret this as a basis for license (60).
At the same time, he treats this as a means for reform: princes should
modify laws to root out corruption and should not "be deceived by the fact
that laws of this kind have grown up almost everywhere and are now firmly
established by long custom . . . the more deeply rooted an evil practice the
more thoroughly it needs to be extirpated" (86). In sum, Aristotle was saying that only gods were an embodiment of law; Erasmus was saying, rather,
that since kings are an embodiment of law it is best to educate them to be
as godlike as possible.

We can see how Erasmus conceives of the distinction between kingship
and tyranny if we look to one of the text's few sustained appeals to scripture: Erasmus discusses the passage from the first book of Samuel (1 Samuel
8) about the establishment of kingship. We recall that the people approach
the judge Samuel to demand a king, and Samuel, at God's behest, warns
them all about what such kings will do to them. The description of the
king that Samuel gives the people by way of warning is treated by Erasmus
as the perfect image of the tyrant; the "judge," Samuel, is depicted by Erasmus

as the image of the "true king, administering the people's affairs for so
many years in sanctity and purity" (30). Erasmus argues that the distinction
between the king and tyrant in the book of Samuel is not one between
regime types, but rather between methods of ruling over people.[28] Samuel
ruled in a "pure" manner, whereas the king made in the image of the
pagans would rule "arrogantly and forcibly" (31). Erasmus insists that there
was no real constitutional shift here—Samuel's position was actually kingship. This is an important claim: a theocratic reading of the passage would
suggest that obedience to a king entails a rejection on the part of the people
of the stringent demands of collective obedience to God. A republican
interpretation (such as that given by Étienne de La Boétie) might suggest
that the people's desire for a king was a desire to relinquish their individual
responsibilities (and in particular their responsibility to bear arms themselves). But Erasmus insists that the people did not actually want a regime
change; they wanted a change in the style of monarchical rule. The "pagan"
style of kingship people demanded was really a shift in temperament: pagan
kings are arrogant and deploy force readily. Once again, as in Seneca, the
distinction between tyranny and kingship is not constitutional but a distinction between ruler's temperaments or manners of ruling. It is here that
the Christian element enters into the picture: Erasmus cites Christ's injunction (Matthew 20:25–26) that Christian rulers must not dominate, but must
make themselves servants. Erasmus propagated this view with courage,
prefacing his commentary to Mark with a letter to Francis I that is as sharp
and powerful a denunciation of the French king's bellicose foreign policy
as could be imagined.[29] But the shift he was calling for was in the prince's
inner constitution; it had nothing to do with the constitution of the country: the state will be transformed when the prince's mind is imbued with
philosophical wisdom and his heart with Christian charity.

   In brief, Erasmus invokes the authority of Aristotle, but he deliberately
avoids the analysis of regimes and the distinction between mastery and
kingship, offering a Christianized version of Xenophontean or Isocratean
character reform. Now, to note this abandonment of classical reflection on
regime form might seem a trivial observation: the mirror of princes must
assume the legitimacy of the monarchical regime, and to enter into the
philosophical analysis of regimes would be both irrelevant and impertinent
given the intended readership. But if we consider the thought of Erasmus's
two most important sources, Plato and Aristotle, we recognize that this
raises serious philosophical problems, for both of those authors insisted

upon the inescapable relationship between constitution and moral
education—ethical reflection that does not include this political component
has a fundamental limitation. Was Erasmus aware of the tension between
the two intellectual sources of his argument, or was he simply an intellectually sloppy compiler of classical pieties?

Teaching Self-Command: Sophrosyne and the City

If Erasmus treats all classical philosophy, and Aristotle in particular, as
unambiguously in favor of monarchy, there are grounds for questioning
Erasmus's political commitments.[30] As we have noted, Aristotle's endorsement of monarchy (*Politics* 1289b1, 1284a4–11) was conditional on the prince
possessing an excellence far surpassing that of his subjects, a state of affairs
that Erasmus, following Aristotle, thought entirely unlikely to obtain (in
spite of his avowed aim of making it so through rigorous humanist education). Hence he called upon his monarch to accept the utility of a mixed
regime: if the prince is a normal man "monarchy should preferably be
checked and diluted with a mixture of aristocracy and democracy to prevent it ever breaking out into tyranny; and just as the elements mutually
balance each other, so let the state be stabilised with similar control" (37).
Erasmus was calling on the prince to recognize the utility of a constitution
in which the rule of one is tempered (our translator has misleadingly translated *temperari* as "checked") by the consultation of the few and the many:
"if the prince is well disposed to the state, he will conclude that under such
a system his power is not restricted but sustained" (37).[31] He even warned
princes that they are not indispensable—Athens and republican Rome are
evidence that states without princes can do just fine (89). Erasmus's appeal
to the mixed regime subtly slips in a call for regime moderation without
actually calling into question the absolute supremacy of the monarch or the
monarchical form. His call for the tempering of princely rule is itself significant in that it appears to countenance even resistance to tyranny (37).
While not, strictly speaking, countenancing revolt, Erasmus offered princes
the prudential admonition that revolt is usually the fruit of tyranny.

If Erasmus points to the mixed regime as a moderating element, he is
obliged by the conventions of the mirror-of-princes model to focus on
moderating the ruler's internal character. Corruption begins at the top and
must be stemmed at the top. Now, between classical moderation and its

modern, institutional variety found in Montesquieu's arguments for power to check power, there is a great gulf. But the mirror of princes' invocation of sophrosyne (temperance, moderation) is also quite distant from the tradition of the concept in both Platonic and Aristotelian political thought, for both classical authors offered accounts of the intimate relationship between city and soul. This is, naturally, a subject that mirror-of-princes tracts are not predisposed to explore, for they must take monarchy as a given. But Erasmus indeed was proposing, in a somewhat subtle manner, that untempered monarchy would craft an immoderate soul. The surface of the text evinces unflappable confidence in the power of humanistic education to curb corruption: "there is no wild animal so fierce and savage that it cannot be controlled by the persistent attention of a trainer" (11). But throughout we note expressions of doubt—Erasmus allows, for instance, that Nero must have been essentially corrupt, for how else might we explain the fact that Seneca failed to reform him (46)? The question is, which of these statements is correct (for they cannot both be)?

In order to address this question, we must consider the method of soulcraft Erasmus proposed. I have indicated the ubiquity of references to Aristotle in the text; the Platonic references are even more numerous.[32] Most of all, the work can claim a Platonic heritage in its constant insistence that the philosophical life is the antithesis of the tyrannical one, and that it is characterized by rational self-command in which moderation of the appetitive and the thumotic elements is the key to a soul's harmony (*Republic* 431). But if this was all that was meant by the Platonic appeal to moderation it would be difficult to distinguish Plato from any of the great classical schools of philosophy. It must be said that while Erasmus cites Plato repeatedly, his text bears a much greater debt to Seneca—and, indeed, large portions are paraphrased from *De clementia*, a text whose entire purpose is royal soulcraft.[33] In his recommendation for princely reading, Erasmus gives, after biblical texts, Plutarch and Seneca, *followed* by Plato, Aristotle, and Cicero (62).

Erasmus declares Plato's "denunciation of tyranny" to be "purer" than Aristotle's, and though he does not say why, we might surmise that it is because Plato placed great weight upon the degree to which tyranny is a disease of the soul and a slavery to the appetitive and spirited elements. The bulk of Erasmus's royal education entails preventing the prince from being corrupted such that he is ruled by base desires for luxury or glorification. But it is here that the inherent limitations of the monarchical regime manifest themselves. The most dangerous source of this corruption—far more than the poets (57)—is the educator who flatters his student. Erasmus devotes an entire section to this problem. Flattery, we learn, can begin even in the cradle, when children are overindulged by their nurses (55). Erasmus argues that a prince must be given "well-bred companions . . . to become his friends but not his flatterers and to create an atmosphere of civilized talk without ever using pretence or lies to gain favour" (55). What Erasmus is claiming—in this passage and in his constant denunciation of titles, vestments, or other glorifications of the prince—is that one is corrupted if one is given the impression that one is naturally superior to others.[34] The key to making the prince virtuous is to raise him with companions who behave as if they are his equals and with tutors whom they respect as intellectual and moral superiors. But it is, naturally, a very difficult task to get people in hereditary monarchies to forget that the young prince will one day wield power. For Erasmus, power tends to corrupt not primarily because the powerful are unchecked, but because the powerful can have no true friends or teachers. Isocrates, justifying his giving advice to the king Nicocles, had written that common people have wisdom the powerful lack because they have been educated without luxury and they have friends who can freely criticize them.[35] Erasmus shares this position that there is something in monarchy itself that weakens the monarch, but he suggests that royal educators can, by art, recreate that experience of equality that common people experience as a matter of course.

Whether this is possible, however, is a very important question. Since *The Education of a Christian Prince* is a text that is itself an example of royal pedagogy, one is struck by a performative contradiction: the dedication to Charles is full of flattery, and the text indulges freely in the trope of the prince as the image of God. Erasmus's *Panegyric for Archduke Philip of Austria* (Charles V's father), which is often linked to the *Education*, is, as befits a panegyric, equally bootlicking. Erasmus, however, thought that this was flattery of a different sort from the corrupting kind—it was a kind of "flattering up" in which one praises a prince for virtues he does not really have in order that the prince will attempt to live up to the praise.[36] In a letter to a friend defending his use of panegyric, Erasmus claimed he was merely following Plato and "tell[ing] a lie in order to do some good."[37] If Erasmus sometimes evinced remarkable candor (as in his jeremiad to Francis I), he was nonetheless aware that royal educators cannot truly approach their students with the candor equality would permit.

Great inequality of power between prince and preceptor overturns the rational inequality of the teacher-student relationship. Tutors become flatterers because their students have power over them. In this sense the one inequality justified equally by Platonic and Aristotelian philosophy—that which derives from unequal wisdom—is undermined in monarchical regimes. Princes require friends who are their equals and teachers who are their superiors; they can have neither.

Erasmus was aware that the radical political inequality of the monarchical regime is itself the greatest threat to royal integrity. This paradox is particularly evident when we consider the difficulty of preventing the prince's educators from becoming his corrupters (the greatest danger that he cites). If Erasmus suggests that it is possible for princes to be rendered paragons of virtue such that they can act virtuously in spite of not being accountable to any but God, he has much less confidence in being able to cultivate such virtue in the prince's tutors: to keep them from becoming flatterers, he prescribes the strictest punishments (including the death penalty) for undermining the prince's dignity (56). The prince's soul will apparently be put in order by people whose own souls might well be so disordered that they need to be threatened with death to behave.

It is perhaps unsurprising that educational servants should be slavish. Classical sophrosyne was essential both to city and soul—a moderate soul in a feverish city is an anomaly. In Plato, moderation has a complex relationship to the construction of the ideal city, something that it loses in its Hellenistic Stoic incarnation, where the city's structure fades in the background. The moderation of the city meant, for Plato as for Aristotle, that the city must be limited in size. But by Erasmus's day, the classical city was not the political model most ready to hand—the dominant model was either the empire or the budding absolutist state. Thus, Erasmus could hint at limiting the possibilities for pleonexia and hubris, but he could not pursue this reflection with the radical implications open to the political philosophers of antiquity. While Erasmus preferred smallness, urging princes to avoid expansion and to prefer improving that territory that they had, he could not reasonably suggest anything approaching the moderate size recommended by Aristotle (i.e., a city ought not to be larger than can be "taken in at a single view" [*Politics* 1326b]).

Nor can radical moderation of wealth be entertained in the text. Once again, Erasmus summons up remnants of the tradition in his argument (which he attributes to Plato) that "citizens . . . be neither too rich nor on the other hand particularly poor" (75, also at 82–83), and his repeated advice to princes is to reduce monarchical expenditure such that they can reduce monarchical income (taxation). But Erasmus certainly never suggested anything along the lines of utopian leveling. David Wootton has suggested that Thomas More was actually working out an Erasmian program.[38] This is entirely plausible, not merely because of the role Erasmus played in the publication of *Utopia*. Erasmus showed great sympathy for the adage that friends have everything in common, placing it at the very beginning of his *Adages* and writing, "It is extraordinary how Christians dislike this common ownership of Plato's, how in fact they cast stones at it, although nothing was ever said by a pagan philosopher which comes closer to the mind of Christ."[39] This reading is strengthened when we consider the degree of sympathy Erasmus evinced for the community of property in Acts 2 and 4 (biblical passages that would be employed quite literally by radical Anabaptists in the coming religious storm).[40] That this is a political proposition on Erasmus's part is equally worthy of consideration: Erasmus wrote that "the apostles . . . were the nobles, so to speak, of this new city, poor in possessions but rich in the gifts of Spirit," and he treated the early community as a kind of spiritually aristocratic, communist republic.[41] That said, Erasmus never indicated a desire to see radical economic leveling in this world—when, for instance, he mentions the agrarian laws, he evinces more sympathy with Cicero than with the Gracchi.[42] The apostles managed this radical state of affairs precisely because they did not establish a temporal kingdom—the kingdom of God was not of this world. Hanan Yoran argues that to suggest, as Wootton does, an Erasmian commitment to common property is an "overstatement"; but Yoran indicates equally the degree to which More's call for communal property "does not contradict the Erasmian reform program."[43] That is to say, Erasmus was awake to Thomas More's argument that corruption had socioeconomic determinants, but he neglected to pursue this thought with the radical, semi-Platonic analysis of regime offered by his friend More.

Plato conceived of moderation as that virtue that created harmony in the city, a condition in which people cease to separate their private interests from the interest of the city as a whole. Hence the *Republic*'s elimination of private property for guardians: private gain at public expense is ruled out in principle because the structure of the city has made members of the city say "mine" and "not mine" about the same things; "all sing the same song together" (*Republic* 432a).[44] Whether Plato thought this ideal could ever be attained or even approached outside of speech—in the imperfect world of human beings—is not important to our reflections here. The point is that Plato suggested that thinking about moral pedagogy depended on thinking about the regime.

In the absence of political change, Plato's oeuvre suggests that soulcraft of the powerful—the taming of the tyrannical soul—might only be achieved through a sustained commitment to the philosophical life. I do not intend to pursue the vexed question of whether Plato thought the political and philosophical lives could be reconciled, but I must insist that Erasmus, despite his pretense that there was no clash between rule, piety, and philosophy, did not think they could. Philosophy is dangerous—Erasmus followed both the Platonic and Aristotelian suggestions that young people would be corrupted or confused by philosophical questioning[45] (a suggestion, incidentally, that Plato only made in the context of an ideal city in which the reigning order itself was crafted according to an eternal model; in the real world, the Socratic attempt to inspire philosophical questioning in the young is entirely laudable). But if Erasmus urged forestalling real philosophical activity until a later age, there is never a point when princes will seek a full philosophical account for justice. If Erasmus appealed to the ideal of the philosopher king, he also insisted elsewhere that "he who is born to authority must exercise virtue readily, not dispute about it at leisure."[46] Erasmus relied much more on hoping that the education succeeded in crafting right opinion, in which maxims have been "fixed in [the prince's] mind, pressed in, and rammed home" (10). But any student of Plato would know that to create self-command in a thoroughly corrupted regime is a project requiring more than a few good tutors or a book of edifying adages. Philosophy could not be reduced to a text, nor could virtue simply be taught, unless that teaching entailed the intense, lifelong pursuit of questioning and dialectic—the life to which the Platonic Socrates constantly tries to win the Athenian youth (with questionable success, if we think of figures such as Alcibiades or Critias).

For neither Plato nor Aristotle could the cultivation of virtue be considered in isolation from the question of the regime: hence moral philosophy is essentially political science. Erasmus was clearly aware of the structural limits imposed by monarchical regimes on the cultivation of virtue in the monarch. He was not a poor reader of classical political philosophy, and he was, in his own way, convinced of the Aristotelian dictum that "Correct habituation distinguishes a good political system from a bad one" (*Nicomachean Ethics* 1103b3).[47] But the difficulty was that the very monarchical system in which the prince's soul is cultivated is one whose inequalities make that cultivation highly unlikely: the one soul that most requires moderation is precisely the soul that is least in a position to attain it.[48] We are thus in a position to return to the question we posed at the outset: why are mirrors of princes such an inadequate bulwark against corruption?[49] The answer is in Erasmus's text itself: the very system that he is attempting to purify is inherently corrupting. This answer could be elaborated with much greater detail if we appeal to Aristotelian sources that Erasmus pretends to meld seamlessly with Seneca, Xenophon, and Isocrates. Virtue is an activity. It is cultivated through imitation of exemplars and repetition; one becomes habituated to reacting to events in a certain way by one's imitation of the people around one. Most of all, this requires a degree of equality, for even the most excellent Aristotelian human being—the godlike, self-sufficient man who would pose such a problem to the city—requires a friend, a second self with whom he can pursue the task of self-knowledge (*Nicomachean Ethics* 1170b). Nero, Commodus, and the great monarchs of Erasmus's day (Charles, Francis, and Henry) were given advice that went entirely against all of their experience and habit by people who were not able to express their views with the candor that equality would permit. (Thomas More tried, to tragic effect.) The mirror-of-princes tract cannot craft the wider context in which virtue is nourished and developed. It cannot break the system's corrupting influence on the prince's soul (or on the souls of his tutors and advisers), nor can it even have recourse to philosophy, a lifelong pursuit whose exigencies would sap the prince's strength for command.

To claim that there is an esoteric argument in a text is a risky endeavor, even when an author indicates clearly his or her willingness to dissemble when addressing the powerful (as Erasmus did). On the subject of Erasmus's awareness of the tension between Aristotle and Isocrates or Xenophon, we can make no firm conclusion (save to note that it would be surprising for one of history's most renowned scholars to have missed one of the central claims with which Aristotle's *Politics* begins). But on the subject of the efficacy of moral education, we may safely assert that his *Education of a Christian Prince* makes a claim central to both Aristotelian and Platonic political philosophy: soulcraft depends on political context. The social pedagogy of virtue requires a degree of political and economic equality without which rulers' souls are corrupted with pride. Power, Erasmus was suggesting, corrupts, not primarily because the unaccountable take advantage of their situation, but because radical political inequality raises rulers too high for their own moral cultivation. Whether or not Erasmus thereby offered a quiet appeal to pursue classical regime analysis, I think we can safely affirm that it is somewhat incorrect to argue, with Fritz Caspari, that Erasmus, "as an educational optimist, . . . fails to see that there are very definite limitations to the effectiveness of education; that it is, after all, unlikely that by it all men can be made good and filled with love for each other as they would have to be in his ideal state."[50] Given the very limitations imposed by the mirror-of-princes genre, Erasmus had little option but to attempt to square the circle with humanistic literary education.[51] The *Institutio* not only makes clear the structural limitations to integrity posed by hereditary monarchy: the very conditions that make the mirror-of-princes tract necessary are precisely those that render its success dubious. And Erasmus's wider goal—making a truly Christian prince whose Christianity is of the sort that Erasmus envisioned—was one that he himself knew to be quixotic. As committed as Erasmus was to moral education, he knew that creating radically humble princes devoted to peace rather than worldly glory would require more than upright tutors and moral treatises. It would require something more along the lines of a miracle. Folly, in her more divine manifestation, would need to speak.

Conclusion: Ethical Leadership

Mirror-of-princes literature is not of mere antiquarian interest. The motivation behind these texts—the cultivation of virtue and dedication to the common good in instances in which power is wielded without oversight and accountability—remains as strong as ever, and the proliferation of professional ethicists is the twenty-first-century answer to mirror-of-princes writing.[52] In the distinctive style of our era, employees, executives, public servants, and elected officials are invited to subscribe to ethical guidelines, to think about ethical behavior, to consult ethics commissioners, to play ethics role-playing games, and the like. To cite just one example, Lockheed Martin used to subject its 130,000 employees to a yearly playing of a board game called "ethics challenge."[53] The "ethics challenge" game, while absurd in many respects, is an exercise in moral casuistry (examination of cases of ethical problems that might arise), which is actually a mark in its favor, since casuistry has the virtue of concreteness. What makes this game risible is that it takes place without questioning the wider context of Lockheed Martin's activities. In order to assess the efficacy of this ethics training, I invite readers to consider Lockheed Martin's practice.[54] This is another example of an appeal to personal ethics in a political-economic context that does not encourage or cultivate integrity.

The appeal to ethical leadership is prevalent in the anticorruption literature today. One insightful critic of an important work on corruption denounces the tendency to relegate corruption issues to a higher authority—ultimately to a deus ex machina in the notion of "leadership," a place where the buck stops.[55] In this sense, such literature from political economy and policy studies is actually weaker than mirrors of princes, which seek to convert the prince—who is by definition *ex machina*, an exception—into a *deus*. Erasmus's technique of producing virtue may be flawed, but at least Erasmus was forthright about desiring a god (or human being who sincerely attempts to take Christ for a model) to save us.

Erasmus looked exclusively to the soul because the literary, discursive, and political context of this text rendered the structure of the city out of bounds. Yet he was quite explicit about the corrupting nature of the regime: in this sense, his project of achieving moral reform through humanistic education alone is as tragic as was his attempt to bridge the divide between Rome and Wittenberg, his attempt to moderate fanaticism, or his ardent crusade for irenic piety. The view that humanistic education can overcome the corrupting influence of a highly inegalitarian society is one that is sometimes offered as an instrumental justification for a liberal education whose utility is being called into question by technocratic and technophilic educational reformers.[56] It is easy to recognize the appeal of this argument—if one could turn humanist education into a technology of virtue it might well increase funding for our apparently self-indulgent pursuit. Without entering into the numerous pitfalls of this argumentative strategy (which both over- and undersells the humanities), I wish merely to highlight the philosophical insufficiency of appealing to a tradition without engaging with the radical possibilities that tradition might offer. Erasmus, attempting to meld Plato and Aristotle with the political realities of his day, both over- and undersold political philosophy, overselling it by treating it as ethically transformative and underselling it by hiding its political and philosophical

radicalism. Erasmus's *Education of a Christian Prince* gives voice to a fundamental insight that integrity in government will always depend on character. But insofar as it is taken on its surface, it falls prey to the vain hope
that cool virtue may be instilled in feverish cities. Below the surface, however, lies the subtle invitation to explore the insights of classical regime
analysis, which conceived of corruption and its cure as at once moral and
institutional.

CHAPTER 3

The Character of Citizens, Part I

Virtue and Corruption
in the Machiavellian Republic of Distrust

The intellectual bankruptcy of the mirror-of-princes genre was due to its flight from political philosophy to extra-political moralism. Its focus on integrity and character was not misplaced but rather decontextualized—its images were drawn without regard to the very structural questions that animated the richest traditions of political philosophy. It was moralism, not political morality. We might be tempted, for the sake of symmetry, to claim that Machiavelli represents the inversion of this one-sided picture, giving us politics without morality. Of course, such a view, for all its glibness, would not be entirely without foundation. But if we allowed ourselves to slip easily into this interpretive stance, we would, no matter how subtle our treatment of Machiavellian normativity, find ourselves wondering what to do with one of Machiavelli's most important terms of art: corruption.

Machiavelli is rightly the *locus classicus* for corruption discourse in modern republican thought. This is not primarily because he offers a disquieting analysis of the "dirty hands" problem, or the distance between political and private morality (though these elements of his thought are extremely pertinent for the study of corruption). It is because he articulated a conception of free and uncorrupted civic life that has held sway over modern republican thought.[1] Machiavelli's story of modernity as a corrupted time in which the vigorous political virtues of the ancient world have been undermined by a spirit of servility has been a constant point of reference. No other figure has so informed modern political philosophy's image of the armed, engaged citizen protecting freedom from within and without. His entire account of history is the story of corruption, and the highest purpose of politics is to stave off decay or to bring about rebirth from within the rotted carcass of a corrupted political order. And throughout Machiavelli issues a call to civic pedagogy—the crafting of civic personalities fit for republican liberty. Machiavelli supplies us with the stylized image of a pure republican character.

To speak of Machiavellian purity, however, appears to be speaking in riddles. For, as J. Peter Euben notes, "Machiavelli mocks the idea of virtue as purity."[2] No doubt. Sexual purity, moral purity, the timorous and dangerous elevation of one's own quiet conscience over the good of one's country, the purity of a regime form—all are subject to withering attacks in his work. But the point must be nuanced, for "good" citizens (as opposed to good founders) have a type of innocence—or, rather, simplicity. "Without doubt," writes Machiavelli, "whoever wished to make a republic in the present times would find it easier among mountain men, where there is no civilization, than among those who are used to living in cities, where civilization is corrupt" (D 1.11).[3] The pure mores of the free Germans are superior to the sophistication of the urbane denizens of the Italian peninsula, who have forgotten the dangers of dependence and decadence (D 1.55). Reverent, austere, committed to the public good: the character of Machiavelli's republican citizen might be confused with humanist models. But this turns Machiavelli into that which he opposed. The richness of Machiavelli's writing derives from the very paradox that Machiavelli the impure has repeated recourse to a language implying purity. In the Machiavellian civic ideal, corruption discourse finds itself straining against its own teleological implications.

Machiavelli's story of purity and corruption is both alien and familiar. One central element of the Machiavellian use of the term has a wide appeal: corruption entails a turn away from public duties, a depoliticization, and a servile complacency about one's own domination. A corrupt republic is rife with faction, personal dependencies, clientelism, and the subordination of the public good to private interests. Machiavelli's concept of corruption captures the types of individual behavior we typically associate with corruption (bribery, nepotism, subversion of law for private gain), while at the same time seeing these as part of a wider societal illness of misaligned dependencies. Free people stand up for themselves, are sufficiently independent not to be bought, and their very virtue enables them to protect their civic condition. S. M. Shumer writes that, for Machiavelli, "when people are corrupt they are privately oriented, apathetic about politics; they have no defenses against the unlimited use of political power."[4] This is a language we can understand, and to many it appears superior to anemic liberal individualism whereby such a private orientation is taken for granted. Indeed, there is something about our age in particular—an age in which so-called "mature" democracies face state capture by oligarchs—that lends itself to a Machiavellian analysis. We are systemically corrupt; we suffer (in varying degrees) from "the liberty of servants" (as Maurizio Viroli titled his Machiavelli-inspired denunciation of civic corruption in Italy under Berlusconi).[5] After all, when one considers the manner in which wealthy power brokers co-opt and control political elites in representative democracies, one cannot be blamed for drawing allusions to the Medici. But when we articulate such republican themes today, we generally think of projects for instilling contestatory politics or generous public-spiritedness;[6] we do not think of the highly regimented, superstitious, violent, poor, and imperialistic people that Machiavelli painted as the embodiment of civic virtue. Attempts to revive Machiavellian republicanism today usually shy away from its violent machismo, portraying its civic spirit in a matter that fits perhaps too comfortably with our mores. Yet it is difficult to disentangle the features of Machiavellian republicanism that make us wince from those that warm our civic-minded hearts. This difficulty is not new to us—no less a reader than Jean-Jacques Rousseau tried simultaneously to revive the heady republican virtues without their bellicosity.[7]

If we have difficulty with the imperialism and martial discipline that are the necessary conditions of Machiavellian civic virtue, we are equally troubled by the harsh measures with which Machiavelli thought freedom should be protected at home. For Machiavelli saw corruption as not merely a product of insufficient public spirit, but of insufficient fear. Hence, bringing a republic back to its origins requires either the shock of external aggression or a stupefying act of internal repression. In addition to having leaders with *virtù*, Machiavelli urges some spectacular executions every ten years or so. Had Rome followed this policy, "it follows of necessity that it would never have been corrupt" (*D* 3.1). I leave aside the enormity of this claim in order merely to point out this disquieting appeal to regular acts of spectacular violence.

That many exhibit mixed reactions to Machiavelli is no proof that his thought is particularly paradoxical: perhaps it is the champions of civic virtue who do not have the courage of their civic convictions, or, conversely, who are thoroughly in the thrall of a false republican ideal.[8] But even if we were to accept this either-or and turn resolutely toward Machiavelli's hard teaching, we would still confront tensions that emerge in his treatment of corruption. Machiavelli conceives of corruption as characterized by faction and calumny, yet he is the apostle of social division and mistrust. He blames inequality for corruption, yet he is equally skeptical of leveling measures. He treats subjection to a prince as the cause of corruption, habituating a populace to servility, yet he places hopes for radical reformation in the intervention of new princes. I suggest that at the root of these tensions is something profoundly modern: Machiavelli speaks the teleological and moral language of corruption, but without anything approaching or even replacing an Aristotelian conception of the realized human life. It is teleology without telos, purposiveness with but a fleeting purpose: renown on the great stage of history.

Readers have tended to line up on divergent sides of Machiavellian paradoxes, pronouncing him a civic humanist pursuing excellence or a subtle teacher of evil, an economic leveler or the liberator of *homo economicus*, a populist or an elitist. I suggest that it is because the concept of corruption as he deploys it has such teleological overtones yet refuses to set up any classical ideal of human flourishing that readers have tended to fill in the blanks. To understand Machiavellian corruption we must come to terms with the fact that Machiavelli offers a soulcraft for the soulless. This is what makes him at once so strange and so appealing: the ambivalence with which we receive Machiavelli is related to our own paradoxical relationship to purity.

In this chapter, we will examine the character of the good Machiavellian citizen and the manner of his corruption. We will begin with a brief discussion of Machiavelli's politics of ethical pedagogy, insisting, against readings that see Machiavelli as offering a proto-behaviorist theory predicated on an unchanging human character, that Machiavelli conceived of character as subject to change and habituation, and that good civic character is both the necessary condition for and the product of a healthy constitution. But though Machiavelli consistently praises certain dispositions (decisiveness, courage, boldness, and the like), he constantly undermines our expectations for an account of the human good. Machiavelli offers no republicanism of civic excellence, but a republicanism of avarice, glory, and distrust. In the following two sections, we will explore Machiavelli's views about the relationship between corruption and inequality and corruption and class conflict. In both instances, I will suggest that the interpretative battles over the

degree to which Machiavelli was egalitarian or elitist are a product of a
desire to overcome the essential tensions that are at the heart of his theory
of corruption and civic virtue. Machiavelli's republicanism fosters neither
the democratic nor the oligarchic character: it fosters both and sets them
in conflict in a thoroughgoing republicanism of distrust. We will conclude
with some reflections on the paradoxical manner in which Machiavelli proposed to reinvigorate civic virtue in corrupted republics, noting a degree of
pessimism in his account of the reformer's power.

Pure and Corrupted Regimes: Machiavelli's Civic Pedagogy

In Chapter 1, we noted a tendency on the part of some studying corruption
to separate "ancient" from "modern" definitions; Machiavelli is often lumped
in with Aristotle as someone who articulated a conception of corruption that
is wider than the dominant understanding today, which deals only with certain types of lawbreaking by individual officials.[9] One can see how, against
the backdrop of liberal individualism, authors who emphasize the common
good might look more similar than different, but such lumping together
obscures much more than it clarifies. One major division in the English-
language literature on Machiavelli is between Pocockean republicans, who see
in Machiavelli an attempt to revive an ancient ideal, and Straussians, who are
wedded to the notion that Machiavelli destroyed ancient wisdom. My irenic
nature would like to assert that they are both right, but a reader of Machiavelli
knows better than to avoid taking sides. Without entering into Leo Strauss's
reading, on the issue of continuity or breach with Aristotelian moral education, we must side with the thesis of a breach. The story of corruption and
human "goodness" in Machiavelli contains no glimmering image of classical
excellence—corruption entails problematic arrangements in structures of
dependence in the city and the affective disposition of the citizens, but there
is no singular notion of an excellent character; the spirit must fit the times,
and by their fruits are the "good" known.[10]

    If, in arguing for a clash with classical ideals, I am taking an anti-
Pocockean position, there is an element of Pocock's argument that it is
important to retain, and this is the manner in which the Machiavellian
republic relates to history. History is the story of corruption and rebirth;
great history is the story of corruption deferred. For Pocock, this is where
Machiavelli broke with the tradition—because the republic finds itself in

secular time, it is constantly subject to the decay that affects all temporal things. Thus it constantly seeks to triumph over this contingent, historical world through the exercise of virtue and the constant reenactment of the founding act—the return to origins is a means of establishing dominion over history. In confronting my question—why and how does Machiavelli the impure employ a language presupposing purity?—Pocock would likely turn it into a problem about temporality and mortality: virtue struggles against fortune, the timeless republic must clash with the ravages of time. I would take this historicist dimension further. The very ideal of the citizen itself is historicized. Against Pocock, who thinks that Florentine republicanism was an attempt to revive a timeless Aristotelian ideal of the *zoon politikon* in a new temporal framework, I suggest that the ideal of civic excellence itself has become unsteady. Human nature is not an end or a standard but merely a set of desires, passions, and propensities to be organized fruitfully.

At the outset of the *Discourses* Machiavelli offers his Polybian account of history as a cycle of regimes and a constant story of corruption (*D* 1.2). In each case, the pure regime grows corrupt when its rulers' private ambitions and desires trump the public good, a position in keeping with the Aristotelian understanding of deviant regimes. But for Machiavelli, the rulers abuse their position because they find their rule unopposed: their natural desire to oppress finds no opposition. Corruption is prevented by fear, which restrains and channels envy and ambition. The corruption that Polybius describes in a popular regime, where "some people began to want to get ahead of everyone else" and there was an "inane hunger for glory,"[11] is, for Machiavelli, part of the human condition (and a desirable part, at that). Machiavelli places all the weight on the manner in which the vicious ambitions themselves can be a check upon one another in a well-structured constitution. It is not that the mixed regime preserves the best of what is in the different regimes, but that it balances the malignancies of all the regimes. For instance, what kept men from corruption in the ancient world, he writes in the *Art of War*, was the fact that when they lost wars they were sure to be killed or enslaved—they retained their military virtue for fear of this.[12] This is another way in which Christianity has corrupted the world, for Christian conquerors, Machiavelli rather untruthfully suggested, are less likely to kill entire cities, and hence to inspire virtuous terror. There is much to say about the role of fear in Machiavelli's thought, but I mean merely to point out that virtue is a product of viciousness, and civic corruption is forestalled in large part by external and internal fears.[13]

But violent disincentives are not the whole story. Machiavelli, no less than Aristotle, thought character was cultivated through habituation. But this cultivation of the passions never presupposed the desirability of making people moderate, liberal, or magnanimous or making politics the realm of classical *homonoia* (harmony), debate, or ennobling leisure. Machiavelli did not merely think such ideals unattainable; he was condemning them as based in a fundamental error about human nature and the nature of political things. The *verità effettuale*—the "effectual truth" that Machiavelli so famously claimed was his alternative to dreamy idealism of previous political thought (*P* 15)—is precisely that there is no settled, ideal state of soul or city that realizes our innermost essence; rather there are varying degrees of health and sickness, and the art of government is the art of pursuing greatness while staving off decline and death (*D* 3.1).

It is for this reason that Pocock's reading is both insightful and unsatisfactory. It is insightful in emphasizing the difficulty that temporality poses, but it does not take the historicist premises to their proper conclusion. Pocock describes the Machiavellian "moment" as a "republican decision to pursue universal values in a transitory form,"[14] but it is difficult to pin down Machiavelli's "universal values." This is the paradox of Machiavellian corruption discourse: the very health or integrity from which the corrupted forms deviate is an unsteady balancing of *umori*.

But for all the celebration of vicious inclinations, there are, to be sure, "virtuous" citizens, and it is important to emphasize that such people are made: the republican citizen has a distinctive character that is both a product and a guarantor of the laws. Strauss asserted gnomically that "economism is Machiavellianism come of age," a point that some have thought means Machiavelli invented *homo economicus*, that unchanging bundle of desires controllable with good institutional design.[15] Certainly, Machiavelli thought people have "always had the same passions" (*D* 3.43), but the universality of this base material nonetheless allows for radical transformation; people's "works are more virtuous now in this province than in that, and in that more than in this, according to the form of education in which those people have taken their mode of life" (*D* 3.43). While it is correct to perceive in Machiavelli an anticipation of the Mandevillean turn in moral philosophy that derived utility from vice, it is somewhat unconvincing to make Machiavelli the father of *homo economicus*; the Florentine argued both that human beings have radically different characters based on their regimes and that good laws, while helping make good citizens, are entirely impotent when the citizenry is corrupted (*D* 1.55). Machiavelli did not think human character an unchanging constant; he certainly thought that there were universal characteristics—malignity and overreaching natural tendencies that must be treated as given (*D* 1.3)—but people's character could be formed and deformed. But good laws both channel and shape the malignity of spirit so that it serves rather than hinders greatness and liberty. Good laws cultivate the type of character necessary for the preservation of a free and powerful city. In free states, people are habituated to freedom.[16]

But if good education and laws can produce virtuous citizens (*D* 1.4), this does not mean that Machiavelli places any weight on people's cultivation of self-renouncing virtues.[17] For one thing, he has no faith in their efficacy; for another, he has no love for their grandeur. Indeed, the opposition between private and public interest that is often invoked by republicans requires some nuancing in the Machiavellian context.[18] Machiavelli's *Discourses on Livy* praises the republican form for being advantageous to private acquisitiveness: "From which it arises that men in rivalry think of private and public advantages, and both the one and the other come to grow marvelously" (*D* 2.2). Self-interest should be a motor for the advancement of the republic, rather than an engine for its destruction. A city without the ambition of the *grandi* or the resentment of the *popolo* would be uninspiring and unhealthy. But if both healthy and unhealthy regimes rely on self-interest, we ought not to conclude thereby that his statements about moral education are merely "a snare and a delusion designed to dupe the inattentive humanist."[19] There is a republican character that needs cultivating. For Machiavelli insists that the things that most characterize corruption—faction, private dependencies, indolence, runaway envy and private vendettas, mercenaries, and the replacement of public duty by private wealth—are the products of a degraded civic character, and the best laws are useless if civic character is corrupted (*D* 1.55). "For as much as it is difficult and dangerous to wish to make a people free that wishes to live servilely, so much is it to wish to make a people servile that wishes to live free" (*D* 3.8). Human beings are susceptible to the education of the passions, and without the correctly aligned passions they will be incapable of freedom.

This is, however, a long way from Aristotelian moral education, which moderates individual and political desire for acquisition. Desires, in Machiavelli's view, are insatiable (*D* 1.37)—or rather they *should be*. Consider Machiavelli's puzzling comparison of limited republics such as Sparta and

Venice to imperialist republics, like Rome. He begins by introducing both types as plausible models, and he even stacks the cards in the favor of the republic for maintenance, according a longer life to Sparta than to Rome. Yet having established that Sparta and Venice were successful and longer-lived than Rome without the class conflict that so epitomized the Roman experience, he proceeds to insist that the very factors that brought them this inner peace (the exclusion of foreigners and the refusal to arm the plebs, respectively) prevented them from being great powers. He then concludes, against the very evidence he has just produced, that remaining small and internally peaceful is impossible because "all things of men are in motion" and there is no middle way between rising and falling. Furthermore, a quiet city would become weak or divided (*D* 1.6) and would fall.[20] How are we to take this outright contradiction with the experience of Venice and Sparta? Clearly, something beyond mere necessity is governing Machiavelli's decision in favor of acquisition: the very spirit of restlessness and insatiability governs his normative stance. Men *ought* to be in constant motion: constant motion is life. Sparta and Venice survived for lengthy periods of time, but the domestic tranquillity they enjoyed was enervating.[21] Machiavelli does not argue for the inferiority of conservative republics like Venice and Sparta; he points out that their inner peace (created by the domination of permanently excluded classes) went along with their outer moderation, and he tacitly invites his reader to feel underwhelmed by their lack of outer ambition and inner dynamism.[22] True, Machiavelli says, Sparta's xenophobic exclusion of foreigners prevented the corruption of its pure institutions (*D* 1.6, 2.3), but it also closed off the avenue to greatness; Rome demonstrated an imperial inclusiveness (*D* 2.3).

Machiavelli's imperialism is troubling because he recognizes the ultimately corrupting nature of expansion: the "prolongation of commands" that Machiavelli thought a central cause of Rome's corruption was due to the very enlargement of the empire; as the armies went farther and farther from the capital, commanders had longer and longer commands, which led them to having armies personally dependent on and loyal to them rather than to the republic (*D* 3.24). Machiavelli nonetheless championed imperialism, appealing to the insatiability of human desire. But in effect, he knew perfectly well that desires—or at least the desires of the many—*could* be satiated and moderated, and he wanted none of it. He did not present insatiable desire as a lamentable fact; he celebrated it. Rome lasted for fewer centuries than Sparta partly due to the very things that made it great.

"Good," then, for city or citizen, cannot be confounded with moderated desire or ambition: it is, on the contrary, a grand desire shaped and focused by institutions. Both the city and the citizen ought to be rapacious and ambitious, desirous of profit and fame (*D* 2.2).[23] This goes as much for the people as for the *grandi*. Machiavelli would have citizens love and hate boldly. Machiavelli says that "in republics there is greater life, greater hatred, more desire for revenge" (*P* 5). This, as much as anything, is what the vaunted *vivere civile* means. Christianity (or at least the Christianity taught by the church)[24] teaches the wrong sort of love and renders people complacent and easy prey to domination. Servitude to a prince is a bad thing because it dampens desires, making the many listless and timid, less avid for gain (because fearful of being able to enjoy it) (*D* 2.2). Good laws make good citizens because they educate and guide their passions; Romulus and Numa imposed such artificial necessities on their people that they remained uncorrupted "for many centuries" (*D* 1.1). But if good laws make good citizens, do they make good people? What is Machiavelli's response to the famous Aristotelian question about the relationship between "the virtue of a good man and of a good citizen" (*Politics* 1276b16)? In Aristotle we see both a civic virtue, relative to the given constitution, and a universal human virtue. The tension between these two is manifest in most real constitutions, though it remains both theoretically possible and politically desirable to bring the two together in a city. Throughout Machiavelli's discussion of republican character, the "good" man appears to be coextensive with the good citizen, but the purpose is inversed: his "goodness" is subordinated to—and even defined by—political ends. This is what it means to love one's city more than one's soul. This is also what it means to think about character in terms of the "effectual truth."

And while there are characteristics that Machiavelli consistently praises in the *popolo*, there is no real fixity in the character of a good political actor. The beauty of a republic is that it has all types at its disposition to answer to the needs of changing times, and there is also no fixed vision of completeness. Rome's harsh founder was followed by a mild one, and each character contributed to the fruitful tension of the republic. Perhaps this helps account for Pocock's hedging on his Aristotelian reading of Machiavelli: "Certainly we can discover areas of [Machiavelli's] thought where he seems to have radically departed from the medieval concept of a teleologically determined human nature, though equally there are moments at which he seems to be using . . . the idea that men are formed to be citizens and that the reformation of their natures in that direction may be corrupted but cannot be reversed."[25] The difficulty is palpable: Machiavelli appears to be speaking in teleological terms and yet he appears to be decidedly against such a mode of thought. Pocock can't decide, so he lets his methodology answers the question for him by lending to Machiavelli the views of some of his contemporaries. The telos seems hard to find precisely because malignancies appear dominant even in the uncorrupted life of the free city, and civic life appears to be less like a kind of fulfillment of human nature than a means to some other greatness involving the type of domination of other peoples that fills the pages of history books.[26]

The Structural and Material Foundations of Civic Goodness: Machiavelli's Love-Hate Relationship with Inequality

I have argued that Machiavelli's politics are centrally concerned with civic pedagogy (corruption is a matter as much of character as structure), but I have insisted that his republican purity is at odds with classical civic virtue, and the "goodness" of citizens and rulers is both somewhat shifting and, in its stable traits, quite far from anything that appears morally attractive to any but thoroughgoing glory seekers. I have also placed weight on the desirability of a certain acquisitive disposition in both the people and the great. But such a disposition might be thought to cultivate inequality, something Machiavelli thought thoroughly corrupting. He wrote, "such corruption and slight aptitude for free life arise from an inequality that is in that city" (D 1.17). But just what healthy equality entails is not clearly explained, and it is a source of much confusion. Machiavelli clearly does not mean an equality of power—he takes for granted distinctions between rulers and the ruled and between plebeian and patrician. Nor can it mean mere formal legal equality, for the very corruption Machiavelli perceived in Florence under the Medici was precisely a product of formal republican equality masking underlying monarchical reality. It has something to do with property relations and the double threat of private dependencies and decadence.[27] But here too we find Machiavelli quite ambiguous, for while he denigrates private dependencies and celebrates a political culture in which the desire for acquisition does not overwhelm the desire for honor or glory, he equally appears to think private acquisitiveness both natural and desirable.

Consider his views on an uncorrupted polis. Machiavelli gives, as an example of civic virtue, the people's reaction to Camillus's order that one-tenth of the booty they captured during the conquest of Veii be given to the god Apollo. The people were incensed at this and contested the order, but Machiavelli insists that had the order been maintained, no one would have cheated the god, in spite of the fact that collection of the tithe would have been left entirely to their discretion (D 1.55). He says the same thing of the citizens of free German cities: they willingly pay, without compulsion or surveillance, what they owe to the city. Now, the argument here is clearly not that people in republics are less self-interested (the Roman people, after all, were violently opposed to parting with the goods they stole from Veii), but rather that they are pious about upholding oaths. To say, with Pocock, that Machiavelli "considered a Spartan rejection of private satisfactions the necessary guarantee of civic virtue" is to make Machiavelli insufficiently Roman.[28] Nor is his argument that civic republics establish trust, for it is the constant distrust of the elites by the people that keeps the republic free. It is rather that the Romans' religious upbringing made them fear the gods more than men, a fear that made up for insufficient love of their country and its laws (D 1.11). Oaths, in an uncorrupted city, are reliable because of the universal eye in the sky (a far cry from the civic trust born of mutual recognition that we shall encounter in the following chapter).

The uncorrupted civic character, then, is not characterized by renunciation of selfish desires. Machiavelli did worry about decadence, for excessive riches encourage passivity and the indulgence in lazy activities such as philosophy. Machiavelli praised Cato the Elder for seeking to ban philosophers from Rome (FH 5.1). Poverty and war prevent such indulgence, maintaining honest martial virtue. Corruption occurs when muscles are no longer tense; hence the danger of mercenaries, for in allowing money to replace martial virtue, one weakens and ultimately cedes control to those who know how to use their muscles.[29] But decadence is not really in the foreground of Machiavelli's argument; indeed, the German cities that he thinks so honest actually come across as a bit boring. They do not desire more than what they have (D 1.55), but that is no recipe for greatness or strength. Machiavelli attributes the continued existence of free imperial cities and of the Swiss republic to a rather aleatory confluence of factors about the actual Holy Roman Emperor (D 2.19) who mediates conflicts for the free cities and who keeps the Swiss afraid yet is insufficiently courageous to crush them.

What is truly impressive about German cities for Machiavelli is less their unimaginative frugality than their abhorrence of gentlemen—idle men who sustain private armies of dependents. Indeed, so harmful is this inequality that the Germans kill gentlemen whenever they see them (D 1.55).[30] This is a rather remarkable practice—all the more so for being obviously untrue. (The story, in fact, contradicts Machiavelli's own account of the German free cities in his report on Germany, where he praises their frugality and simplicity, but also indicates that they have a class of gentlemen; he even argues that this is the source of their friction with the more egalitarian Swiss.)[31] Machiavelli's cheerily vicious exaggeration allows him to emphasize just how useful equality is to a free people.

Inequality is the source of corruption because it engenders personal dependencies. Rather than having their interests tied to the public good, people have their interests tied to a particular person. They become weak and unfree, and their relationship to the city becomes one of gain at the city's expense. Dependencies in a republic—factions—come to be like little principalities, with people learning all the habits of servility in their cultivation of their private patrons. This had been the fate of Florence, where republican forms had been a mere veneer over a reality of a moneyed monarchy. Machiavelli applauds the punishments of wealthy populists who employ their wealth and station to purchase dependents and set up factions. Inequality undermines the public good because it renders particular what should be general—allegiance is diverted from the public to private individuals, and the state appears more as a prize over which leaders of factions fight. It raises the specter of envy, one of the most pernicious sentiments (D 3.30), it places the wealthy above the law, and it even perverts the law itself. A city with such inequality is one in which the very laws that once served the public good become pernicious tools for private advancement. Free speech on political issues, for instance, was praiseworthy in an equal republic because "it was always good that each one who intended a good for the public could propose it; and it is good that each can speak his opinion on it so that the people can then choose the best after each one has been heard. But when the citizens have become bad, such an order becomes the worst, for only the powerful people propose laws, not for the common freedom but for their own power; and for fear of them nobody can speak against them. So the people came to be either deceived or forced to decide its own ruin" (D 1.18). The corruption invoked here is not some simple moral failing—there has been a psychological shift with a material basis.

The ambitious and wealthy can deceive without fear, and the rest of the people are dupes or cowards. They are, in fine, slavish, and the institution of freedom of political expression is rendered a source of unfreedom. When inequality has corrupted the people, even good laws become pernicious.

But if inequality is the cause of corruption, it is hard to understand Machiavelli's assertion that among the advantages that the Roman republic had over the Florentine was the fact that the diversity of humors in Rome "brought the city from equality in the citizens to a very great inequality, those in Florence reduced it from inequality to a wonderful equality" (*FH* 3.1). Surprisingly, Machiavelli associated this *mirabile ugualità* with Florence's lack of virtue. And if inequality were so deadly to virtue, one might expect Machiavelli to have been more adamant about protecting a certain economic balance—in the manner, say, that his future disciple James Harrington would be. But Machiavelli had little faith in the ability of republics to fix property relations. For, in spite of repeating on several occasions that the ideal condition is to keep the public rich and the citizens poor "so that they cannot corrupt either themselves or others with riches" (*D* 3.16; see also 1.37, 2.19, 3.25), he equally articulated disapproval in the Roman attempt to do just that, the agrarian laws.[32]

Machiavelli attributed the death of Rome to two factors: the prolongation of commands and the agrarian laws. The battle between patricians and plebeians had given birth to a number of institutions intended to contain the power of the elite—most important, the tribunes. But there remained a long thread of simmering conflict over wealth that had produced laws intended to spread more evenly the advantages of empire.[33] Specifically, these laws were intended to distribute captured lands to plebeians and to limit the amount of land that could be accumulated in order to limit inequalities. Machiavelli's treatment of these attempts to reduce inequality of property is mixed. While he was sympathetic to the intent of the agrarian laws, he thought the attempt of the Gracchi (Tiberius and Gaius Gracchus, tribunes of the plebs in the second century BCE) to revive them foolish, so entrenched were abuses such as the accumulation of public lands. As Edward Andrew has noted, Machiavelli not only blamed the agrarian laws for the civil discord that eventually destroyed the republic, but he was also hostile to a number of classical defenders of the plebeian economic interests, Spurius Maelius, Manlius Capitolinus, and Spurius Cassius.[34] These are difficult examples, for they speak both for and against Machiavelli's egalitarianism. Spurius Maelius, for instance, was a rich grain dealer who attempted to feed the plebeians from his own stores during a famine (in 439 BCE). Machiavelli (following Livy) interprets this as an attempt to gain private dependents; thus, he concludes that Spurius Maelius was rightly punished for ambition (*D* 3.28). Equally interesting is the case of Spurius Cassius, who was the first author of an agrarian law. Spurius Cassius lost his life (in 485 BCE) for seeking to court the plebeians with a gift of money. For Machiavelli, the fact that the people rejected the gift was a sign that they were not corrupt—they knew that Spurius Cassius was trying to buy them, and they valued their liberty more than the bribe (*D* 3.8). As for Manlius, he was not only a hero of Rome, but also a patrician who took the side of the plebeians, trying to reduce their debt burdens, and who accused the senate of corruption; Machiavelli, however, charges him with courting faction and applauds his punishment.

How egalitarian, then, was Machiavelli? On the one hand, he was clearly arguing that the inequality that allowed the rich to court popular faction was the greatest source of corruption, and the fact that these leaders failed—as later leaders did not—to cultivate factions is evidence that the republic at that time was still uncorrupted. Nonetheless, in each case we see a strong patrician hand contributing to the downfall of these populists, and Machiavelli appears pleased with the patrician containment of popular demands. The same difficulty arises in the interpretation of Machiavelli's denunciation of the agrarian laws. Of the Gracchi he writes that their "intention one should praise more than their prudence" (*D* 1.37). Now, when Machiavelli praises one for good intentions it is weak praise indeed. Still, it is quite clear that he thinks the Gracchi were attempting to deal with a very real problem: dependencies are a product of wealth inequality; their method was simply foolhardy since it attempted to revive a very old law, such that it truly seemed a dangerous innovation.

This ambivalence had led to competing interpretations: some, like John McCormick, have argued that Machiavelli is basically on the side of the Gracchi; others have followed the likes of Harvey Mansfield and Leo Strauss, thinking that Machiavelli is more oligarchic. But Machiavelli is both things, for this is the meaning of his mixed republic. "Corruption," writes Claude Lefort, "does not hang on a perversion of mores; it indicates, as a permanent possibility, a mode of resolution [*dénouement*] of the conflict between the classes."[35] I would respond that it is both—the denouement of class conflict itself entails and engenders the very shift in mores Machiavelli deplores. Let us expand on Lefort's insight: corruption occurs

when one side wins and the salutary tension between the classes is eliminated. Radical inequality leads to corruption, but imposing moderation is
akin to imposing stagnation. The radical economic equality established in
Sparta by Lycurgus made everyone poor (D 1.6), but this salutary condition
only persisted because of the very lifeless fixity that defined the Spartan
condition—a fixity that included inequality of rank, something that closed
off avenues to ambition. Alternately, the radical equality that Florence experienced, which entailed a plebeian desire to expel nobles or exclude them
from office, simply led to constant factional struggle (FH 3.1) as opposed to
virtuous class tensions.

Machiavelli's praise of poverty is not an attack on the desire for gain;
poverty is meant to keep the people hungry for foreign spoils. His praise of
mores that do not despise poverty—think of Cincinnatus, who saved his
country and then returned to his measly four jugera of land (D 3.25)[36]—is
due to their salutary effect of not turning poverty into a source of violent
political envy.[37] One must give the poor means of finding social approbation and glory through military success (and giving their avarice an outward focus).[38] But he never wanted the poor to be satisfied with their lot.
On the contrary, the desire for profit is a source of grandeur: Machiavelli
praised the desire for gain that causes people to conquer foreign lands and
to cultivate their own. As we have seen, rivalry and desire for honor and
glory are spurs to greatness (D 2.2; see also 2.1 on the unsurpassed profits
of Rome). Inequality is a requirement of virtue even as it is a source of
corruption.

Corrupt and Purifying Social Division: Civic Enmity and Anticivic Friendship

Citizens are good, then, when they are in a state of perpetual tension, simmering mistrust, and competition. This praise of tension is, of course, one
of Machiavelli's most famous innovations. On a classical understanding, corruption and division go hand in hand, for both are illustrative of a breach in
civic harmony and devotion to the public.[39] Machiavelli offered social division as the antidote to classical delusions of unity; and yet he participated
equally in the denigration of faction as the epitome of corruption.

What types of division keep republics pure and what types corrupt?
The short answer is that class distinctions are healthy, while factions are

unhealthy. But to say this is to explain little; after all, the depressing spectacle of Florentine history is a story of class conflict spilling over into factionalism and civil strife. The Roman defenders of the plebeians whom Machiavelli characterizes as ambitious demagogues are all examples of figures who, on Machiavelli's reading, sought to recuperate healthy class cleavage for the purpose of unhealthy faction. Faction entails the raising of personal dependencies over public dependency: "a free way of life proffers honors and rewards through certain honest and determinate causes . . . and when one has those honors and those useful things that it appears to him he merits, he does not confess an obligation to those who reward him" (*D* 1.16). As noted above, clientelistic dependencies are the soul of corruption. Those figures are the most corrupting who are the greatest givers of private gifts.[40] "The private ways [of seeking glory] are doing benefit to this and to that other private individual—by lending him money, marrying his daughters for him, defending him from the magistrates, and doing for him similar private favors that make men partisans to oneself and give spirit to whoever is so favored to be able to corrupt the public and to breach the laws" (*D* 3.28; exactly the same argument is made in *FH* 7.1). This is a thoroughgoing indictment of the clientelistic dependencies that defined political life in Renaissance republics.[41]

Machiavelli wrote that the difference between divisions in Florence and in Rome is that Florentine divisions were always settled by the sword in a lawless fashion. It is those divisions "accompanied by sects and partisans" that are harmful; "those are helpful that are maintained without sects and partisans" (*FH* 7.1). Where Rome institutionalized class conflict, Florence saw it emerge in fits of populist tyranny followed by oligarchic repression. In the *Florentine Histories*, Machiavelli has a group of unnamed citizens lament that Florence and other Italian cities had become (in the late fourteenth century) places of perpetual intrigue and faction: there is "neither union nor friendship" (*FH* 3.5); rather, there are merely conspiracies. Everything is corrupt: laws are not enforced, "goodness" is termed folly, faith is only kept when it is useful, and people destroy liberty, all the while dressing their actions up as honorable defense of the nobles or the people. It might seem surprising that Machiavelli, famous for calling clemency cruel and liberality avaricious, should object to such terminological inversions. But these leaders' cruelties are not well used: they merely generate clientelistic hierarchies. The citizens are entirely devoted to the capture of the state and the destruction of their enemies. Factions are always destructive; people think they will be happy when they have wiped out their enemies, but they simply find themselves generating new factions.[42]

We should not be misled by the classical overtones of this appeal to harmony; Machiavelli's mixed regime is not characterized by *homonoia*, and he presents those who promise unity on the classical model usually as deluded or hypocritical.[43] The unity that Machiavelli advocates with such deceptively conservative language is one created by an institutional structure that prevents the establishment of personal dependencies. We noted above the distinction between public and private ways of attaining reputation. Note that the same desire for reputation is at play in both of these manners of behaving: there is no disinterested motivation in the "good" mode. But the two manners have radically different effects. When one or the other mode is dominant, ambitious citizens are tempted to imitate that which is crowned with approbation.

Consider Machiavelli's comparison of the harsh Manlius Torquatus and the humane Valerius Corvinus (*D* 3.22). Both figures, we learn, attained glory, so there is no real basis to favor one mode of ruling soldiers over the other. Nonetheless, Machiavelli concludes that Manlius's bloody spectacle of executing his own son for disobedience was, in its very lack of humanity, so stunning that it had wondrous effects on discipline and was a significant cure for corruption. Indeed, Machiavelli claims that a republic that has frequent recourse to figures like Manlius Torquatus (who, like Brutus, committed filicide) might well avoid corruption *indefinitely*. Why is this so? After all, Valerius seemed to manage just fine without killing his own children. The real difference between them is that Manlius's harsh modes are guaranteed to prevent him from being loved: "showing oneself always harsh to everyone and loving only the common good, one cannot acquire partisans; for whoever does this does not acquire particular friends for himself, which we call . . . partisans. So a similar mode of proceeding cannot be more useful or more desirable in a republic, since the public utility is not lacking in it and there cannot be any suspicion of private power" (*D* 3.22). Friendship itself is corrupting; the violence that severs particular links of family or friendship for the sake of the law and the common good is particularly purifying. These virtuosi are not merely sources of fear, but of example; real citizenship means entertaining the possibility of filicide and fratricide. Manlius, like Romulus, Brutus, or Caterina Sforza (whose willingness to sacrifice her children so pleased Machiavelli that he recounted the story on several occasions)[44] belongs to a long list of figures who acquire reputation in public modes and whose desire for reputation makes them disdain all private affections.

This aspect of republican virtue has often been described as sacrificial, but Machiavelli did not think in those terms. Torquatus was harsh by nature and principally desirous of being obeyed. He exercised his passions—but in a public manner. For when private means reign, envy finds itself armed with partisans, and internecine conflicts abound; but when people seek honors through public means, their lack of private partisans means that the hatred they engender will not be harmful. In a healthy civic condition citizens, to achieve station or glory, must "attempt to exalt the republic and to watch each other particularly so that civil bounds are not transgressed" (*FH* 7.1) Mutual surveillance is a key source of purity. And if an uncorrupted city contains people who willingly pay precisely what they owe without surveillance (*D* 1.55), it is because they have a fear of divine wrath instilled by their civic religion. Divine surveillance serves where human eyes are absent. If we can term Machiavelli's civism "civic friendship," it is one paradoxically founded on mutual suspicion, a common detestation of kings, and a commitment to public laws as a means of furthering personal and class interests.

In a corrupted regime, social division manifests itself in plots. It has the aspect of a fight for the spoils of government. The key to keeping division from becoming corruption is to make it official: public accusations turn resentment into a public good. In the same way that civic religion co-opts religious passions for public use, so too do public accusations co-opt the passions of envy, greed, and hatred for a general good.

This is not a call for transparency as a means to justice. What Machiavelli celebrates here is a public performance of accusation and punishment —an ongoing staging of a collective revenge that sates the wrath of the people and reenacts the violence with which the state was founded.[45] Machiavelli is undisturbed by unjust results: "For if a citizen is crushed ordinarily [i.e., through this legal process], there follows little or no disorder in the republic, even though he has been done a wrong. For the execution is done without private forces and without foreign forces, which are the ones that ruin a free way of life; but it is done with public forces and orders, which have their particular limits and do not lead beyond to something that may ruin the republic" (*D* 1.7). The important thing is for violence to be sanctioned by the laws, not for it to be just.[46] The purpose of public accusations is to channel the inherent violence of political life so that it strengthens the laws rather than undermines them.

Machiavelli's love of division and the politics of open accusations should thus not, then, be understood in the light of the principle of publicity at the heart of liberal free-speech regimes. Public accusations are about *attenuating* the dangers of free speech: "put up or shut up" is the governing principle. If a person cannot convince the judges that his accusation is true, Machiavelli says that he should face being cast off the Tarpeian Rock (*D* 1.8). The widespread celebration of whistleblowers in our political culture, which sometimes goes so far as to protect their anonymity, would have been thought by Machiavelli a recipe for calumny. Anonymous accusations of corruption are themselves a manifestation of corruption. He says of Florentine degeneration, "Of one individual they said that he had stolen money from the common; of another, that he had not won a campaign because he had been corrupted. . . . From this it arose that on every side hatred surged; whence they went to division; from division to sects [parties]; from sects to ruin" (*D* 1.8). Calumny is corrupt; accusation is pure.[47] Paradoxically, the most corrupt polities are those in which the charges of official corruption fly thickest and fastest. In such societies, these charges might well usually be true, for there is a generalized disdain for the public thing, but the very manner in which the charges emerge foments faction rather than abating abuse of the public good. It is incorrect to assert, as Danielle Allen does, that "Machiavelli places more emphasis on efforts to reduce the cost of making accusations through formal channels than on the effort to increase the cost of acting outside formal channels of accusation."[48] He places equal weight on *both* elements, the danger of calumny and the utility of accusation. Public accusation is the cure for private calumny, encouraging speech that keeps the great from getting too confident, but discouraging speech that makes for armed civil conflict.

Allen reads Machiavelli as arguing for the epistemic value of the adversarial mode, but the Machiavellian city lives in the world of appearances. There is much to be said about the people's capacity to judge: Machiavelli both praises the people as having godlike perspicuity (*D* 1.58) and a credulity that can be both dangerous (*D* 1.53) and salutary (*D* 1.12). Without resolving these tensions, let me merely insist on the well-understood point that where truth is concerned, it is only the "effectual truth" that matters.

Public accusations, then, channel energies that would otherwise become private feuds and vendettas. The spectacle of public accusations, while born of unprepossessing self-interest, nonetheless transforms a civic vice into a civic virtue. And the event itself transforms the souls of the participants/spectators. We mentioned above the case of Manlius Capitolinus, the great savior of Rome and populist who was subsequently thrown from the Tarpeian Rock (in 384 BCE). Manlius was punished, among other things, for calumniating his enemies with the charge of having misappropriated public funds (D 1.8). On Machiavelli's presentation, Manlius's populism was mere ambition. Machiavelli writes that when Manlius was forced to substantiate his libel publicly, he was unable to do so, and hence he was imprisoned. Machiavelli argues that it was the people's lack of corruption that turned them against someone they so greatly admired. In a corrupt city, Manlius would have done very well because he would have managed to gain a private following of plebeians (D 3.8); as it was, the virtuous plebeians sided with the senate to condemn someone who had been their benefactor. Now Machiavelli ascribes this to the lack of civic corruption, but it is worthwhile noting the precise institutional mechanism by which this salutary end was achieved. It was because the people themselves were permitted to be the judges that the judgment turned out to be so salutary:

> Although the people of Rome, very desirous of its own utility and a lover of things that went against the nobility, did very many favors to Manlius, nonetheless, as the tribunes summoned him and delivered his cause to the judgment of the people, that people, from defender having become judge, without any respect condemned him to death. . . . Love of the fatherland was able to do more in all of them than any other respect, and they considered present dangers that depended on him more than past merits, so much that with his death they freed themselves. (D 3.8)

The teaching of this chapter is that civic culture is stronger than one man's attempt upon it: the desire to live freely is persistent, and a virtuous people can only be corrupted over generations. "Love of the fatherland"—or rather, fear of a future tyranny—motivated the people. But the institutional mechanism that reinforced the plebeians' attention to the public good was the very fact of having the people themselves judge. The passage in Livy (which Machiavelli follows closely) places great emphasis on the fact that as Rome was gearing up for a violent civil war between patricians and plebeians, the tribunes of the plebeians suggested avoiding a war by instituting legal proceedings against Manlius. In Livy's version, a tribune says, "as soon as the multitude shall perceive that the contest is not with them, and that instead of advocates they are to be judges; and shall behold the prosecutors plebeians; the accused a patrician [for Manlius was a patrician who had set himself up as the defender of indebted plebeians]: and that the charge is that of aiming at regal power; they will show more zeal in defence of their own liberty than they will attachment to any person whatever."[49] The extra-legal class war that was about to break out was prevented by co-opting class prejudice and by making the plebeians themselves the judges. Machiavelli condenses but does not alter this argument: it was the plebeian possession of the office of judge that made them judge in the public interest; had magistrates attempted to do it, they would have faced civil war.

The fact that the plebeians were clearly manipulated to act against their class interests here is no argument against their civic virtue for Machiavelli: they exercised their decision within the confines of a public outlook rather than in open disregard for law and public order. Had they pursued class interests with Manlius as their head, their desire not to be oppressed would have slipped over into dependence on a great man and the quest to make the state a basis for dominating their enemies. But they were not corrupt— which is to say, their prejudice against Manlius's class and their fear of being someone's dependent had not abated. The well-ordered republic finds channels for the desire to dominate that do not result in domination —these channels are mostly the profitable and glory-providing practice of war, but they are also through the contestatory nature of a mixed govern-ment. Well-ordered regimes prevent corruption by allowing institutional-ized social division to power the state. When populist and elitist readers of Machiavelli try to line him up with one class or the other they impute to him an oligarchic or democratic conception of the good life; but the condi-tion of civic piety is a product of their institutionalized, persistent mutual distrust. Unity is a product of division, and "goodness" entails a ceaseless and perpetually unfulfilled striving for domination.

Curing Corruption Through a Return to Origins:
Improbable Princes, Servile Liberation

We have seen that the Machiavellian republic's purity entails soulcraft, but those souls are characterized by a balance of malignities. But what is to be done about systemic corruption? When one overindulges in the metaphor of corruption and pollution, it is a short step to adopting the metaphor of radical purification. Certainly this is the case in Machiavelli's work; Italy is a festering wound; the domination of the barbarians stinks (*P* 26). Such illnesses demand radical cures. We are familiar with Machiavelli's response: return to origins. But this is easier said than done. The most troubling teaching in Machiavelli's oeuvre is no doubt the call for violent founding and refounding in which the entire society is turned upside down, the poor are made rich, the rich poor, whole populations are moved around, and order is remade.[50] If contemporary anticorruption efforts often appeal to the vague remedy of "good leadership," Machiavelli makes the matter explicit: systemic corruption will only be overcome by means of a new prince, or what the tradition understood as a tyrant.

If a complete renewal is not yet possible (or necessary), Machiavelli urges extreme punishments, bloodletting, and the establishment of a dictator, who is authorized by law to behave arbitrarily. For Machiavelli rejects the view that the Roman office of the dictatorship led to Caesar's rise; on the contrary, the office was salutary, and it would not have had negative effects if Caesar's time had not been so corrupt and if he had not attained such enormous private authority previously due to the prolongation of his command (*D* 1.33–34). The beauty of the dictatorship was that it allowed for exceptional powers to be exercised in a manner that strengthened the law (since it was a legal power). If dictators serve paradoxically to uphold law, they do rather undermine Philip Pettit's thesis that republicanism is systematically opposed to the exercise of arbitrary power.[51] But as Caesar's example shows, dictatorship is insufficient when a society is truly corrupt. In such a case, there is nothing for it but to start over with a new prince, the armed prophet who can redeem a fallen people.

There is something antirepublican in such appeals to individual leaders: beyond the obvious question of who polices the police, these proposals raise the question of whether top-down anticorruption measures are not directly implicated in the very reproduction of corruption itself. For Machiavelli's teaching is that societies are ultimately corrupted by the lack of liberty. This tendency toward inertia is both a protector of free republics (good habits caused the Romans to withstand the dangers of Manlius) and a hindrance to reform. This is why Machiavelli thinks Milan or Naples are incapable of freedom no matter what shocks one applies to them (*D* 1.17). People become dependent upon leaders, unable to oppose and incapable of fulfilling the duties that make societies free; they turn inward to their now-anticivic pursuits, or they become groveling courtiers. And they cannot cure themselves: "most men are more apt to preserve a good order than to know how to find one for themselves" (*FH* 3.6). Florence did not succeed in reforming itself, for its reforms were always based on factional interests (and conspiracies) rather than the general good (and public accusations) (*D* 1.49). Perhaps the most famous paradox of Machiavelli's oeuvre is his attempt to grapple with the problem that rule by one corrupts, but only rule by one can reform (*D* 1.18). And "ethical leadership" in the context of a new prince is a contradiction in terms: "Because the reordering of a city for a political way of life presupposes a good man, and becoming prince of a republic by violence presupposes a bad man, one will find that it rarely happens that someone good wishes to become prince by bad ways, even though his end be good, and that someone wicked, having become prince, wishes to work well, and that it will ever occur to his mind to use well the authority that he has acquired badly" (*D* 1.18). Readers have been divided on how to interpret Machiavelli's hope for a new prince who will transplant populations like so much livestock and kill the sons of Brutus; who commits genocide and filicide in order to found an age of liberty; and who does evil for the purpose of achieving good. The fact that a great leader who has these conflicting impulses is rarely found outside of scripture and myth is an interesting problem for interpretation;[52] certainly, on Machiavelli's account the Roman experience entailed not one godlike legislator but good fortune in having a succession of founders of different, complementary characters. But this does not undermine the fundamental claim that the cure for corruption requires the bitter pill of tyranny, shock, and refoundation. On this, some have found him to be cleverly devilish in turning republican talk to the good of *uno solo*.[53] Others have seen in this figure a popular emancipator, though in their enthusiasm for Machiavellian civism they downplay this purifying violence (or, in some cases, to give it an unduly cheery radical-democratic interpretation).[54] But the paradox remains: given everything Machiavelli says about the corrupting effects of one-man rule, how can we understand the move from the "civil prince," whose power rests on personally dependent soldiers and popular approval, to a condition of a mixed regime, in which the aristocratic and the democratic elements are in a fruitful tension?

The standard reading is that princes found and people maintain free republics. But if we consider the manner in which Machiavelli describes

how a new, civil prince must consolidate his position, we see not an education of the people to civic independence, but a cultivation of personal
dependency. Consider the advice to a new prince to arm his subjects (*P*
20). Readers often emphasize the anti-oligarchic aspect of this position
(new princes must crush old nobility). But Machiavelli is quite clear that
the purpose of the move is to turn "subjects" into the prince's "partisans";
just as in chapter 9 of *The Prince* he insisted upon the need for the new
prince to cultivate personal dependency in the people, so too does he advise
here the cultivation of personal dependency in his army. Still, one might
think that the advice is a trap: perhaps Machiavelli knows that the armed
people will ultimately use their power to dispossess the prince of his authority.[55] But if Machiavelli was setting the prince a trap (and it is clear that he
did not think one-person rule admirable for any end other than founding),
it is hard to see how the trap will be sprung. After all, he does not actually
say that all subjects should be armed; on the contrary he says that "all
subjects cannot be armed" (*P* 20), so one must make the armed subjects
into one's partisans. "The difference of treatment that they recognize
regarding themselves makes them obligated to you" (*P* 20). And when the
unarmed part of the people, who generally are content with not being
oppressed, see themselves in some security, they will be grateful, passive,
and dependent. The new prince's creation of partisans can even, if the
prince is sufficiently virtuous, be at the expense of the people. Severus,
lauded by Machiavelli for his leonine and foxy qualities, managed to be a
fine and admirable prince (*P* 19) even as he indulged his friends, the soldiers, at the expense of the people. Doubtless Machiavelli did not think this
a model for lasting reform, and Severus's heir is indeed a textbook case
of the corruption of monarchies. But this only reinforces our troubles in
reconciling the new prince who must establish a personal order with the
free republic that, while in need of leaders (*D* 1.44), cannot be entirely
dependent on one man without becoming corrupted.

Salutary extralegal founders, then, are highly improbable, and the methods they must use to gain power are corrupting. The extraordinary confluence of events that brought about the Roman mixed regime was more a
product of good luck than good planning. All of which is to say that it took
that unpredictable goddess fortune to save virtue from the virtuous. But
however much the return to origins engenders paradoxes, the reviving of
virtue through spectacular shocks is largely about breaking the relationships
of dependency and friendship that have been allowed to build up. It is

about restoring the public good by reinstituting the tensions, ambitions, and distrust that are the hallmarks of civic life.

Where does all this leave good republicans? What does the Machiavellian republicanism of distrust tell us about the regaining of civic virtue in our atomistic, oligarchic age? And is the virtue of the free Machiavellian citizen worth having? I have argued that Machiavelli's use of the concept "corruption" is so perplexing precisely because it entails all the soulcraft that we have come to associate with perfectionist Aristotelian teleology, yet it refuses to orient itself according to any compelling conception of human flourishing; rather, it cultivates democratic and oligarchic characters and sets them in tension, and the tension itself must stand in for the good. This mode of civic pedagogy encourages and channels certain appetites for gain and glory. The classical ideal of civic friendship gets a radical alteration, and the political life aimed at leisure and justice appears through Machiavellian lenses to be feeble and unambitious.

Machiavelli's deployment of the term "corruption" invites us to think of an ideal, upright form of civic life and human being, yet Machiavelli constantly undermines our expectations of that finality, presenting the character of the good citizen not as an ideal of flourishing but as a teetering, unstable thing, forever in need of stimulants such as fear, envy, ambition, and the pleasure of bloody spectacle. To be corrupt is to fail to experience these passions in the right way. A city is corrupt when such passions are no longer filtered through public offices, contained by public laws and productive of public greatness. Statecraft is the crafting of restless souls.

In placing emphasis on the less attractive elements of Machiavelli's civic virtue, I might be accused of exhibiting the moralism he so derided. I am not, however, crying out in moral horror, though I am hinting that Machiavelli's republicanism is perhaps not the ideal that champions of civic virtue wish to evoke in pronouncing his name.[56] Machiavelli's acquisitive, striving, ambitious, distrustful, and courageous citizens are the product of their laws and orders; their civic personality is both the cause and consequence of their legal and religious institutions. Without such civic personalities, good orders will avail nothing; without good orders, such personalities are rare and their actions rarely fruitful. But the whole is precariously balanced, in spite of Machiavelli's incredible suggestion that decennial bloodletting can prevent corruption indefinitely (D 3.1).

For the antiessentialist radical democrat, Machiavelli's lack of teleology is quite attractive. Chantal Mouffe, distancing herself from neo-Aristotelian republicans, asserts that Machiavelli "incontestably represents a fundamental point of reference for those who want to think politically today, and if it is important to renew intimacy with the tradition of civic republicanism, it is essential that it be under his aegis."[57] She is correct to see a kindred spirit: Machiavelli's notion of the political is agonistic, and like her he seeks to find ways of keeping civil division without allowing it to become civil war. Also like Machiavelli, Mouffe wishes to maintain the importance of external enemies as a necessary condition of civic identity.[58] She does not, it is true, adopt Machiavellian imperialism, but one sees a similar machismo in her insistence on the necessity for international enmity. Others claiming the mantle of radicalism do hold up the more disquieting moments as exemplary: Miguel Vatter, for instance, argues that Manlius Torquatus's killing of his son was an "event" of republican revolutionary freedom.[59]

Perhaps such suggestions are the product of Machiavelli's canonization as an author—killing the sons of Brutus has become a literary cliché rather than a visceral reality. Still, some readers have confronted this legacy. Hanna Pitkin attempts to separate the bellicose, insatiable Machiavelli from Machiavelli "at his best," the Machiavelli who reconciles social division and plurality with common striving.[60] In her reading, it is as if Machiavelli was never quite able to live up to his own discovery of our mutual vulnerabilities, and thus took refuge in his own worst instincts for radical independence, self-sufficiency, and machismo. Others have sought to have their republican purity without the icing of violence: Iseult Honohan, for instance, writes, "There need be nothing quite so martial about civic virtue in a republic which is not under constant threat of external attack."[61] Perhaps. But for Machiavelli, the notion that civic virtue could be maintained in such conditions would have been fanciful: goodness required sufficient fear from the outside and the inside—and sufficient public channels for attaining gain and glory. Contemporary thinkers are drawn to Machiavelli's civic virtue as a counterweight to the apolitical, servile apathy that allows people to think liberty consists in a politics composed of factional struggles between oligarchic groups for the capture of state resources; at the same time, he is attractive precisely because he does not deploy "a premodern view of the political community as organized around a substantive idea of the good life" (to quote Mouffe's dismissive characterization of neo-Aristotelians).[62] But the dismal conception of civic integrity driving Machiavelli's thought and its essential attachment to imperialism, superstition, mutual surveillance, the bloody spectacle of public accusation and purge, and the ultimate recourse to tyranny when the city has grown too decadent are matters from which sympathetic readers flee into abstraction, euphemism, or literary flourish. I suggest, however, that these two sides of Machiavelli are inseparable. Machiavelli serves as an important counterweight to those who, nostalgic for a premodern solidarity, would deny the importance of division and discord. But if Machiavelli liberates us from the specter of solidarity, he does so at the expense of a polis characterized by contestatory speech about the just and the unjust—what I would term "the political." This is what it means to employ the discourse of corruption in the absence of teleological conceptions of human flourishing.

CHAPTER 4

The Character of Citizens, Part II

Étienne de La Boétie on Corruption, Transparency, and the Republicanism of Trust

Machiavelli's ideal entails a paradoxical civic personality of impure purity: his conception of civic freedom, which is a product of unease and ambition, cultivated and channeled, might be characterized as a republicanism of mistrust. "It is not good," he insisted, "if magistrates lack somebody to observe them and make them refrain from actions that are not good."[1] Machiavellian public accusation, we noted, is salutary spectacle. It is both discipline and pageant, and it both requires and cultivates a particular type of civic character. In this chapter we will examine another direction in which republican thought has gone: the republicanism of trust.

Let us begin with the cliché heard every time the issue of corruption arises: "sunlight is the best disinfectant."[2] It speaks to a widespread view: the gangrene of corruption can be cured by exposing it to the light of day. Corruption thrives in secret; we must eliminate the shady deals in back rooms. And transparency itself *creates* trust. Of course, for all that political figures parrot the phrase, most concede that politics requires some degree of opacity: to insist that there ought to be no secret negotiations is akin to insisting that there be no feathered birds. But even though the principle of publicity sometimes must cede to the grubby world of politics, we remain generally receptive to the idea that corruptible human beings require mutual surveillance to keep them honest. This view is strongest in a modern, liberal philosophical tradition that is skeptical about human perfectibility and that seeks to control cities of devils through the mutual checking of powers. It is equally present in the Machiavellian call for mutual surveillance and public accusation. This call for transparency is an outgrowth of distrust.

Of course, transparency is not synonymous with integrity; when there is no capacity for enforcement, a transparent abuse of power merely makes a bad situation worse. Nor does transparency render legitimate those actions that, while legal, are widely mistrusted. Until recently American campaign financing was transparent (some might say brazen), but it still raised significant concerns about systemic corruption. Nonetheless, the increased opportunities for secrecy in the funding of campaign advertising cannot be seen as a step forward: transparency is widely seen as a necessary, if insufficient, condition of integrity.

But there are grounds for ambivalence even here. Foucauldian objections to transparency suggest themselves: the transparent world is the world of the panopticon, the nanny cam, the constant surveillance of oneself and others that serves to reinforce dominant relationships of power.[3] We are rendered transparent even beneath the skin; our very souls are observed and configured with scientific tools. "Transparency" is a word that hides a move to uniformity—in shining their light into every dark corner, the champions of transparency subject the world to control, strengthening the power of those who play the transparency game best. One polemical author (less subtle than the Foucauldians) has gone so far as to equate the call for transparency with totalitarianism: "George Orwell has already described the place where the fanaticism for transparency leads."[4]

Appealing as this iconoclastic argument is, however, it cannot allay well-established—even ancient—concerns that those who conduct political affairs in secrecy will be tempted to turn public goods to private purposes. Nor is the worry about shadows merely a liberal concern. We recall Rousseau's enthusiastic praise of Geneva, "a state where, with all private individuals being known to one another, neither the obscure maneuvers of vice nor the modesty of virtue could be hidden from the notice and the judgment of the public."[5] Given our mixture of moral intuitions in this matter, it appears that the first place where we should be seeking transparency is in the conceptual contours of transparency itself.

The difficulty is that "transparency" is a metaphor that defines a number of possible phenomena. What is being made transparent, to whom, how? If transparency cures corruption, how does it do so? What is the pure state of integrity that is preserved by this visibility? Does transparency engender trust? What is seen and what is concealed in situations of transparency? This chapter explores one civic humanist response to these questions: Étienne de La Boétie's *Discours de la servitude volontaire* (*Discourse of*

Voluntary Servitude).[6] A classic in French political philosophy, this
sixteenth-century text has somehow fallen below the radar of the English-
speaking world.[7] La Boétie, famous friend of Montaigne and member of
the Parliament of Bordeaux, wrote a youthful paean to liberty arguing that
subjection to tyrants is the result of corruption—not primarily of the
tyrant, who is indeed corrupt, but of the subjects, who lose their desire for
liberty and equality and come instead to will their own subjection. The
story that he tells is of a human falling away from a natural, healthy condition of radical mutual transparency and civic equality to a corrupted condition of estrangement, inequality, and subjection. This chapter seeks to
highlight the manner in which La Boétie conceives of a healthy, uncorrupted political community as one in which there is complete mutual
transparency—but it is a transparency of a different sort than that with
which we are most familiar. My main purpose in reading La Boétie is to
draw out two competing conceptions of how members of a polity are
known to one another, two models of transparency: transparency as political friendship and transparency as mutual surveillance. These models are
mutually exclusive, and they have radically different effects on trust. Those
with civic republican sympathies would do well to consider La Boétie's
reflections on the links between mutual transparency and civic freedom.

An objection might well be raised at the outset, however: is this not a
question of comparing apples and oranges? On the one hand, I have spoken
of the desire for citizens to know what their governments are doing, and
on the other I have spoken of government surveillance of citizens. Surely
these are radically different phenomena that cannot be unified under one
general term "transparency." I argue, however, that they are intimately
linked. Indeed, the dialectic between trust transparency and surveillance
transparency is precisely that which is revealed in a reading of La Boétie.
To watch someone like a hawk—as Machiavelli had urged—is to foreclose
the capacity to watch him like a dove. Calls for transparency and openness
attempt to have things both ways; I intend to point out some social-
psychological trade-offs. In addition, I suggest that the view that one can
cultivate openness above and secrecy and privacy below requires a capacity
for constant compartmentalization of public and private disposition—a
compartmentalization that runs against the grain of classical civic republicanism. The battle between the two competing models of transparency that
I am highlighting here is ultimately a battle between competing conceptions
of the public good, and the social psychologies of trust and distrust are tied

to wider regime considerations, a fact that comes clearly into view when one engages with La Boétie and the classical traditions that so informed his analysis.

In many respects La Boétie represents an exception to the story of modern corruption discourse. A thoroughgoing humanist, La Boétie appealed directly to classical authorities invoking a teleological civic tradition. But—for reasons probably having to do both with the youthful exuberance of literary erudition as with his political circumstances, which were unpropitious for republican politics—he did not offer an account of the good or the political means of achieving it. La Boétie's notion of the good is a kind of radical transparency itself. But this relational ideal—mutual transparency as the good—is without positive content. The reader must fill in the blanks. In the following interpretation I propose to do so with elements from La Boétie's political-religious context and elements from the classical tradition to which he appealed. In so doing, I will be highlighting the ambivalences of this heady ideal.

The first section of the chapter outlines the relationship between tyranny and corruption in the *Discours*, pointing out the manner in which appeals to narrow self-interest keep people in a state of subjection and mutual enmity. The subsequent two sections outline the nature of the healthy Boétian community based on full mutual transparency, arguing that its greatest debt is to a classical conception of political friendship. Against some dominant interpretations of the *Discours*, I insist that La Boétie does offer a republican political ideal that, while vague on institutional details, entails extreme solidarity. The final section bolsters this interpretation and offers some significant reservations about La Boétie's stirring civic ideal by turning our attention to his late reflection on French confessional strife, the widely neglected 1561 *Mémoire sur la pacification des troubles*. I will argue that his call for a strict and violent reinstatement of confessional uniformity is not a complete volte-face but is intelligible in light of his insistence on radical solidarity—and it suggests that there is a high price to pay for extreme civic friendship. We will conclude with some reflections on the comparative utility of these competing models of transparency.

Systemic Corruption: Tyranny and the Bribe

The central civic humanist worry was about the corruption of *citizens* such that they neglect the public good; decadent individuals abandon their civic duties for personal ends inimical to free civic life. This leaves them prone to subjection. Étienne de La Boétie's attack on tyranny as a product of the corruption of citizens follows this humanist line quite closely. But the *Discours de la servitude volontaire*, widely referred to as the *Contr'un* (or "Against one"), equally appears to have a foot in many other camps: classical philosophy, modern state of nature theory, and even anarchism. A masterpiece of Renaissance rhetoric, the book's success lies in its fruitful ambiguities.

The question that La Boétie poses is the following: why do masses of people persist in obeying tyrants? Why would multitudes of reasonable beings obey a single individual who has no particular merit of which to speak and who even appears determined on courses of action that run counter to his subjects' most basic interests? It is particularly perverse that people would allow themselves to suffer a thousand cruelties "by neither a Hercules nor a Samson, but by one little manikin [*un seul hommeau*], who is most often the most cowardly and effeminate of the nation."[8] It cannot be that subjects are mere cowards, following tyrants because they fear for their lives; on the contrary, some show resolute courage in war, giving their lives for this very cretin who oppresses them. Why, then, do they obey? The entire essay's argument will flow from the manner in which La Boétie has phrased this question. For the essay's brilliance is to have posed this question at all; it was certainly a rhetorical coup in sixteenth-century France to make obedience to one's monarch appear to be an odd, unhealthy anomaly in need of explanation. Only someone steeped in classics—Cicero, Livy, Plutarch, Tacitus, Xenophon—could so pose the question as to make the very notion of servitude to a single ruler appear illegitimate from the outset. What is clearly implied in the question is the conclusion that La Boétie is going to draw: authority always derives from the consent—indeed, the *desire*—of the governed. People obey tyrants willingly. The real question is one of social psychology: why do people will such a strange thing?

The response is that people allow themselves to be tyrannized because they have become slavish. Servitude itself corrupts subjects—habituated to their condition, they no longer seek freedom. For, La Boétie argues, if people wish to be free, they need merely to stop obeying tyrants. But regrettably, people have lost that love of liberty that was so common among the ancients. La Boétie seeks to shake his readers, awakening them to their misfortune: "Poor, miserable, idiotic people, prejudiced toward your own harm, blind to your good," he harangues, why do you allow yourselves to be dominated? Tyrants are but little men with two arms, two eyes—"Where has he gotten all these eyes with which he spies on you if you haven't given them to him? How is it that he has so many hands with which to hit you unless he gets them from you?" (*OC*, 12–13). Subjects of tyrants are complicit in their own subjection.

The Payot paperback edition of the *Contr'un* bears the frontispiece from Hobbes's *Leviathan*. It is in some ways an apt image of La Boétie's claim that the power of the "one" is, in fact, the power of all who obey him. The "little man" who seems individually so contemptible is actually the head of a massive artificial man. La Boétie appears equally to be Hobbesian *avant la lettre* in conceiving of the sovereign's power as a product of his subjects' consent and the sum total of the subjects' power united. But La Boétie is, naturally, thoroughly anti-Hobbesian in decrying as tragic this loss of natural liberty. And if one can feel a certain civic republican thrill in this heady cry of liberty, one also can conceive of a sensible Hobbesian reluctance to break one's bonds. Indeed, La Boétie's suggestion that regaining one's liberty is perfectly easy—a mere question of wanting it and of ceasing to lend one's hand to one's own oppression—comes across as an unforgivable rhetorical excess. But La Boétie's account of our servitude is more complex than this, and the text is more than a mere exercise in humanist composition. While the beginning of the *Discours* offers an optimistic, empowering message, the later sections paint a bleak picture of group psychology.

The great question is, what makes a people will so perverse a thing as its own domination? The apparent paradox here is derived from the double manner in which La Boétie is considering his audience—they are at the same time collectivities and individuals. In brief, La Boétie's argument is that in the situation of subjection there is no true collectivity, hence no public-spiritedness; the state's power—the eyes with which it spies and the arms with which it strikes—is born of radically atomized individuals each in their own little way serving, through active participation or passive acquiescence, to buttress the power structure that is so inimical to liberty. People are co-opted into a system of servitude by being individually and collectively corrupted.

His story of collective corruption follows the typical civic humanist story of decadence undermining virtue. The emperors bribed the people collectively, intoxicating them with spectacles, coliseums, festivals, and other populist measures that made the people forget their subjection or come to think that the lack of freedom is in their best interests. Second, he argues that tyrants typically corrupt religion, turning the honest worship of God into a superstitious devotion to the tyrant's person. He quotes a passage from Virgil approvingly in which a sibyl suffers "cruel torments," "for wanting to imitate the thunder of the sky and the fire of Jupiter" (OC, 42), and he damns to hell contemporary kings who cultivate such superstitions in their people.[9]

But if the people are corrupted collectively through populism, luxury, and superstition, the main source of slavery, "the spring and the secret of domination" (OC, 44), is the system of individual corruption that the tyrant establishes. La Boétie describes a pyramidal power structure in which a small group of advisers, sharing in the tyrant's dissipate desires, join him in pillaging the public. They each have under their control a hundred clients who maintain the system for rank and profit; they, in turn, have the power of purse, places, and rank over their clients, and so on (OC, 45–46). The entire system reposes on the cultivation of a tyrannical/servile sensibility in people; they seek individual profit and the joy of possessing power themselves: "these lost souls . . . are happy to endure suffering in order to inflict it, not on the one who harms them, but on those who suffer like them" (OC, 48). This is the way in which people actively become their own enemies: they are charmed by the idea of wealth and power represented in the dominant figure of the king and his counselors—like moths seeking some inexplicable pleasure in the flame of the candle, they are drawn to that which destroys them (OC, 55).

Identifying with the source of repression, people make themselves its servants. They do not recognize that the system that they are reinforcing is merely the principle of piracy rendered political; the state becomes entirely dependent on the desire for domination and individual enrichment joined to a constant terror of losing not merely what they have gained, but their lives as well. La Boétie completes his treatise with a classically inspired tableau of horrors decrying as ephemeral the pleasures of the courtier, client, and tyrant. With a mixture of erudition and outrage, he illustrates the folly of accepting the tyrant's bribe and the dreadful uncertainty in which both the clients of the tyrant and the tyrant himself live. Simply put, the bribe is not worth it; the dependency of the patron-client relationship both habituates people to a slavish condition and renders their existence entirely precarious.

Nature, Community, and Communication

So far we have a familiar, classical picture of tyranny as a product of total corruption—a system in which servile people are entirely dependent on a chain of personal dependency in which the public is merely a source of wealth to be pillaged for private gain. This civic republican picture of corruption as a loss of civic virtue is fully consonant with our contemporary picture of corruption as patron-client networks preying on the public. And, indeed, La Boétie's description of the tyrannical state, in all its horrors, would not appear out of place in a description of twentieth- (and twenty-first-) century totalitarianisms and kleptocracies. Nor is its relevance limited to these extreme conditions—the phenomena described as the springs of tyranny are the types of social pathology (clientelism, state capture) that are central in any account of contemporary corruption.

If La Boétie is both classical in his allusions and in the philosophical sources, there is something surprisingly modern about his call for liberty: the *Discours* offers what appears to us to be an embryonic theory of the state of nature. Human beings, he argues, were made to be free. As children, we have a natural inclination and duty to follow our parents, but this is a mere preparation for adulthood when we can follow nothing but our own reason. And, he suggests, at some point in the past we lived in a condition of radical equality, in which each was free from domination.

The Rousseauian dimension of this is striking, and we might wonder whether La Boétie is pointing to some prehistoric condition akin to that found in the *Discourse on the Origins of Inequality*. Pierre Clastres suggests that La Boétie differs from Rousseau only in that La Boétie believes the original condition actually existed.[10] In Clastres's view, La Boétie wrote an anarchist text that envisaged a pre-political society, a society before the state, taken as an institution in which some rule over others. This is an influential reading, and one that has some textual justification, but it overlooks the examples of free societies to which La Boétie refers his readers: Sparta, republican Rome, and democratic Athens. (I hesitate to mention the nonhistorical example he gives, Plato's *Republic*. To laud the "liberty" in Plato's Kallipolis is surely a strange thing, and no clear explanation is offered in the text. We will return to this puzzle later.)

If a Spartan and an Athenian can be said to enjoy liberty, we can hardly conclude that the Boétian ideal is pre-political. It is not a "state of nature," understood as a pre-political society; it is a "natural" state, understood as a political system in which the human telos is realized. Far from being prehistorical, it is a historical reality one can encounter when one enters into discourse, by means of books, with Xenophon, Cicero, Aristotle, and Plutarch. But it is difficult to pin down precisely what type of rule he wishes to celebrate. Sparta is not Athens, after all. And if La Boétie appears to be the consummate democrat, he exhibits a thorough disdain for the demos, whom he thinks easily duped by populists. Equally perplexing is the question of whether La Boétie means to condemn princes in general, or whether the text merely attacks tyrants.[11] In some editions of the *Contr'un* one can read a clear distinction between the two: "There are three sorts of tyrants—*I speak of evil princes* [*mechans princes*]" (*OC*, 19; this variant is in the footnote, n. 41; italics mine). This qualifier, however, is widely considered to be a later insertion meant to water down the text's radical conflation of prince and tyrant. If the Aristotelian conceptual distinction between a king and a tyrant is never questioned in the text, La Boétie clearly suggests that it is difficult to see "anything public in a regime where everything belongs to one" (*OC*, 3), and he articulates the standard republican concern that living under a good prince is bad for citizen virtue.[12] Ultimately, any attempt to determine the precise nature of the republican regime championed in the *Discours* is bound to be speculative; the text simply does not have enough determinative content to support a full political philosophy. But this is not the text's purpose; its purpose is to awaken a dormant passion for equality. It is meant to awaken the feelings of a *citizen*. To establish the precise institutional arrangements entailed by the ideal of nondomination requires us to go beyond this brief display of literary virtuosity to the sources animating La Boétie's passion. The burden of the philosophical duty is carried by the ancient philosophers and historians to whom La Boétie points. That is, while some readers (notably Claude Lefort) would have us understand this text's vagueness about regime types as indicating a break from the philosophical tradition, I suggest, on the contrary, that it is only comprehensible in light of a tradition of civic thought to which it points. Its antique references are not ornaments; they are signposts.

La Boétie claims that the love of liberty (defined as obeying nothing but one's own reason) is a natural human passion, and the strange condition of his fellows—their desire for their own subjection—is a corruption of their fundamental nature. This claim is far from self-evident, and La Boétie defends it with several arguments that hinge on his readers' aversion to slavery. But ultimately his case rests on a teleological claim: nature has made us for the *purpose* of friendship and mutual aid. "Our nature is such that the common duties of friendship make up a great part of the course of our life" (*OC*, 4). Friendship requires equality and the absence of compulsion, things that are incompatible with a situation of subjection. "Nature, the minister of God, the governess of men, has made us all in the same form, and, as it appears, of the same mold, in order that we may all know each other [*de nous entreconnoistre*] as companions, or rather, as brothers" (*OC*, 15). Friendship is our natural telos, and because friendship requires a degree of equality and reciprocity, the subjection of some to others is unnatural. Inequalities in talents and strengths exist, of course, but they exist that we might use them to help each other, not to dominate over one another. Most important, we were made to *know* one another ("de nous entre-connaitre tous pour compagnons"): "this good mother [nature] gave us all the earth for a home, and lodged us all in the same house, made us all on the same model in order that each might be able to be mirrored in another, and recognize ourselves in the other; for she gave us this great present of the voice and the word [*la parole*] in order that we might better be acquainted and fraternal, and that we might make, by the common and mutual declaration of our thoughts a communion of our wills" (*OC*, 16). Language is not the essentially human trait because it enables us to discuss the just and the unjust (as in Aristotle, *Politics* 1253a10); language is essential to our nature because it is the manner with which we become *transparent* to one another. With the capacity to express our wills, we can not only make promises (a preoccupation of later social contractarians), but we can *know* one another.

It is important not to mistake this for a proto-Hobbesian claim. La Boétie writes, "What makes a friend certain of the other is the knowledge he has of his integrity" (*OC*, 53). The Hobbesian trusts his fellow citizen's word because the sword of the sovereign, established by mutual consent, is there to back it up. Such a situation is the antithesis of La Boétie's ideal: "between evil people, when they gather together, there is a conspiracy and not a companionship; they do not love one another, but fear one another; they are not friends, but accomplices" (*OC*, 53–54). Hobbesian human beings are naturally distrustful of others and can attain confidence only under the overawing sword. The very existence of sovereignty is due to individuals' fearing one another. La Boétie is suggesting that we are naturally gregarious and that it is the artifice of subjection that makes us mutually distrustful.

La Boétie speaks of our natural friendship as something that is both philosophically and temporally prior to servitude: it is both an Aristotelian final cause and a real historical condition. People can be habituated to servitude, much as horses can be habituated to the bit, but this is an unnatural condition and a corruption of their original state. He laments (in a phrase whose Rousseauian overtones have misled modern readers into identifying La Boétie's nature with a *pre-political* historical moment): "What evil occurrence it was that could so denature man, the only creature truly born to live freely [*franchement*], such that he lost his memory of his original condition and his desire to regain it?" (*OC*, 19).

One source of our initial fall is, paradoxically, our natural penchant for friendship itself. Because our capacity for friendship draws us to and makes us grateful to virtuous people, we have a tendency to accord respect and authority to benefactors that can slip ever so dangerously into servitude (*OC*, 4). We thus tend to seek out our own domestication—we so easily slip from a rational obedience to outright servitude. It does not take long for people to thus become habituated to servitude and to lose their memory of equality and liberty. Thus, the people La Boétie insists on browbeating for their servile natures are in a sense not responsible for their condition—like fallen man afflicted with original sin, they are both inculpated and exculpated. But if La Boétie thinks the mass of people can be domesticated and, in a Machiavellian sense, lose their civic *virtù*, he insists equally that there are always some individuals in whom the yearning for liberty is strong (*OC*, 29–30). Custom—habituation to servitude—denatures people, but it never entirely drowns out nature's voice. What prevents these people from acting is their solitude. And their solitude is ensured by eliminating the means of communication.

The sovereign closes down communication in two ways. First, he prevents the free communication of ideas. La Boétie, the enthusiastic humanist, knew the thrill of—and the radical political inspiration in—reading about ancient liberty.[13] (This is precisely why Hobbes would later warn his readers about the dangers of allowing young people to read classic texts.)[14] By barring access to texts, the tyrant isolates people in their own time such that they can no longer imagine anything better outside of it.

But it is not enough to erase communication with tradition; one must also erase any form of solidarity. The final isolation is achieved by preventing communication between subjects:

> The zeal and affection of those who kept, in spite of the times, their
> devotion to liberty [*la franchise*], however great they are in number,

remains without effect because they do not know one another: under the tyrant they are entirely deprived of the liberty [*la liberté*] to do, to speak, and almost to think: they become all isolated in their imaginations [*tous singuliers en leurs fantaisies*]. Thus, Momus, the God of Mockery, was not joking when he lamented of the man made by Vulcan that he had had not placed a little window in the heart such that one might see the man's thoughts." (*OC*, 31)[15]

This isolation is not merely the means by which people are kept in bondage; it is itself the negation of their essential communicative nature. Momus's lament is a fair one—if we were automatically transparent to one another we could not be so easily divided. But we require speech to reveal ourselves to others, and kings have the power to bridle the tongue.

The greatest corruption for La Boétie, then, is the destruction of our capacity to *know* one another. We are rendered atomized, isolated individuals: our natural penchant for communication and friendship is broken down. "Abuse of public office for private gain" is the entire modus operandi of this regime—public office exists *for* private gain because there is no longer a *public* good to speak of. Indeed, there is no *peuple*, but merely a collection of separated individuals spying on one another. Hence the enormous difficulty involved in renouncing one's servitude: when La Boétie tells his readers that they are responsible for their own oppression he is addressing the people as people, that very collectivity whose existence depends upon reciprocal knowledge of one another's character. He may berate the cowardly people as much as he will—there's no "people" to address, for they have been rendered atomized individuals, prevented from mutual self-revelation. In the condition of subjection, rare are the instances of friendship—each is to the others a terrifying specter, an eye watching their every act, an arm waiting to strike.

Transparency and Corruption

Let us notice what a fine contrast this makes to the Hobbesian story about human nature. In the Hobbesian world, we are naturally strangers. The only way to bring us together is to force words—the windows on our wills—to stay in place. Both the keeping of our word and the keeping of words become the duty of the sovereign, whose sword guarantees contracts and establishes the limits of our rights. The Hobbesian subject is corrupted when his mind is corrupted—he fails to see that justice and obedience are in his interests. This is a result of excessive freedom of communication and the dangerously unclear use of concepts such as the ancient use of the term "liberty," or dangerous religious opinions, the product of aberrant, uncontained priestcraft. Rational clarity and mutual transparency are produced when the meaning of words and the connection between words and wills are firmly fixed by the force of the sovereign's sword. In nature we are strangers; in the commonwealth, under the authority of an absolute and arbitrary sovereign, we can finally know one another. The *Discours* gives the inversion of this teaching—it is the sovereign that breaks down our natural knowledge of one another, thus breaking apart our solidarity. Much depends here on their contrasting views of language: for Hobbes, language is artifice; for La Boétie, it is natural. The art directors at Payot ought to have printed *Leviathan*'s frontispiece in photo negative.

Let us push this comparison further by considering the Foucauldian complaint about the link between transparency and control. In a sense, the Hobbesian project is about both establishing transparency through force and establishing force through transparency. But it is a limited transparency: our wills become transparent to one another because we state them in commonly established terms and the law makes sure that our wills conform to our words. The law (and the sword upholding it) thus places fetters on our acts and words (for speaking is an act), thereby eliminating the terrible uncertainty that a state of anarchy engenders. But in the deepest recesses of our minds, we remain impenetrable. This is important, for one of the most important and salutary consequences of Hobbesian solipsism is that the holy inquisition is thereby rendered illogical. Acts of hand and tongue must be regulated; the dark recesses of our thoughts are no more visible than they are governable. But the commonwealth makes a community with words, thereby making us predictable to one another.

But if we attend to La Boétie, we will question the cost of this attempt to pin down words and wills with swords. Atomized individuals purchase their security with subjection, but conformity in word and deed must be assured by surveillance. Hobbes himself wrote of the necessity of spies: "For *discoverers* to Ministers of State, are like the beames of the Sunne to the humane soule . . . and therefore are they no lesse necessary to the preservation of the State, than the rayes of the light are to the conservation of man."[16] But La Boétie is suggesting that this surveillance model is inimical to mutual self-revelation. Either we are all transparent to one another—through friendship—or we are made the object of a tyrannical gaze. On La Boétie's analysis, the insecurity of the ruler's position leads to an unquenchable interest in the souls of subjects. No ruler can assume that the subject means what the subject says; no subject can trust the insecure ruler. In the condition of radical hierarchy, the tyrant must deploy the most invasive techniques of surveillance—the many eyes that spy. Of course, this is never entirely possible—hence the ruler's perpetual unease and perpetual resort to violent threat and example (horrors La Boétie describes with flourish).

So we find ourselves with two radically opposed conceptions of political health as transparency—Hobbesian surveillance and Boétian disclosure. The surveillance model, in its Hobbesian form, is content to rest on the surface of things (you can think whatever you want); the Boétian suggestion is that this is not possible—the psychology that reigns in such a situation of inequality will make the ruler perpetually distrustful and ever in greater search of certainty. Nor does La Boétie suggest that it is desirable, for it undermines the *entre-connaissance* that he thinks is the hallmark of free social existence—note, indeed, that this is a level of mutual knowledge that Hobbes thought impossible. What I'd like to argue is that there is a tradeoff between these ideal types, transparency through surveillance and transparency through reciprocal self-revelation. When we all lend our eyes to the sovereign, spying on each other, we occlude the possibility of friendship.

This leads me to the much debated question of La Boétie's ideal regime. Claude Lefort tells us that the *Discours* is clearly a response not merely to tyranny, but to all principalities,[17] and it is difficult to disagree with this assessment given the necessary inequalities that exist in a monarchy, and indeed in any form of hierarchy that does not involve some sort of shared ruling and being ruled in turn. The implication for Lefort is that the text breaks entirely with the traditional Aristotelian distinction between corrupt and uncorrupted regimes. Some have gone so far as to see in La Boétie's vague natural condition of liberty a ground not for a republican political project, but rather for the radical revolt against politics itself, against the fact of domination that exists in all states. Eric Voegelin sees this as a weakness, arguing that La Boétie's spirit of revolt represents the quintessential example of courage without wisdom; a similar claim about his institutional vagaries is made with more celebratory intent in Miguel Abensour and Marcel Gauchet's declaration that La Boétie's revolt forces us "à penser la liberté contre le pouvoir," that is, to think of liberty as the antithesis of power itself.[18] At the same time, it is difficult to reconcile this with his praise of Sparta (or yet of Plato's *Republic*). Lefort argues that while La Boétie mentions these ancient (and ideal) cities he fails to identify the good regime precisely because he is claiming that all instantiations of political unity, all regimes, manifest this perverse desire to be dominated.[19] If La Boétie addresses himself to a *peuple* and attributes agency to a *peuple*, his back and forth on the collective and yet plural nature of this entity is intended to undermine the view of a unified people.[20] For Lefort, La Boétie is offering a stark warning about the desire for a unity that erases the distinctions between people: it is this "singular" that so bewitches and "enchants" us.[21] It is in La Boétie's appeal to our linguistic nature that we learn both of our unity and of our separation: "When we think of language, we think already of the political, delivered from the illusion of the One."[22]

Philosophically fruitful as Lefort's use of La Boétie is, I suggest that it is not entirely faithful to La Boétie, being largely a product of Lefort's project of illuminating the symbolic form that mediates between the (plural) people and their political unity. In the *Discours*, language does, indeed, provide us with a means of uniting disparate individuals. But that unity is an extreme unity. According to the *Discours*, the fact of language demonstrates that nature "has shown in all things that it does not merely want to make us all united, but all one" (*OC*, 16; ne vouloit pas tant nous faire tous unis que tous uns). Lefort's take on this phrase is the following: "to affirm that the destiny of men is to be not merely *tous unis*, but *tous uns* is to bring the social relation back to communication and the reciprocal expression of agents; it is to recognize as a principle the difference of one from another, and to let us understand that this difference is only reducible in the imagination, and at the same time . . . it is to denounce the lie of the governors who make of the union of their subjects or that of citizens the sign of the good society."[23] This is a rather large *sous-entendu*, and it stems from a line that is capable of being read in a different manner. Surely La Boétie's claim that nature did not "did not want merely to unify us, but to make us all one" could be read as a call to *radical* solidarity of the sort that Lefort thinks illegitimate.[24]

For Lefort, the name of the "one" conjures up an image of a massive power that the people, perversely, desire. La Boétie, he tells us, is breaking from traditional political philosophy in that he is not offering any conception of an uncorrupted polity—we shouldn't try to fill in the blanks with utopian images and collapse society into politics. I do not wish to dissuade readers from attending to Lefort's reflections, but I would like to suggest that La Boétie was proposing precisely what Lefort wants to warn us about: a radical civic unity. This is a republicanism that has its origins in ancient philosophy. The text's vagaries about institutional matters are due to its pointing outside of itself to a classical literary tradition (precisely the tradition tyrants wish to silence). The free people who existed prior to the great descent into servitude were free precisely because they were able to establish radical solidarity through mutual transparency. The tyrannical regime corrupts their souls because it makes them incapable of friendship and thus incapable of solidarity. The artificial unity that tyranny creates is violent and inherently exploitative: it exists at the expense of solidarity. Lefort has rightly noticed that there is something curious in La Boétie's addressing of a unified *peuple* at all, but we are not thereby to understand that the unified "people" is a dangerous fiction or that the text cannot conceive of any "free people." The *Discours* is arguing, rather, that domination has been rendered possible because the "people" has been broken down into a collection of individuals. La Boétie is saying to the *peuple*, "you each individually feel the weight of this domination to which you each individually contribute." It is as if the will of all runs counter to the general will: the "you" is the collective subject that, could it will collectively, would never will its own subjection, but because people will separately, each in his own cocoon, the wills combine to support an insufferable condition.[25] The ruler, in his turn, is rendered more than the weak little individual that he is: he is transformed into an image of power.

The type of unity that Lefort would have us see in La Boétie's ideal is one of unity in difference. The nature of language, for Lefort, entails differentiation—by claiming that our mutual communication of our natures requires the mediation of language, La Boétie is implicitly arguing for human plurality against the dangerous fiction of unity. Lefort's is an Arendtian ideal, in which people make themselves known to each other in great speech acts in the civic realm. Hannah Arendt celebrates respect, which, in distinction to love, does not erase the difference between people: "Respect, not unlike the Aristotelian *philia politikē*, is a kind of 'friendship' without intimacy and without closeness; it is a regard for the person from the distance which the space of the world puts between us."[26] But, however accurate this is as a description of Aristotelian political friendship, it is not the model that La Boétie offers; rather, he offers something closer to a perfect Aristotelian friendship of virtue. He writes, "Friendship is a sacred word, it is a holy thing. It is never found except between people of quality, and it only is achieved through mutual esteem. It is nourished not as much by good actions, but by good living." But what most cements friendship is, as we have already noted, "the knowledge that he has of the other's integrity" (*OC*, 53). There is an epistemological element to this friendship. We can see how appropriate it was for Montaigne to want to preface his publication of La Boétie's article with a paean to friendship heavily inspired by Aristotle. Montaigne cited approvingly Aristotle's view that friendship is the preeminent concern for legislators,[27] and he celebrated a kind of virtue friendship that went perhaps further than Aristotle would have wanted, bordering on the complete effacing of differences between friends: "In the friendship of which I speak, they [the souls of the friends] mix and confound one in the other in a mixture so total that they erase and can no longer find the seam that has joined them."[28] This is a version of what Aristotle called "perfect friendship," though it posits much more unity than Aristotle would have approved of (recall his insistence on heterogeneity in *Politics* 1261a). Indeed, Aristotle himself might be seen as closer to Lefort's view that language presupposes heterogeneity, insofar as it is that which permits us to discuss the just and the unjust and to deliberate together (*Politics* 1253a). La Boétie sounds even closer to the civic ideal of Plato's Kallipolis, where the guardians all say "mine" and "not mine" to the same things (*Republic* 462c). For all the rarity that Aristotle and Montaigne—and even La Boétie—see in virtue friendship, for all that it seems to describe the unity of great souls, the *Discours* treats it as the dominant principle in the pre-servile condition. The ideal is one of extreme unity through *entre-connaissance*, where mutual beneficence is a product of mutual knowledge of one another's integrity; it is this very knowledge that is undermined in the tyrannical condition.

This mutual transparency is a product of a radical openness to one another—an openness that requires language as a medium and equality as a condition.[29] That is, La Boétie shares Momus's complaint—since we cannot see one another's hearts, the only way to feel confident in our neighbors is if they reveal themselves to us. Pointing to the linguistic medium of our mutual recognition does, as Lefort suggests, imply an assumption about plurality, but this is a plurality that La Boétie thinks can be overcome with radical reciprocity. Nature "has tried with every means to tighten and solidify the knot of our alliance and society" (*OC*, 16). Such a bond cannot occur in conditions of domination; it requires equality. Equality and unity are inseparable; we are offered here a politics of friendship that ultimately transcends division, and thus that runs counter the Lefortian and Arendtian project of preserving plurality.

In short, La Boétie's *Discours* offers us, in its ideal types of the tyrannical and free conditions, two social psychologies, one based upon mutual knowledge and trust—a version of classical civic friendship—and another based upon mutual suspicion, where each is a possible enemy to each, and all are held in the chain of shortsighted self-interest; for the ignorant part of the people have a tendency to be corrupted and learn to love the very chains that bind them—because they are no longer in a condition of being able to understand civic friendship. They become "distrustful of those who love them" (*OC*, 36). They spy on one another because their natural mutual transparency has been broken down.

Friendship and the Pacification of Troubles

There is much in the *Discours* that can stir the heart of the modern civic republican or egalitarian. La Boétie's commitment to a generous form of civic friendship based on equality and mutual recognition is extremely appealing, but its utopian dimensions might appear fanciful. When political thinkers seek to transform politics into friendship, they generally face the charge of obscuring or eluding the political itself. We can picture a knowing Florentine smirking at this attempt to found a republic on affection. But if the *Discours* is a text that warms our hearts as it raises our eyebrows, what are we to make of this parlementaire's 1561 *Mémoire sur la pacification des troubles*, offering political advice in the face of violence between Huguenots and Catholics? For here, La Boétie—ever faithful to his king and church—argued that the tolerationist policy favored by Catherine de Medici and her chancellor Michel de l'Hôpital was inacceptable for political reasons, and he urged a two-pronged strategy of accommodation and repression. Like many Catholic humanists, La Boétie was convinced that serious reforms were needed in the church—ecclesiastical corruption, he thought, not doctrinal questions, had been the main basis for the popular appeal of the Protestant cause. But he was also convinced that tolerance was an untenable policy and that those Protestants who had manifested violence towards the king's law should be violently suppressed and a bloody example should be made of the leaders. "You would be amazed to see to what degree, after this terror, the people will be more tractable, easier to control, and more easily contented."[30] It is clear from his condemnation of the counterproductive efforts to convert people with the sword that he would not have supported the Saint Bartholomew's Day Massacre (1572) that came eleven years later, but his advocacy of terror here seems remarkably like the type of behavior we might expect from the tyrant who is so thoroughly denounced in the *Discours*. One almost wonders how both texts could be the work of the same person.

One response to this tension would be to suggest that La Boétie was no longer the same person: in contrast to the *Discours*, the *Mémoire* is the work of a mature man directly implicated in the political life of his province. Certainly he was young (La Boétie was thirty-one at the time, but this was a very ripe thirty-one); La Boétie, having spent the previous decade serving as a counselor at the Parliament of Bordeaux, was not the enthusiastic student of the *Discours* writing odes to the liberty he found in classic literature. Another possibility would be the suggestion, which has recently resurfaced after a long period of being considered disproven, that the *Discours* was actually penned by Montaigne—the case for this claim is made by several authors in the collected volume *Freedom over Servitude*.[31] This attribution, while based on a fair amount of conjecture, gains some plausibility when one notes the murky origin of the *Discours* and Montaigne's playful use of misdirection in the *Essais*. It remains, however, a suggestion that has not caught the imagination of the vast majority of La Boétie and Montaigne scholars.[32] One of the things that push these authors toward this interpretation is the apparent distance between the *Discours* and the *Mémoire*. But I would like to suggest that the gulf between these two texts is not as great as one might think, even if it does somewhat reflect both the distance between youthful extravagance and mature cynicism and between theory and practice. Without entirely reconciling the texts, I wish to suggest that the primary concern animating his advice in the *Mémoire* is equally that animating the *Discours*: the importance of mutual transparency and social unity.

La Boétie argued that the main causes of popular Protestantism were not the subtle theological matters that preoccupied Luther, Zwingli, or Calvin, but merely the abuses of the church and the comparative probity of the reform leaders. The second cause of the troubles had been the obstinate and violent response to this cry for reform. Trying to root out unbelief with violence backfired, causing people to flock to the new church not only for its tempting novelty but also out of a sense of respect for martyrs. Things had thus been allowed to fester to such an extent that there were effectively two forms of religion being established in the realm. In response, he championed what in England would later be called "comprehension," a type of doctrinal compromise that would prevent the church from fracturing by weakening the main causes of division. (Somewhat naively, he gave some theological and sacramental propositions that he thought would be widely acceptable, and he proposed some ways of papering over divisions.) At the same time, those engaged in violent sedition must be punished in an exemplary fashion. For if it had been foolish of Kings François I and Henri II to pursue heresy with fire and sword, it was equally foolish for Catherine de Medici to tolerate the establishment of two churches within the state.

Note that while La Boétie offered an anti-tolerationist teaching, he did not support any type of holy inquisition. On the contrary, his call for the moderation of church doctrine derived from his commitment to respecting (within limits) Protestant consciences. Indeed, as Malcolm Smith has pointed out, La Boétie thought that one was *not* duty-bound to obey one's sovereign in matters of religion.[33] Nor ought the sovereign to attempt to enforce opinion with fire and sword. Aside from being a tactical error (*Mémoire*, 43), it is simply useless to try to burn one's way into someone's mind. La Boétie displays the awareness of the observation, most associated with Hobbes, that one can only legislate deeds, not thoughts. (Though the *sous-entendu* here is always that thoughts will follow practice.)

But why should religious diversity be so untenable? Some of La Boétie's responses are typical of his age. Like many of his contemporaries, he did not regard tolerance as a virtue but rather perceived policies of toleration to be mere cease-fires, and not real peace (*Mémoire*, 57). And like many, La Boétie had difficulty countenancing the idea of allowing falsity to flourish—and he was no different from the bulk of his fellows in thinking it untenable that truth and falsehood should both have rights (and his *Mémoire* suggests a naive simplicity on the nature of theological truth that is surprising from one so close to Montaigne).[34] But La Boétie's intolerance was largely based on a political concern about the effects of religious division on social unity. He wrote, "No other dissention is so great or so dangerous as that that comes out of religion. It separates citizens, neighbors, friends, parents, brothers, the father from his children, the husband from the wife; it breaks alliances, parentage, marriages, the inviolable rights of nature, and penetrates to the depths of hearts to rip out friendships and plant irreconcilable hatreds" (*Mémoire*, 49). Now, he was particularly

worried about how this division makes the state an easy target for its enemies.[35] But he did not say that this condition of division is inconsistent
with obedience to a king: "it is still possible that in the face of all of this it
could nonetheless not remove anything from the obedience a subject owes
to his sovereign" (*Mémoire*, 49). No, indeed. For division, we know, is no
enemy of obedience—we have seen that divisions are exploited by tyrants,
and this is precisely what makes this division so inviting to invaders.[36] Religious divisions have split the body politic, leaving "a dismembered republic" (*Mémoire*, 44),[37] where there is "a near universal hatred and ill will
between the subjects of the king" (*Mémoire*, 36).

His call for uniformity—indeed, his incipient Gallicanism, for La Boétie
intimated that the French church should reform itself—was political rather
than theological. La Boétie was expressing the view, quite commonly held,
that religious pluralism would lead to the demise of social cohesion.
Implausible as this seems to us, it speaks to a widespread sixteenth-century
fear, felt by many who had no necessarily strong views on the theological
details of salvation by works or faith, that the reformers' breaking away
from the church entailed the destruction of all social bonds. To understand
this point, it is important to remember the centrality of the church in
ordering and facilitating communal life. Attending mass was widely held to
be something requiring a clean, repentant soul—to take Eucharist one must
have reconciled with one's enemies; similarly, the pax, or "kiss of peace,"
one of the more important lay experiences in the mass, offered a powerful
experience of neighborly reconciliation and purification. As Virginia Reinburg writes of sixteenth-century worship, "For lay congregants, the mass
was less a ceremonial representation of eucharistic doctrine or Christ's original sacrifice than a sacred rite uniting them with God, the Church, *and
each other*."[38] The common practice of worshipping was not merely unifying in the way that national festivals or cultural activities are unifying; it
was conceived of as itself being the glue that held communities together,
and there was a fear that if people worshipped separately they were not
merely endangering their own salvation, but were breaking the social bond.
Simply put, it was thought to be essential for *everyone* to come together
repeatedly, reconciling any differences through the kiss of peace, forgiving
one another their trespasses, reconnecting on a weekly basis with the source
of communal trust.

In arguing for the civic importance of uniform worship, La Boétie was
not offering anything novel but was rather giving voice to a commonplace

opinion. But I wish to stress the connection between this view and his earlier claim about the importance of mutual transparency for social cohesion and liberty. Religious uniformity, like language, serves as a medium for the mutual revelation of our character to one another. That is, uniform public worship serves to cultivate civic trust and mutual transparency. To split this institution was to undermine trust and friendship.

This is a view with a heritage in the sources La Boétie and Montaigne so admired. The classical opposite of civic friendship is, naturally, not confessional strife, but rather faction and division of opinion. Cicero, in his treatise on friendship, has Laelius argue that "friendship is in fact nothing other than a community of views on all matters human and divine, together with goodwill and affection," and he exclaims, "What house is so well established, what state is so strong that it may not be entirely torn to pieces by hatred and division?"[39] "Concord," Aristotle insisted, "also appears to be a feature of friendship." This concord (*homonoia*, otherwise translated as "harmony" or sometimes "unanimity)" is not the unanimity of opinions about factual matters that are not causes of mutual concern, but about the common itself: "a city is said to be in concord when [its citizens] agree on what is advantageous, make the same decision, and act on their common resolution" (*Nicomachean Ethics* 1167a). This is the nature of "political friendship" (1167b). The opposite of this unanimity is faction, discord over the nature of justice and who ought to rule. Aristotelian civic friendship is possible between good people—hence it has an element of virtue friendship to it. Those who are not good "cannot be in concord, except to a slight degree, just as they can be friends only to a slight degree; for they seek to overreach in benefits [to themselves] . . . the result is that they are in conflict, trying to compel one another to do what is just, but not wishing to do it themselves" (1167b). Note how these two conditions appear to mirror respectively La Boétie's natural (free) and unnatural (servile) conditions in the *Discours*: the one condition entails mutual transparency, the other entails distrust and exploitation. Now, I do not propose here to answer the thorny question of whether Aristotle's *philia politikē* is a friendship of virtue or utility (it appears to share elements of both). What I wish to suggest is that something akin to—or even more extreme than—Aristotle's ideal is the inspiration for the political friendship that La Boétie thought the defining feature of the political condition that accords with human nature.

It is in this context that we might understand his perplexing reference in the *Discours* to the "liberty of Plato's Republic." Is it possible that La

Boétie did not throw this in as a mere learned reference, but rather that he intended his readers to consider the Platonic unity created by the strict control over the stories told about the divine? But this raises a significant tension. How can La Boétie, on the one hand, condemn both the censorship that deprives people of ancient texts and the political usurpation of religion and yet support a policy of civil religion?[40] First, we can dispose easily of the usurpation of religion—there is no question of kings pretending to any divine power here. La Boétie's concern is not to sneak supernatural justification into the justification of rule. The civic interest in church unity is due to its importance in achieving communal unity. Put differently, it is not about ideological legitimation of the ruling order. The Machiavellian desire to invest citizens with fervent, superstitious civic piety is not the desire animating La Boétie. Indeed, the dispute is not primarily about doctrinal opinion: "one is greatly mistaken if one thinks that so many men have separated from us out of a mere difference of opinion" (*Mémoire*, 64). It is the exterior forms of worship that most offend normal people, and it is here where common ground must be found. La Boétie expressed optimism that these could be sufficiently altered that most people would think matters solved—particularly if preachers are prevented from stirring up divisions. Thus, when he insisted that once the church was reformed no one be permitted—on pain of death—to preach or administer sacraments outside of the church, it was not because of the theological content of the preaching, but because this was the creation of a separate church, which split the population into hostile camps (*Mémoire*, 89).

Common worship, like a common language, serves as a means of keeping people open to one another and cultivating social trust. La Boétie's religious intolerance is based on the view that confessional unity is the minimal condition of civic friendship. But there is also a paradox here. It is as if a dirty secret is let loose in the *Mémoire*: mutual transparency, the most natural thing of all, requires some artifice to maintain it, a civic religion; but the means required to maintain this might well lead us back to the surveillance society. For, after all, how else would one prevent the type of ecclesiastical splitting if one did not engage in surveillance of some sort?

The trust and mutual self-revelation that La Boétie thought to be the natural human telos were the products of a political project—just as people could be habituated to obedience, so too could they be habituated to liberty and mutual trust. But this requires institutions, and his mature political reflections led him to the disquieting suggestion that trust required ecclesiastical uniformity, even going so far as to grant the king rights to reorganize the church in order to preserve this source of mutual trust. Again, this is not a question of doctrinal content, but rather the maintenance of a common cultural practice that, like language, permits us to overcome the problem of not being able to see into one another's hearts. But the business of achieving "natural" friendship of a free society entails habituation through well-constructed laws and institutions. Lycurgus, noted La Boétie in the *Discours*, "with his laws and his police [i.e., his social order] nourished and made so well the Lacedaemonians, that each and every one of them would rather have died a thousand deaths than recognize any other lord than reason and the law" (*OC*, 25). Note that Lycurgus did not merely habituate Spartans to love liberty—he *made* them what they were; he constituted them as a people.

Conclusion: *Homonoia* as the Medium of Transparency

In exposing the distance between the type of mutual knowledge entailed in civic friendship and the closed, watchful condition of the tyrannical client-patron network, La Boétie's *Discours* can be read as powerful indictment of the surveillance society. The ubiquity of cameras, audits, wiretaps, whistle-blowers, "vigilant" citizens inquiring into the nature of their neighbor's piety—all these thousand eyes that seek to open up the soul have the effect of closing us up within ourselves. For all that they can insure some degree of conformity in outward behavior, these are systems that undermine the very unity they seek to create—people are corrupted by the surveillance society, rendered incapable of trust and more likely to seek out opportunities for private gain at public expense. This is akin to shining a searchlight into a dark room—one side of the objects within appears illuminated, but they cast the darkest shadows behind them. But if we allow our eyes to be accustomed to the dark, the objects in the room will disclose themselves to us. The nature of our neighbors will be disclosed to us if we allow ourselves to listen. We are truly transparent to one another when we are friends. Reading La Boétie alerts us to the fact that there is an essential conceptual difference between transparency through mutual surveillance and transparency through mutual friendship. And when comparing the ideals it is surely difficult not to find appealing La Boétie's *philia* both in principle and in practice—is one's relationship with one's neighbors rendered more secure through friendship, or through having video cameras trained on their front door? In the attempt to cultivate civic virtue through transparency it is worthwhile paying attention to what manner of openness we wish to cultivate. For La Boétie, to be in a position of having to watch one another like hawks is to be already in a corrupted condition.

But surely, it will be objected, this surveillance model is only disturbing when it comes from above. If there is sufficient surveillance from below ("sousveillance," as the ugly neologism has it) things will balance out and civic life will not be allowed to erode completely. Certainly, this is an element of the Machiavellian project—the constantly tensed muscles of the plebs and their perpetual distrust of the patricians assure the preservation of free civic life. But such a stance might come at a price, and if the emerging social science literature on the utility of generalized trust is any indication, it may be a price too high for the benefit it confers.[41] It is a commonplace observation that corruption undermines trust in institutions; the reverse is also true—lack of trust is corrupting. The two models of transparency we have drawn from La Boétie are ideal types—no country or organization can be founded on total surveillance, nor yet on pure friendship. My point is that it is important to reflect on the trade-offs between these two psychological dispositions of friendship and distrust.[42]

This is not to suggest that we can cure corruption simply by according blind trust to the powerful. I must emphasize that the key to La Boétie's republican ideal of mutual *entre-connaissance* is some form of civic equality—radical inequalities are incompatible with friendship and trust. Attempts to undermine oppressive networks of political clientelism need to attend to the regime contexts in which such networks thrive. That is to say, civic republican conceptions of corruption as the loss of civic virtue and the increase of dependence are not mere anachronisms in contemporary debates about corruption, in spite of the irretrievable nature of the ancient polis. The importance of attending to inequality should not be forgotten by those who seek purely cultural determinants of corruption; if the reader will permit the Putnam reference, La Boétie is not merely saying that subjects of tyrants are bowling alone, but that they are pushing and shoving for access to the bowling alley. La Boétie does not spell out the nature and extent of the equality that he thinks congenial to trust and friendship, but he is insistent that friendship is based "in equality, where there is never a clash, where all is always equal" (*OC*, 54).[43] It is worthwhile for students of political corruption to give greater attention to the effects of material inequality and zero-sum competition than is often done.

But if we are thereby offered a powerful defense of equality and friendship, we are also apprised of their great difficulty. The radical virtue friendship that underwrites La Boétie's natural ideal is presented by Montaigne and Aristotle as the rarest of things. Indeed, one wonders if one can ever even approach such a complete *entre-connaissance*; after all, as a reading of Montaigne himself would remind us, it is hard enough to know ourselves.[44] What guidance can this ideal—this radicalization of a lost classical vision of harmony—offer us in our quest to render political life nonexploitative? This goes beyond the administrative studies' question of how to cultivate trust in large bureaucratic institutions: it challenges us to think about citizenship anew, all the while raising disquieting questions about the relationship between pluralism and equality. Can we think of nonexclusionary forms of social interaction that nonetheless retain the functions that La Boétie ascribed to the church? We are fortunately at some distance from the communalist view of uniform public worship as a necessary condition of social harmony, but a wider question remains open about what types of uniformity are required for *philia politikē* and whether these forms of uniformity recreate the exclusions and homogeneity that have come to be associated with the liberty of the ancients.

CHAPTER 5

Corruption, Social Change, and the Constitution

The Case of Viscount Bolingbroke

In the previous two chapters we examined corruption and purity as they emerged in two competing modern republicanisms that offered quite distinct models of human depravity. But those two visions do not in the least exhaust the possible ways in which the language of virtuous freedom and servile corruption can decline. In this chapter, we will advance two centuries to another era in which the language of corruption had pride of place. The reader should not take this as a sign that the intervening time is without interest—recall, we are not pursuing a history of the concept in all its literary and discursive byways, but an analysis of what I am arguing constitutes distinct and important deployments of the term that have contemporary analogues. The eighteenth century is a particularly fertile ground for corruption discourse. It abounds with anxieties over standing armies, credit, debt, and decadence, giving birth to endless tirades against the age and not a few nostalgic glances toward ancient Rome, a fact that led J. G. A. Pocock to make a number of important claims about the affinities with Renaissance civic humanism. But eighteenth-century discourse contained a number of varieties, some of which are quite a long way from Florentine political thought.

The conception of corruption that we will examine in this chapter is one that could be politely (and somewhat imprecisely) termed "conservative." It has been impolitely (and somewhat more accurately) termed "nostalgic," but that predicate will need unpacking. Henry St. John, 1st Viscount Bolingbroke (1678–1751), was one of the most important corruption-mongers of the eighteenth century, and his treatment of the subject bears some similarity to several of the traditions we have canvassed. He certainly was a reader of Machiavelli, and he learned a great deal from the latter's insistence on the importance of the mixed regime. Yet he was equally influenced by the mirror-of-princes tradition, and his own foray into that genre evinces some of the naive moralism that we discussed in Chapter 2. Consider his direct appeal to the Machiavellian call for radical reform from a new prince. Having cited with approval Machiavelli's appeal to a prince who will bring a constitution back to its origins, Bolingbroke proceeded to suggest that the "patriot king" can, in a corrupt society, "easily to himself and without violence to his people, renew the spirit of liberty in their minds" by setting a good example and rewarding virtue.[1] One can hardly imagine a less Machiavellian moment. I would like to suggest that Bolingbroke is not best understood by linking him to the mirror-of-princes tract or to the Florentine political tradition, both of which he referenced. He is an example of the term being employed by a threatened elite decrying a shift in power. Corruption discourse here is the expression of an ideological objection to an unprecedented phenomenon, the modern bureaucratic fiscal state. To study Bolingbroke's deployment of the concept of corruption is to study a phenomenon that we have seen repeatedly in modernity as global commerce has altered traditional monopolies of hierarchy and influence.

Bolingbroke is an ideologically baffling creature: a free-thinking deist, sometime Jacobite, a raging partisan who disapproved of party, and a Francophile critical of excessive monarchical influence in England's mixed constitution (yet calling for a patriot king to restore virtue to his people), it is not surprising that so many have thought him little more than an opportunist. Yet there is a consistency to his jeremiads that is revelatory of an excluded elite grappling with the meaning of its exclusion and finding the cause in innovations reshaping the political landscape. For radical changes were afoot; the sociopolitical results of 1688 and the wars and commercial expansion were of such a nature as to raise serious worries about decline and decadence. The country developed a massive debt with the use of new financial institutions, its standing army grew drastically, as did its military engagements on the Continent, and a new unlanded wealth appeared to be holding sway over the traditional gentry. For Bolingbroke and the so-called "country" opposition, these changes were a corruption. Indeed, the threat to liberty was greater now than it had been under James II or Charles I. This corruption was both moral and political, and it began at the top: "friends of liberty see that the greatest masters of tyranny have judged the form, without the spirit, of free government more favourable to their schemes of oppression, than all the authority that absolute monarchy can give; and that they made an innovation in the form of their government on this very motive, and for this very purpose" (151). Corruption, innovation, and tyranny are three unholy sisters.

The early eighteenth-century explosion in accusations of corruption was a reaction to the systemic alterations in Britain's social and political fabric. The place of money in politics seemed inordinately high, and the ministry of Robert Walpole—Bolingbroke's inveterate enemy—was widely derided as the epitome of corruption. "Every man has his price," Walpole was reputed to have said, though his sympathetic biographers argue that he merely said of some of his enemies, "all *these* men have their price."[2] But it is more important that he was *thought* to have said that every man has his price. For the apoplectic opposition, only corruption could permit such a man as Walpole to reign for two decades. But what did the country opposition mean when they decried corruption? In this chapter we will see that their primary concern was with a shift in the locus of wealth and power—corruption then, as now, indicated abuse of the public for personal gain, but it had a wider, systemic aspect: it entailed a fundamental shift in the constitution. Bolingbroke—the most philosophically consistent opposition ideologist—deployed the term "corruption" to describe not only a kind of personal dependency indicating a lack of individual virtue and self-command, but equally a societal imbalance of power and property. I will suggest that there was a tension between the moral and institutional aspects of his argument.

Isaac Kramnick termed Bolingbroke "nostalgic," and there is much to be said for the designation.[3] Bolingbroke offered an idealized vision of a historical English constitutional balance that was being undermined by the centralized bureaucratic state. Political discourse in Augustan England is a case study for the way in which the language of corruption is a convenient way to articulate personal enmity and resentment in universal terms. Such widespread accusations and counteraccusations are a sign of a polity in a state of profound distrust. But it is more than this. The particular Bolingbrokean articulation of it offers a paradigmatic view of corruption as the loss of a traditional civic order and its replacement by alignment of individual interests through the coordination of the centralized financial bureaucratic state. Bolingbroke offered a view of corruption that continues to have parallels in contemporary responses to the bureaucratic state.

Bolingbroke was an insightful observer of the financial and bureaucratic revolution of the late seventeenth and early eighteenth centuries. He was equally a class ideologist. Both of these elements make his denunciation of corruption particularly instructive. There is a paradox in the emergence of Bolingbroke's virulent anticorruption talk in early eighteenth-century England. As John Brewer writes, "The effectiveness with which the British state taxed its subjects was in large part a direct consequence of a major transformation in the British fiscal system that occurred gradually between the Restoration and the mid-eighteenth century, as England moved from a fiscal system marked by heterogeneity and amateurism to a tax administration characterized by the orderly collection of public moneys by a predominantly professional body of state officials."[4] The paradox is that the very hallmarks of what many today would term corruption are precisely what Bolingbroke was harking back to as a period of constitutional purity. What Bolingbroke was lamenting was a shift from the patronage relationships that defined governance in early modern England to the party clientelism that is so prevalent in the modern state. Alarmist and shrill, his cry of corruption has incredible staying power as a language of a class that is seeing its prominence slide, and we hear echoes of it in many lamentations of the rule of finance in our world of perpetual national debt. In such lamentations there is the explicit assumption that power follows property, but only a quiet or implicit statement about what the healthy forms of dependency are. What Bolingbroke shared with the Machiavellian tradition was the tendency to see corruption in terms of relationships of dependency; he broke from the Florentine, however, in his espousal of a harmonious vision of the proper order of dependency in the ideal constitution. But if he was, in this respect, distant from Machiavellian republicanism he was equally distant from the "Weberian" form of bureaucratic integrity that we shall explore in Chapter 8.

We will begin this chapter with a brief foray into the political context of early eighteenth-century Britain, for Bolingbroke's theoretical claims cannot be understood without understanding his practical political positions. The second section will outline the meaning of corruption in his thought. The third section will discuss the reforms he wished to enact in order to reclaim independence. The final section considers the nature of the dependency relationship he sought. We conclude with some reflections on some of the enduring aspects of Bolingbroke's thought.

Corruption and Augustan Politics

The relative political stability that we associate with the Hanoverian period was largely a product of a delicate maneuvering, control of patronage, and outright bribery. Eighteenth-century English politics functioned in a manner foreshadowing the spoils system that we associate with party machine politics of the nineteenth and twentieth centuries, though there was a surprising number of permanent, professional civil servants that lent a stability to administration.[5] The Whig oligarchy cemented its power in the reigns of George I and II, and their rule was heavily based on the careful cultivation of interests. Robert Walpole, in addition to lining his own pockets, was able to employ pensions and positions to secure pliancy in Parliament, cooperation in the country, and a steady set of electoral victories in boroughs where every position of importance was heavily influenced by patron-client networks and where, in cases of boroughs with few electors, electors themselves were susceptible to the influence of gifts. Change of ruling clique meant a serious shift in the allocation of public goods.[6] This explains the great anxiety after the death of Queen Anne and the change of ministry: Jacobites were not necessarily all blind devotees to the Stuart cause and divine right, but were often looking to see a shift in which their friends could effectively capture the state and its various rents. We see equally clearly in the years following the 1715 Jacobite uprising a thorough attempt by Walpole to root out Tory influence throughout the country; he found that where people could not be shifted, loyalties could.

Since Bolingbroke's political writings are in large part propaganda, it is necessary to review his biography. Born in a wealthy gentry family, he had a good career before him despite a reputation as a libertine.[7] He began his political life as a member of Parliament in 1701 in a seat previously occupied by his father and grandfather, and he endeared himself to the Tory, Robert Harley (later earl of Oxford); his early success was tied to that of Harley (though he ultimately would scheme against him). He served as secretary of war in 1704, leaving the post several years later when Harley's position slipped. In 1710, however, Harley was back in and Bolingbroke was given the post of secretary of state, where he helped negotiate the Treaty of Utrecht to end the War of Spanish Succession (against Whig pressure and with some secret negotiations with France). In his time in power under Harley, he managed to root out his opponents from positions of prominence, and he was also instrumental in impeaching the young Robert Walpole (who had just held the post of secretary of war) for corruption. St. John was given a peerage (becoming Viscount Bolingbroke). The late years of Queen Anne were marked by her favor of Tories, but her health was failing, and since some Tories had entertained objections to the Hanoverian succession, the arrival of George I was not a good sign for Bolingbroke's political career. Certain that his enemies, back in power, would seek revenge for having been sent to the wilderness (or the Tower, in the case of Walpole), Bolingbroke fled to France, where he became secretary to James Francis Edward Stuart, claimant to the British throne, known as the "Old Pretender." Bolingbroke would later denigrate Jacobites, but he served the Old Pretender during the attempted rebellion of 1715 (though he sought all the while to convince the unbending James to convert to the Church of England). The failure of the rebellion made Bolingbroke reconsider his position, and he abandoned the Pretender and sought a pardon, which he eventually received in 1723 (Bolingbroke bribed the king's mistress with £11,000 in order that she might lobby on his behalf).[8] While not permitted to return to the Lords, he was able to return to England, and he spent the next twelve years engaged in a political campaign of vilifying Walpole as the devil incarnate. (He received a secret pension from France in support of his opposition work.)[9] In 1735 he returned to France and continued writing philosophical, historical, and political texts, never abandoning his campaign against Walpole and the corruption he saw in his country.[10]

One can experience a degree of familiarity when one reads about Augustan politics today. Long wars had placed the state in massive, seemingly permanent debt, a credit bubble had been created—and burst—by unscrupulous financial interests who were subsequently screened from prosecution by the government (because many were connected to the powerful). Ideological suspicions were rife, elections were heavily influenced by money, and the opposition politicians spent endless time demonizing the ministry, calling for the reduction of taxation, and fulminating about tyranny at every turn. The price of contesting elections rose dramatically in the thirty years after the 1688 revolution. "Many families beggared themselves," writes J. H. Plumb, "trying to maintain an old family interest which had cost their forefathers little more than a glass of beer and a side of beef."[11] And hopeful candidates in the early eighteenth century often had to placate electors not merely with private gifts and clientelistic appointments but with gifts to the borough or county itself: "Lawrence Carter provided Leicester with a piped water supply. Sir Cloudesley Shovel and Sir Joseph Williamson built Rochester a town hall and Sir Joseph threw in a grammar school for good measure."[12]

The price of elections rose with the Septennial Act of 1716: since the prize was larger, the cost of contesting elections was higher.[13] Election costs were an investment in future gains from places and perquisites. The most radical difference between the purchasing of Augustan elections and their purchase today is, of course, that we live in the world of the mass franchise and the cultivation of public opinion. But though the electorate was much smaller and much more subject to individual pecuniary motivation than today's electorate, it would be wrong to discount the place of public opinion in eighteenth-century electoral politics. Mass opinion mattered, and the newspaper as an organ of party interests was very much a living institution. Walpole had his propaganda paid for by the Treasury: in a ten-year period he spent £50,000 on journalists, and further public money was spent on the free distribution of these papers.[14]

Another important difference was the nature of party. We speak loosely of Whig and Tory, but there was—and continues to be—considerable debate on what the parties were and what they stood for. For Walpole, Tories were inveterate advocates of divine right who were intolerant of dissenters, champions of "passive obedience," and closet Jacobites. For Bolingbroke (post-1715), the old Whig-Tory division was out of date. Everybody accepted the principles of 1688, he insisted, and the only real division in the country was between the "country," which stood for liberty and the ancient constitution, and the nefarious "court" faction, whose purpose was to install tyranny through systematic corruption. Bolingbroke's theory that the terms "Whig" and "Tory" were out of date was not entirely risible. There is significant debate about the degree to which party groupings in the early eighteenth century were ideological, but where ideology fails, interest glues together coalitions. Political "friendships"—clientelistic networks—were of central importance, and Walpole's stable parliamentary coalition was very much like rudimentary forms of party "machine" politics.

Bolingbroke's insistence that there was only one real party distinction between patriotism and corruption is difficult to read without rolling one's eyes (one can sympathize with Samuel Johnson's quip about patriotism being the last refuge of the scoundrel). This is neither the first nor the last historical occasion in which someone attempted to press sour grapes into the wine of virtue.[15] Nor was it clear that Jacobitism was dead, as 1715, 1719, and 1745 would make clear. Walpole's press expressed incredulity about the decline of old Jacobitism that Bolingbroke professed, but that too was self-serving: Walpole wanted the gentry to see a Jacobite behind every opposition lament.[16] But beyond this elite rivalry there was a serious foundation to their quarrel. Bolingbroke's lamentation that the battle was between a corrupt court faction and the patriotic, post-partisan country party contained, in spite of its general hypocrisy, some perceptive observations about the manner in which large centralized bureaucratic administration altered the constitution. Let us turn to the meaning of his rhetoric.

Bolingbroke, Walpole, and the Meaning of Corruption

I have said that eighteenth-century politics were characterized by patron-client relationships ("friendship" or "connection"). Now, in our day, the term "political patronage" has become near synonymous with corruption, but in the eighteenth century it was not generally seen that way. The use of the term "corruption" to denote bribery was commonplace, but few contested the power of the well-placed to select trustworthy people for posts of importance. Certainly the ideals of merit, virtue, and civic duty were always asserted, but everybody knew the importance of influence, and Bolingbroke's complaints about placemen and crown patronage should not be taken to be about patronage in general,[17] but about patronage's descent into bribery. We can understand Bolingbroke's lamentation as a horror at the spectacle of classic patronage giving way to quid pro quo clientelism. In an important work on the concept of patronage, Edward Andrew notes that there was a distinction between the type of "friendship" denoted by the patron-client relationship (in which the patron pays a kind of homage to the genius of his socially inferior client) and the "placeman," who was simply a purchased agent. Andrew quotes the second Duke of Argyll complaining of his brother that he "wants to make all his friends tools of Walpole. . . . My Brother Ilay prefers his Places to all other Considerations; friendship, Honour, Relationship, gratitude & Service to his Country Seem at present to have no weight with him."[18] As much as this sounds like high-minded cant, it does refer to a serious difference between two types of subordination. When Bolingbroke raged against placemen, he was not objecting to personal relationships of support that wealthy gentry and nobility might cultivate with less wealthy but more talented dependents. He was lamenting a mercenary quality in which straightforward subordination was bought, particularly the subordination of one estate of the mixed constitution to another. Some political scientists have adopted a distinction between *patronage* as a highly personalized relationship and *clientelism*, which entails mass-based politics and the party machine.[19] This terminological distinction is not ideal—both terms originate in the classical Roman relationship between the *cliens* and the *patronus*, a relationship of personalized protection and service between free men of unequal social position. But artificial as it might be to split these two terms into two different phenomena it is important to recognize that there are two different phenomena at play. If one is local and particular, part of a gift economy and a personal connection, the other is part of a mass phenomenon featuring the party machine that delivers mass support through "bosses" and parliamentary support through the control of offices. All mass democracies in the modern age have passed through (or remain in) highly clientelistic conditions. Eighteenth-century England was experiencing a shift from the one form of dependency to the other, and Bolingbroke's lamentations were an attempt to come to terms with this shift.

The most famous avenue of opposition writing under Walpole was the *Craftsman*, the opposition newspaper written by Bolingbroke, Nicholas Amhurst, and William Pulteney.[20] The paper was an endless torrent of abuse upon Walpole and the government and a constant accusation of corruption. One of the more widely cited contributions of Bolingbroke is the *Craftsman* no. 16, "The First Vision of Camelick,"[21] a "Persian" allegory on English history. Not one of the most subtle examples of this genre (nor terribly "Persian" in its aesthetic—it describes pontiffs and a senate), Bolingbroke's vision nonetheless gives a clear picture of his ideological position. It begins with a king who comes and signs a holy document that is the source of all peace, justice, and happiness in the kingdom. But later kings break the charter occasioning civil war—there are conflagrations in which the holy document, while obscured or broken, remains a kind of guiding light. Eventually a king truly bows down before this constitution, and the land is happy: "industry, commerce and liberty danced hand in hand throughout the cities." But just as the king and nobles are gathered round celebrating the sacred nature of the great document, a rich parvenu "dress'd in a plain habit, with a Purse of Gold in his Hand," comes in and

throws money around. Everyone is so desirous for the money that the rich
man is able to pocket the constitution.[22] And so he entirely corrupts
the country, and people become slaves. But the vision has a happy ending—
the Walpole figure runs out of money. And so the document rises once
more to its earlier prominence and all is right in the world. The great source
of corruption—the corruption that undermines the sacred covenant
between king and people—is born of money. But there are grounds for
optimism in the tale: as soon as the nasty little rich man disappears, "every
chain dropped off in an Instant. . . . Heaven and Earth resounded with
Liberty!" Get rid of Walpole and his ilk—particularly the moneyed interests—and all will be well.

This, in a nutshell, is Bolingbroke's theory of English government—a
sacred constitution has, for time immemorial, been the guarantor of peace
and justice, but the struggle for its preservation has entailed much bloodshed.
Post–Glorious Revolution, it has been realized, but it is threatened by new
money that can buy the very arbitrary power that one civil war and a subsequent revolution had been fought to prevent. The new scourge of the age is
corruption: "Corruption is a more deadly weapon than the highest prerogative, in the hands of men who are enemies to such a constitution of government as ours is" (184). Bolingbroke's writing brims with moralism, as if the
mere replacement of a Walpole with one of more solid virtue would solve the
problem. He wrote a brief description of honest ministers, men "in their
descent noble and generous; full of the virtues of their ancestors; educated in
the knowledge and study of our constitution, its laws, settlements, dependencies and interests; always faithful to the crown, when consistent with their
duty to their country . . . easy in their fortunes; . . . more careful to preserve,
than to aggrandize a family; making virtue the foundation of their friendship,
and merit the title of their favor."[23] And on it goes. But character is something
that has systemic components. Bolingbroke fully bought the tale that decadence had "enervated" once-virtuous people (the Persians, Spartans,
Romans). Pericles "debauched" politics and made Greeks slavish and easy
prey for Philip; Hannibal's very successes led to the destruction of Carthage;
and Bolingbroke cites the story from Herodotus that Cyrus had pacified the
Lydians by introducing vice and luxury.[24] Ethics is a civic concern, and a
general lassitude is connected to the most insidious form of tyranny known
to mankind—the tyranny of money.

If Bolingbroke's allegory has a happy conclusion, it remains disquieting,
for the demise of the wealthy parvenu minister is occasioned by his running

out of money. Channeling Machiavelli (but perhaps anticipating the policy of "starving the beast"), Bolingbroke wrote: "Distress from abroad, bankruptcy at home, and other circumstances of like nature and tendency, may beget universal confusion. Out of confusion order may arise" (221). But it will arise only if a "patriot king" is there, founder-like, to recognize that crises are opportunities and to help establish virtue (242). And if Bolingbroke hoped the "patriot king" could cure corruption, he had also learned from Machiavelli (and from experience) that one can rarely expect to see a succession of kings sharing virtue. The patriot king's job is to "restore good government" (252); it is the people, returned to virtue under virtuous institutions, who will have the duty of preserving it.

We will not focus on the "patriot king"—we may simply repeat that appealing to the deus ex machina of a virtuous prince is a recurrent vice of anticorruption reformers. We have noted that Machiavelli offered a self-consciously paradoxical account of leadership as a cure for corruption. Bolingbroke did not have the same subtlety of vision. One can envision Bolingbroke salivating as he counseled his patriot king not only to "purge his court" (253), but also to pursue the old gang "not to sate private resentments" but "to make satisfaction for wrongs done to their country." As to the difficulty of choosing virtuous counselors, Bolingbroke points out that good princes simply wouldn't choose bad counselors (254). Virtue begets virtue.

Bolingbroke is often termed a civic republican due to his worries about corruption, his call for public-spirited virtue, his defense of the rule of law, his haranguing on the dangers of tyranny, and his call for a return to origins. Certainly, Rome serves his purposes, as does Machiavelli. There is a danger, however, of allowing the appearances of these themes to place Bolingbroke in a company where he would be uncomfortable. Bolingbroke admired Machiavelli, but he was no Algernon Sidney, and he had a horror of republicanism. He wrote of the 1650s, "There was a time, our fathers saw it, when the House of Commons destroyed, instead of supporting, the constitution, and introduced tyranny, under pretence of excluding slavery" (140). Rome, for Bolingbroke, had a faulty constitution because it was a mixture of democracy and aristocracy without monarchy. He did not agree with Machiavelli's view that the consulship constituted a monarchical element (143).

David Hume wrote (possibly thinking of Bolingbroke), "The Tories have been so long obliged to talk in the republican stile, that they seem to have made converts of themselves by their hypocrisy, and to have embraced the sentiments, as well as the language of their adversaries."[25] Bolingbroke appealed to numerous arguments that had been staples of republican writers, but as Shelley Burtt correctly indicates, "Bolingbroke blames the social mobility created by the market in public debt for completely demoralizing England's landed gentry. But the danger identified is not that these men can no longer lead lives similar to Aristotle's publicly involved Greek citizen. It is simply that they cannot be trusted to preserve the icon of virtue—the balanced constitution—against political pressure to the contrary."[26] It would certainly be incorrect to see Bolingbroke's praise of civic virtue as Greek—and I do not think it terribly Machiavellian either. Bolingbroke complained of luxury and decadence, but he was not truly keen on frugality. On the contrary, he thought the purpose of government was to protect liberty and commerce (274). Riches were necessary for national well-being. Bolingbroke cited Sallust quoting Cato's lament, "Luxury and avarice, public want and private wealth abound" (183), but he did not actually agree with the civic-republican ideal of private want and public wealth; it was when the public was *rich* (as we shall see) that Bolingbroke thought it tended toward tyranny.

Nor was Bolingbroke in favor of the highly militarized populace that Machiavelli favored; unlike red-blooded republicans, Bolingbroke did not think civic life consisted in developing the martial virtues through good laws. His opposition to professional standing armies ought not to be confounded with the Machiavellian opposition to mercenaries. Bolingbroke placed the country's liberty in the hands of its sailors, not some fired-up militia. Indeed, his opposition to the standing army had (as Pocock has pointed out) much more to do with the large, centralized systems of taxation and appointment such an institution entails than with its tendency to undermine the active martial virtues in citizens.

The real basis for freedom was the mixed constitution. But Bolingbroke's mixed constitution is neither Aristotelian nor Machiavellian. Bolingbroke saw the mixed constitution as something that emerged from conflicts of interests over time, but it was an ultimately harmonious agreement of interests: "as our government is now constituted, the three estates have not only one common interest, which they always had; but they have, considered as estates, no separate, contradictory interest" (163). He deprecated the class tensions that Machiavelli had thought the source of Roman strength: "the want of a third estate in the Roman system of government, and of a

representative body, to act for the collective body, maintained one perpetual ferment, which often increased into a storm, but never subsided into a
calm" (130). Or again, "the true image of a free people, governed by a
Patriot King, is that of a patriarchal family, where the head and all the
members are united by one common interest, and animated by one common spirit" (258). There will be no opposition in a virtuous state—neither
partisanship (the faction that so worried Machiavelli) nor class conflict (the
tension that so appealed to Machiavelli).

Now, trumpeting the mixed constitution as the source of English liberty
was commonplace—almost everybody thought the mixed constitution was
England's heritage, and none wanted it corrupted, but there was disagree-
ment about how that mixture functioned. Dr. Johnson thought corruption
had occurred because the Parliament had too much power since 1688: "the
want of inherent right in the King occasions all this disturbance. What we
did at the Revolution was necessary: but it broke our constitution."[27] Walpole, in a parliamentary response to Bolingbroke's friends, wrote, "It is
certain that ours is a mixt government, and the perfection of our constitution consists in this, that the monarchical, aristocratical and democratical
forms of government are mixt and interwoven in ours," but the proposal
of the opposition—frequent elections—would itself upset the balance and
throw the country into democracy.[28] Frequent elections would make ministers less likely to think of the long term; they would rather pursue short-
term projects bent on gaining them immediate reelection. As for corruption, Walpole denied that it was widespread and insisted that if it took place
anywhere it must be in instances where real interests were not at stake, for
no English landowner would sell his birthright so cheaply.[29] Hume went
further, arguing that placemen were a boon to the mixed government, preventing it from slipping into democracy.[30] Maintaining that the influence
of the crown in Parliament was necessary for the constitution, he suggested
that the term "corruption" was an "invidious appellation."

But Bolingbroke thought such people had not fully understood their
ancient constitution: the three orders must not be allowed to invade each
other. "Our constitution is no longer a mystery," he wrote (78); the previous generation's conflict had been born of partial understandings of the
constitution. "A spirit of liberty, transmitted down from our Saxon ancestors . . . preserved itself through one almost continual struggle, against the
usurpations of our princes, and the vices of our people" (82). Things must
not slip too much in the democratic or the monarchical direction. Nor

ought one to fall into the Roman error of having two estates: the genius of the English constitution was the place it accorded to the intermediary bodies of the nobles. Here we can see a view that would have some resonance with Montesquieu's aristocratic liberalism: the peers "are properly mediators between the other two [estates]"; liberty depends upon their—and the Commons'—being independent and not "tools of faction, or the vassals of a minister" (140).[31]

The most important element of this claim is Bolingbroke's view that the constitution was determined by the balance of property. Bolingbroke shared a view of English history that we have (thanks to Pocock) rightly grown accustomed to term "Harringtonian." The view is that the nature of the constitution is dependent upon the underlying balance of property. Like Harrington, Bolingbroke thought that the constitution had been rendered more popular by the shift in property occasioned by Henry VII's abolition of feudal retainers and Henry VIII's appropriation of church lands that had subsequently entered the market, creating a larger class of freeholders. Unlike Harrington, however, Bolingbroke thought the Elizabethan constitution was a masterwork of balance. Now, the harmony of the three orders depended upon their mutual independence, which had been created by these shifts in the balance of property.[32] The independence that Bolingbroke thought the Commons and Lords could exhibit was due to their possessing greater estates; in the past the many had been dependent on great lords who had feuded among themselves or against the king in a spirit of faction. The Tudor balance of property, in contrast, forced all to pursue goals in the public interest and brought back that state of "perfection" that Bolingbroke located, nostalgically, in an ancient Saxon past. The civil war had been fought to bring the country back to its balance, though it had witnessed a dangerous republican moment. But the greatest danger now was the manner in which, post-1688, the monarchical power had grown at the expense of the other orders, making all financially dependent on it. Bolingbroke thought that the "corrupt" system that he perceived had been erected under William and Mary, born of a mixture of political considerations and self-serving interest:

> The notion of attaching men to the new government, by tempting them to embark their fortunes on the same bottom, was a reason of state to some: the notion of creating a new, that is, a moneyed interest, in opposition to the landed interest or as a balance to it, and of

acquiring a superior influence in the city of London at least by the establishment of great corporations, was a reason of party to others: I make no doubt that the opportunity of amassing immense estates by the managing of funds, by trafficking in paper, and by all the arts of jobbing, was a reason of private interest to those who supported and improved this scheme of iniquity, if not to those who devised it.[33]

Whatever the motives of its devisers, the system had created dependencies that had upset the balance, weakening the integrity of the state and the personal integrity of its gentry. Bolingbroke saw the new centralized military-bureaucratic-financial state as entailing a shift of the balance of property to the court and a radical shift in morality.

Integrity and patriotism entail a devotion to the constitution over any attachment to particular people. Hence personal dependencies cultivated by ministers are suspect. "The integrity of Parliament is a kind of Palladium, a tutelary goddess, who protects our state," and this "integrity . . . depends on the freedom and the independency of Parliament" (94). The phrase "freedom and independency" is redundant in Bolingbroke's usage: to be free in the civic sense means to be free not merely from violent control but also from having one's judgment and one's civic duty clouded or influenced by other actors promising personal advantage. This means being proper-tied. Corruption was the danger of the age because it could achieve through gifts what was previously attempted through prerogative. The court could capture Parliament with wealth and place.

What particularly disturbed Bolingbroke was that corruption was no longer recognized for what it was. In the past, corruption "hath been always kept under by the shame and danger, that attended both the corrupter and the corrupted," but now people seem to think it perfectly acceptable for the crown to undermine the independence of Parliament (185). What we witness in Bolingbroke's conflict with Walpole's ministry is the clash of contested visions of corruption: the court faction did not see its activities as corrupt and was thus not clandestine about the bulk of them.[34]

Indeed, Walpole and his friends insisted that it is normal to entrust office to people who are sympathetic to the ministry's goals and reasonable to reward service to country with positions. Bolingbroke thought the defenders of such action were mere apologists for vice:

> They plead . . . private dependency, as an essential part of our con-
> stitution. When they have perplexed . . . our ideas of dependency

and independency, they reason, if I may give their sophisms so good a name, as if the independency of each part of the legislature, of the king particularly, arose from the dependency of the other parts on that part. . . . It is false, because the constitutional independency of each part of the legislature arises from hence, that distinct rights, powers and privileges are assigned to it by the constitution. . . . This independency . . . consists properly and truly in the free, unbiased, uninfluenced and independent exercise of these rights, powers and privileges. (120)

The only dependency that should exist is the interdependency that arises when one estate presents its views to the others in their public setting (i.e., in the conjoined action of Commons, Lords, and king).

Free people are to be uninfluenced. This is the case for electors, members of the House of Commons, and Lords. The formal structure of the constitution is such that this is possible: peerages are made by the crown but cannot simply be taken away on a whim, so the peers are independent (164). Members of Parliament are equally independent in law because they owe their place to their electors. But in practice both members and the electors themselves can be rendered slavish if the court has too much wealth. Now, there is something disingenuous about Bolingbroke's claim that elections and members' votes were simply for purchase. Walpole would have been very happy if they had been, but, as he realized on numerous occasions, his grip was never complete either on members or on electors. While some members were buyable, writes Jeremy Black, "it is also necessary to note the role of issues and of political independence. . . . Patronage and political management alone were insufficient to keep governments in power."[35] Black points out that Walpole's policies were popular—he kept the peace, which had strong fiscal implications, he kept the land tax low, and he gave no more ground to dissenters. Would Bolingbroke truly have denied the ministry the power to make appointments based on loyalty to its program? He wrote that the many "entries to corruption" must be closed up, but there are some that could not be wholly eliminated, and indeed were less dangerous than others: "there is a just distinction to be made because there is a real difference. Some of these entries are opened by the abuse of powers, necessary to maintain subordination, and to carry on good government, and therefore necessary to be preserved in the crown, notwithstanding the abuse that is sometimes made of them; for no human institution can arrive at perfection" (209). Bolingbroke, then, did not disapprove of patronage in itself. The power simply must not be "abused." But abuse was a product of structural conditions and would only be curbed with certain reforms, to which we now turn.

Curing a Corrupted Regime

The main reforms to be taken were the following: frequent parliaments, a reduction of national debt, an end to "placemen," and the elimination of a standing army, the reduction of the excise—all traditionally Whiggish positions whose adoption by the opposition was somewhat embarrassing to the government. Let us take Bolingbroke's complaints one by one.

The Frequency of Parliaments

The Septennial Act had a certain unpopularity, but moves to have it repealed were unsuccessful; opposition opinions remained somewhat split due to the different effects its repeal would have in different types of constituency.[36] In theory, however, more frequent parliaments would mean that MPs would be called to account for their actions, and hence depend on their electors, rather than on ministers (103–105). Elections would cost less, and most important, corrupt members would be gotten rid of in a peaceful fashion so that people need not do as Jephthah did and appeal to heaven (104).[37] Bolingbroke also hoped frequent elections would force aspiring MPs to be members of their communities. Freeholders should prefer solid landed men who are from their county.

Most important, frequent elections would make members dependent upon their constituents and prevent them from combining into solid parliamentary blocks. With frequent elections, Bolingbroke wrote, "there is not time sufficient given, to form a majority of the representatives of the people into a ministerial cabal," or if there is, "such a cabal must soon be broken" (104). Note that what he is describing as a cabal is, in fact, the basis for stable party government as we have come to know it in parliamentary systems. A stable majority is treated here as inherently corrupt.

Placemen and Pensions

The existence of parliamentary representatives who were financially dependent on the crown because they held offices or pensions was a subject of repeated lamentation and periodic legislation. Bolingbroke was ever in favor of weakening their importance. But though he supported bills limiting the number of placemen, he ultimately thought the greatest danger was the very property imbalance that gave the government so many places and pensions to dole out in the first place.

Debt and Finance

The size of the sovereign debt was a universal concern, but Bolingbroke's worries were quite specific. Being able to carry large debts is a necessary condition of centralized bureaucratic states, but for Bolingbroke that ability was a source of general corruption. The large national debt was part of a general system that had seen the rise of novel financial instruments like the Bank of England and the South Sea Company. The latter, originally set up by Harley in 1711 as a vehicle to take on some government debt, got creditors to trade their government debt for stock. Since the company was granted a monopoly on trade to Spanish South America (largely the trade of slaves),[38] it appeared to be a good bet. But as with the Mississippi Bubble in France, the South Sea Company saw wild speculation based on fraudulent reports of the company's prospects. Walpole managed to get out in time (though recommending the stock to others).[39] Bolingbroke himself, while he would later express righteous contempt for stockjobbers, was involved in the beginnings of the scheme, though he was well clear of the matter when the bubble burst—one of the few advantages that exile brought him.[40] Walpole was not at first associated with the company, and his political career took off when he managed to patch the company together, protect the reputation of the royal family, some ministers and some directors of the company. The rampant speculation and the wild shifting of wealth that took place in the period made it a popular symbol of the age's social and political corruption.[41] For Bolingbroke, there was something entirely vicious about the power being wielded by "stockjobbers": "the landed men are the true owners of our political vessel; the moneyed men, as such, are no more than passengers in it."[42] The new financial instruments not only allowed people of low birth and morals ("the meanest grubs on earth" [182]) to rise to undeserved prominence, but they also encouraged the tendency to compare oneself to others, creating an artificial sense of impoverishment among the objectively wealthy and pushing the culture in ever more venal directions (183). The radical inequality created by this was giving birth to radical dependency: "immense wealth of particular men is a circumstance which always attends national poverty, and is in a great measure the cause of it" (183).

It was galling that the tax-paying landowners and merchants were being sucked dry to feed unproductive lenders and speculators. (This was hyperbole—landowners and merchants were doing quite well, but Bolingbroke was cultivating resentment.) Worse, the central power to which it gave rise was breeding a culture of dependency on the court: "the establishment of public funds, on the credit of these taxes, hath been productive of more and greater mischiefs than the taxes themselves, not only by increasing the means of corruption, and the power of the crown, but by the effect it hath had on the spirit of the nation, on our manners and our morals" (180). The result was a constant resort to debt: "In times of peace, in days of prosperity, as we boast them to be, we contract new debts, and we create new funds" (181).

Now, Walpole would have pointed out that such funds were useful methods of restructuring and lowering the existing debt. But Bolingbroke was not reconciled to the notion that states should carry such substantial debt at all, for these debts not only fostered a financial elite of unprecedented power, but they also permitted the executive to continue for quite some time without depending on parliamentary funds. Long parliaments (infrequent elections) and large sovereign debts were two elements of the same illness, increasing the center's independence and power at the expense of the country. This was a fundamental change to the constitution weakening the king's dependence on the commons (105).

Standing Armies

The standing army (as opposed to a citizen militia) had often been decried as a despotic institution (particularly, though not exclusively, by republican writers). English observers liked to point to absolutist states such as France and Spain as places where large standing armies were a menace to liberty. But from the 1690s onward the English had started to look much more continental in their military arrangements. Bolingbroke worried about this, but less because of the oppression such an army entailed than because of the opportunities it gave for patronage. The larger the force, the greater the number of commissions to dole out, the more opportunities for profit in equipping the forces, and so on.

Excise

The taxes required to finance the new fiscal-military state were quite high—and, more to the point, they were regular. Walpole had, we have pointed out, kept the land tax low—indeed, he had placed most of the tax burden on the excise. Throughout his rule, the excise constituted the greatest source of tax revenue.[43] Bolingbroke disliked all taxes, but there was something particularly disturbing about the excise, for it entailed its own centralized administration (the land tax was administered locally). Bolingbroke thought excise officers meddled in elections, and he thought that "this change in the state and property of the public revenue hath made a change in our constitution . . . since it gives a power, unknown in former times, to one of the three estates" (176). The excise was a particular ill that was part of the wider problem of the continuous taxation required for a centralized state: "As we have annually increased our funds, and our taxes, we have annually increased the power of the crown."

Independence for Whom?

We have, then, a portrait of systemic corruption in which freedom is bought and sold; this has been brought about because of a systemic shift in property relationships. For all Bolingbroke's moralism, he had a strikingly determinist account of virtue. The structure of a constitution has "a proportional influence on the reasoning, the sentiments, and the conduct of those who are subject to it" (77). That is, if power follows property, virtue is a synonym for financial independence. This is not the Aristotelian vision of property as a basis for ennobling leisure; rather, it is a much more mechanical theory suggesting that most people are for sale. For all his cant about the salvation to be found in a virtuous patriot king—and for all his demonization of Walpole—Bolingbroke thought every man had his price, and he thought corruption had systemic causes.

> Should angels and arch-angels come down from heaven to govern
> us, the same danger would exist, until the springs, from whence it
> arises, were cut off; not because some angels and arch-angels have
> fallen . . . [and] become tempter . . . , but because, as private liberty
> cannot be deemed secure under a government, wherein law . . . is

> dependent on will; so the public security must be in danger, whenever
> a free constitution, the proper and sole security of it, is dependent on
> will; and a free constitution . . . is dependent on will, whenever the
> will of one estate can direct the conduct of all three. (170)

Bolingbroke was reacting to the incipient bureaucratic administration that
is the necessary condition of the modern fiscal-military state—but he was
not reacting in the manner of the nineteenth-century reformers, who would
succeed in reducing "Old Corruption" through thorough civil service
reform.[44] The notion of a professionalized administration did not conform
to his ideal of sturdy landed gentry exercising their virtue (and protecting
their interests) in positions of authority. In the civil service, he could never
see anything but a cipher for the insidious will of a prime minister. Consider the excise administration, which Bolingbroke decried as an army of
"dependents on the crown" exercising their authority in an "arbitrary"
manner (175). The excise was, indeed, intrusive, and its employees were
numerous, but John Brewer describes them as extremely professional, their
professionalism being ensured by a most rigorous series of controls, including the tendency to move them around so that they would not build up any
fixed, corrupt connections in a community.[45] The excise did have enormous
power that appeared almost arbitrary, but officials generally exercised this
power efficiently (which is why the nation's credit could be so good in spite
of its cumulative debt).

Was Bolingbroke simply cultivating resentment with his attack on the
excise? Not quite, or at least not only. He correctly noticed that something
radical had changed. But what he was calling corrupt were those elements
of modern state power that later theorists of bureaucracy and good governance would come to see as the bulwark against corruption. He thought
dependency was a product of lack of wealth. This is why he thought (like
many eighteenth-century Britons) that the poor could not be trusted with
the franchise. But he went further than many would have. In 1710, under
Harley, Bolingbroke was involved in the passage of the Parliamentary Qualification Act (9 Anne, c. 5), with the full title of the "Act for securing the
freedom of parliaments," which ensured that eligibility to stand for Parliament required £300 per annum in land for boroughs and £600 per annum
for counties, "a Law," wrote Bolingbroke, "which was intended to confine
the Election to such Persons as are *independent in their Circumstances*; have
a valuable Stake in the *Land*; and must therefore be the most strongly
engaged to consult the *public Good*, and the least liable to *Corruption*."[46]

Making *landed* wealth the exclusive criterion was an obvious attempt to privilege the landed interest at the expense of commercial or financial elites. But Bolingbroke was not anticommercial, and his main preoccupation was to insure independence. He quite insightfully noted that in a highly unequal society formal equality and personal dependence could be a recipe for a type of servility every bit as dangerous to liberty as that found under absolute princes. But his solution to this was not some Harringtonian agrarian law—it was, rather, to reset hierarchy back to its previous arrangement in which local grandees maintained their power at the expense of the crown and the burgeoning administrative state. Equality was never Bolingbroke's ideal— indeed, while he saw the Roman agrarian laws as a fully understandable result of the unequal division of property, he deprecated them as a source of class conflict that had ultimately sunk the republic (129ff.). Corruption was the undermining of the balance of power and property that had been established between the three estates. Imbalance bred dependency in those who ought to have been too well bred to be grasping and too wealthy to be bought.

In brief, his cry of "independence" was a call for a return of control to wealthy country gentry and nobility. The most important part of Boling-broke's thought is that part that is the least trumpeted on the surface of his writing, the type of dependencies that obtained under the properly balanced constitution. Power follows property, and the crown's command of the purse was overpowering the country. The purity Bolingbroke perceived in the ancient constitution was merely the condition in which a different class held the reins of local power and patronage. Bolingbroke's tireless tirades illuminated the manner in which corruption and dependency were kin, but the purity to which he pointed was merely a different form of dependency. Representative parliamentarianism and the centralized bureaucratic finan-cial state, with its need for the cultivation of stable majorities, with its stable financial independence, and with its powers of place, undermined the cozy relationships that Bolingbroke experienced in his youthful rise to office under the patronage of Queen Anne.

Conclusion: The Politics of Nostalgia and the Ambivalence of Independence

To term someone nostalgic might appear straightforwardly uncomplimen-tary, but cultivating a longing for an imagined, lost condition can be a politically fruitful rhetorical stance. Everything depends on the lost ideal that is conjured into imaginative existence. But in the case of Bolingbroke, the injurious valence of the appellation is merited. His historical ideal was both self-serving and idealized. But class ideologist though he was, the pressure he and his fellow "patriots" brought to bear—pressure backed up by an intermediary body that felt itself squeezed—might well have had a somewhat salutary effect of slowing the rise of a centralized state with dangerous ambitions. There is, however, something quixotic about Bolingbroke's tirades against the bureaucratic state. The desire to have commercial empire without the trappings of large administration was a fundamental contradiction in his thought. Nonetheless, it was a desire that would have considerable ideological traction. And, indeed, it may be that terming his views "quixotic" exhibits an unwarranted optimism about the permanence of the fiscal-bureaucratic state: Bolingbroke's analogues today continue to fight it as the soul of corruption, and their victories have not been meager.

Bolingbroke rightly saw that domination could enter into a polity when radical inequality and financial speculation established new centers of power, but his response was to frame the corruption in terms of an idealized historical condition in which the radical independence of the estates guaranteed civic integrity. His agrarian, gentry ideal would go on to have great influence on political thought not only in Britain but also on the American continent. And, for all that the ideal of landed gentry has ceased to be part of our imaginative furniture, his animus against central government and the bureaucratic financial state continues to echo in contemporary politics. There is an important dimension of his attack on clientelism that needs retaining, for the crafting of stable coalitions through the manipulation of financial dependencies is one of the more persistent traits of representative politics in inegalitarian societies. But as in Bolingbroke, such lamentations often emerge in bursts of resentment and nostalgia about previous periods in which electors and representatives were independent. And as in Bolingbroke, such denunciations are often less than direct about the types of dependencies that existed prior to the bureaucratic state. Independence is an ideologically promiscuous ideal. Bolingbroke saw that independence was determined by material conditions and he viewed financial dependency as the soul of corruption. But purity required not state intervention to promote universal independency; rather, it called for a return to earlier patterns of dependency. Whether Bolingbroke's attempt at an aristocratic response to oligarchy entails a distinction with an insufficient amount of difference is a question I leave to the reader.

CHAPTER 6

"La vertu même a besoin de limites"

Montesquieu on Moderation and Integrity
in the Modern Commercial Republic

In our study of corruption's various faces so far we have drawn a number of parallels between deployments of the concept in early modern political philosophy and manners of thinking about corruption and integrity in contemporary political discourse. But it is truly with Montesquieu that we encounter an argument about the exact nature of corruption that appears to speak directly to our social-scientific mores, for Montesquieu offered an analysis of corruption that ties its definition to the institutional and social-psychological dimensions of regime types. At the same time, Montesquieu deployed the concept of corruption in a universal manner employing it as a basis for evaluating competing regimes.

We have seen that contemporary debates around the meaning of corruption often flounder on the plurality of modes in which the term is deployed. This gives birth to endless battles between universalists and particularists, where the first express misgivings at relativistic political morality and the latter decry cultural imperialism. Cross-cultural deployments of the term appear to run roughshod over difference (just as transhistorical definitions appear to run roughshod over historical particularity), but studies that attempt to explain differences in political morality by appealing to cultural particularity often run the risk of cultural essentialism. Montesquieu (in spite of his somewhat unprepossessing foray into climatic determinism) manages an extremely fruitful reconciliation of particularity and universality, drawing our attention to the fact that the historical and cultural diversity of political cultures can be understood according to a logic of regime forms.

Of particular importance in Montesquieu's account of regime forms is his assessment of classical republicanism, about whose political virtue he expressed a profound ambivalence. In this he serves as a healthy corrective to a great deal of contemporary political thought. The turn toward republicanism both in the literature on the concept of corruption and political theory more generally is born of a displeasure with the liberal incapacity to speak the language of the common good and collective civic decay. But reviving republican civic virtue in the world of the modern commercial state is a project that has been fraught with tensions and contradictions since the eighteenth century—tensions that are particularly manifest in contemporary "neo-republican" thinkers who redescribe liberal norms with language and imagery derived from republican Rome. Montesquieu offers us a reflection on the varieties of corruption that simultaneously appeals to and undermines republican ideals. It is a position that embraces the moral dimension of corruption discourse, but it does so with highly moderated ethical ambitions that make it appealing to a world wary of "perfectionism." But as much as his view of corruption and the limits of purity sits comfortably with trends in contemporary liberal political theory, it nonetheless relies upon two tenets that are inaccessible to the anti-perfectionist: the first is that even the moderately corrupt regime that emerges as the most hopeful model for the modern commercial state retains a commitment to the crafting of certain ethical and affective dispositions in its citizens. The second is that the normative basis for Montesquieu's qualified celebration of this regime is an account, however thin, of a fundamental human nature, a touchstone we have grown increasingly reluctant to touch.

This chapter is structured as follows: the first section looks at both relative and absolute corruption in Montesquieu's thought. It indicates that the type of relative corruption—that which causes a regime to change form—is linked to the absolute corruption that Montesquieu sees in the "principle" of despotism. All these forms of corruption entail a shift in the affective basis of the regime away from that which turns citizens' and subjects' energies toward the public good. We will see that the two passions that most detract from human sociability are fear and avarice—those passions that are most in evidence under despotism. The second section will demonstrate that Montesquieu's view of natural sociability has its anchor in his brief foray into natural law. Montesquieu's imaginary construction of the state of nature offers a thin but normatively important conception of purity, but it equally points to the essential corruptibility of human beings in political society. The third section turns to his portrayal of England, exploring the manner in which Montesquieu thought corruptibility could best be contained and moderated. Here we will note the degree to which England is awash in the corrupting passions; its moderation is a result of an extremely precarious balance of corruption. For Montesquieu, the price of heroic Roman purity was too high, bloody without and stifling within; the solution of commercial modernity is a pact with corruption—not a pact with Mephistopheles, but a pact with a grubbier, duller, more English demon, perhaps one resembling Robert Walpole.

Montesquieu's Varieties of Corruption

In *The Spirit of the Laws*, Montesquieu deploys the term "corruption" in the same manner that he employs other moral terms, straddling the descriptive and the normative. Corruption is at once something purely relative to a given regime (a loss of that regime's dominant passion) and universal, a degradation of human nature. Both these dimensions—the relative and the absolute—speak equally to individual character and political structures. With a classical unwillingness to separate city and soul, Montesquieu offers a series of sociopsychological analyses of different regime forms and the requisite character of their respective citizens or subjects. In this section, we will attempt to flesh out the link between the relative and the absolute.

Let us begin with the relative: corruption can be defined differently based upon the given regime. If the reader will permit a brief reminder of Montesquieu's basic schema, there were three types of constitution and three corresponding types of corruption. Each type entails an alteration of the affective source of the regime—not its constitutional structure, but the dominant passion that "makes the regime move," what he terms its "principle" (3.1).[1] That is, every political arrangement has some sort of dominant social-psychological force that makes individuals behave in such a way as to preserve the regime—the principles are the affective basis on which people's energies turn toward obedience. The principles are what make the public possible; without some sort of affective motivation, there would be no public at all. As we will see, if the types of corruption differ with regard to regime, they all share the quality of rendering people less public-spirited. We recall that the three regimes, republics (split into democracies and aristocracies), monarchies, and despotisms have, as principles or animating passions, virtue (love of the *patrie* and of equality; moderation is added to the aristocratic republic), honor (love of distinctions and prerogatives), and fear, respectively. Let us look at the manner in which these principles are corrupted.

Republics are of two sorts, democracies and aristocracies. In both cases, corruption entails a diminution of virtue. "The principle of democracy is corrupted not only when the spirit of equality is lost but also when the spirit of extreme equality is taken up and each one wants to be the equal of those chosen to command" (8.2). Citizens are all equal, but citizenship entails strict duties to obey the legitimately constituted powers. In this classical republican conception, the individual's liberty is not individual license but rather a product of a juridical condition of being a citizen: one can speak of a free city. A civic virtue akin to (but somewhat more self-renunciatory than) that praised by Machiavelli ties people to their city. Aristocracy, another form of the republican regime, is corrupted when the elite cease to have that moderating virtue that causes them to rule according to law—and hence it becomes arbitrary government, or despotism (8.5).

This "political virtue" makes people place all of their energies in the service of their city. Political virtue is "l'amour de la patrie," the "desire for true glory, self-renunciation, sacrifice of one's dearest interests" (3.5). Montesquieu expresses clearly the relationship between public and private in a classical republic:

> Though all crimes are by their nature public, truly public crimes are nevertheless distinguished from private crimes, so called because they offend an individual more than the whole society.
>
> Now, in republics private crimes are more public, that is, they run counter to the constitution of the state more than against individuals; and, in monarchies, public crimes are more private, that is, they run counter to individual fortunes more than against the constitution of the state itself. (3.5)

The very conception of crime differs according to constitutional form. When people have virtue, they consider all of their actions to be for the republic. Hence, lax behavior in their "private" lives is a sign of corruption. If the dominant definition of corruption today is the abuse of public office for private gain, we can see that all crimes in Montesquieu's ancient republics are corrupt, for the passion for private gain is a corruption of virtue.

(Note, in passing, how distinct this is from Machiavelli.) There is no crime that is not equally an instance of political corruption. The converse is true of a monarchy. In a monarchy, these private ambitions are not rejected. They are moderated by a sense of honor that regulates ranks and makes people act with a degree of public-spiritedness (3.7), but their motivation is individualistic and, from a republican perspective, corrupt. Possessions and even governmental offices are private things, and many public crimes are therefore more particularly crimes against particular nobles. The prevalent definition of corruption today that we have often mentioned (the abuse of public office for private gain) appears to strain against this constitution, since public office serves the private interests of officeholders (within the confines of an honor system), and any "abuse" of public office tends to be more of an abuse of other nobles or the monarch himself.

"Political virtue" entails that one's love and ambition is thoroughly linked with the good of one's city. It is, from a liberal perspective, stifling, and Montesquieu points out just how difficult it is to understand from the outside: "When that virtue ceases, ambition enters those hearts that can admit it, and avarice enters them all. Desires change their objects: that which one used to love, one loves no longer. One was free under the laws, one wants to be free against them. Each citizen is like a slave who has escaped from his master's house. What was a *maxim* is now called *severity*; what was a *rule* is now called *constraint*; what was *vigilance* is now called *fear*" (3.3). When this virtue is corrupted, one is no longer motivated by a love of the laws, but rather by *fear* of the laws. One's relationship is altered toward public things—they begin to be seen as extrinsic to oneself, and thus as oppressive, alien. We can imagine a degree of utilitarian calculus on the part of people such that they accept some laws out of self-interest, but this entire way of thinking entails a profound shift in attitudes. From the perspective of the cities without republican virtue such ancient respect (*attention*) for the laws is perverse and can only be a product of fear. For how else can we explain (the liberal might exclaim) such monstrous stifling of the individual?

Montesquieu admired this austere, republican "political virtue," but there is some debate as to the degree to which he thought it ought to be resurrected in the modern world. Certainly he argued that the English experiment with republicanism proved an abject failure because the principle of virtue was not firmly established in the people (3.3). Montesquieu appears to lament the fact that modern political thinkers no longer speak of virtue, but rather of "manufacturing, commerce, finance, wealth, and even luxury" (3.3). Yet he himself suggests that this shift is permanent, particularly given the size of modern states (virtue is appropriate to smaller republics). He also hints that this shift away from ancient virtue is somewhat desirable. Montesquieu treated the martial spirit of the ancient republics as noble, but also inhumanly cruel, and he equally thought that virtue required excessive self-abnegation. In an oft-cited passage, he compared republican virtue—the passionate love of their city and laws—to the love of monks for the rule of their order: being deprived of all normal objects for their passions, monks direct all of their love toward the very rules that restrict them (5.2). This virtue is a kind of self-flagellation (presumably these monkish citizens would rather will their own subjection than not will). Nor is such virtue terribly amenable to liberty—on the contrary, it is stifling. A free regime must temper such virtue: "Who would think it! Even virtue has need of limits" (11.4).

Montesquieu's second regime, monarchy, is corrupted when princes centralize at the expense of other loci of power. In a monarchy, we recall, the principle of honor provides a limitation on the abuse of power. When this principle is corrupted, the laws of honor are no longer obeyed—the various ranks cease to play their role. Rather, the monarch devolves into a despot—one man who governs according to his own whim rather than according to established law and custom. A monarchy relies on honor because it relies on the principle that makes the nobility act in the interests of the state. In other words, a monarchy is not truly one-man rule, but is rather the rule of one supported by a vast array of nobility who are dutiful because they have prerogatives and honors that separate them essentially from the people, but that equally make them an independent, if subordinate, source of power.[2] This moderates the regime, preserving its law-abiding qualities, since nobles will insist on preserving their prerogatives and will refuse to do anything beneath their dignity. Montesquieu tells the heart-warming story of a viscount who refused to take part in the Saint Bartholomew's Day Massacre of 1572 because it was beneath his dignity to act in such a way (4.2).[3]

Honor is a brake on the power of the monarch because it cultivates individual ambition among nobles. At the same time, honor turns the nobles' interests toward the state and even makes them do heroic acts that verge on selflessness. Entirely bound up in their own *amour-propre*, these nobles seek glory. Since honor can make people sufficiently courageous to have contempt for death itself, it is a principle that is most dangerous to despots, whose entire method of control depends on threatening people with death (3.8).

Montesquieu conceived of "selfless," virtuous political action as something constituted through a very rigorous education and set of laws that proscribe all avenues for personal interest at the expense of the city. That is to say, the "renunciation of oneself" (4.5) that republican virtue entails is actually a cultivation of only one passion, love of the city, at the expense of the others. The self and its passions are still the source of a person's actions, but the passions are so constricted by laws that one directs one's energies toward the public good, and, in this sense, against what one would have more readily desired had one not been so denatured by political education. Montesquieu portrays this republican cultivation of people's love as highly unnatural and even "painful" (4.5). A sense of honor is much less painful and difficult to cultivate, since it appeals to passions that are easier to deploy because they are more directly self-regarding.

It is for the same reason that Montesquieu thought despotism the regime requiring the least amount of educational effort, since the principle of despotism—the passion of fear—is extremely easy to manipulate. If virtue is as difficult to cultivate as fear is easy, we get a sense that there is something highly artificial in courageous public-spiritedness, and something natural in fear. But should not despotism, then, be considered the most natural of regimes? On the contrary, if Montesquieu considers timidity a natural human trait, so too are affection and sociability. Despotism actually undermines our friendships and all of our natural relationships, all the while elevating our fears to unnatural levels. "It is useless to counter with natural feelings, respect for a father, tenderness for one's children and women, laws of honor, or the state of one's health; one has received the order and that is enough" (3.10). Despotism, in Montesquieu's account, does violence to our very nature by placing unhealthy psychological burdens on us, taking away our natural familial affections and our wider sense of community.

If the "principle" of despotism is fear, we might think that its corruption will entail confidence, but Montesquieu here leaves the realm of relativity—despotism, he insists, is *essentially* corrupt, for fear is its "principle," and fear is an essentially corrupting principle: "Other governments are destroyed because particular accidents violate their principle; this one is destroyed by its internal vice if accidental causes do not prevent its principle from becoming corrupt" (8.10). This is a difficult passage—fear itself must be "corrupted" for corruption not to be total. Montesquieu is arguing that despotism only works when it is actually moderated by some accident of religion or climate. Voltaire wrote that there was no such thing as "despotism" as Montesquieu defined it, there being no regimes on earth that existed without some law.[4] But this is precisely Montesquieu's point— despotism is an ideal type. It cannot subsist without some moderating element. In the "oriental" despotism, Montesquieu acknowledges the degree to which religion moderates the regime (5.14; 12.29; 26.2). No society can exist on fear alone, and fear itself is fundamentally corrupting.

Moderate, lawful government is a fundamental good for Montesquieu because of its effects on the souls of its citizens. Montesquieu insists that there is no problem if one sociable principle is exchanged for another—a corruption of virtue into honor (or vice versa) does not alarm him, as the regime will retain some principle tying people to the public good (8.8). Arbitrary government is so harmful not because self-rule is a fundamental good or because arbitrary rule entails a usurpation of natural rights, but because the despotic regime's principle, *fear*, does fundamental harm to the human psyche.[5] Human beings are corrupted by fear because they are rendered less capable of fellow feeling or of any solidarity.[6] In Montesquieu's imaginary natural state, fear is precisely that which drives people away from one another; it is that which leads them to think primarily of their individual good. A society based on such a principle will be entirely fragmented. When one perceives oneself subject to overwhelming force of arbitrary rule, one retreats into oneself. Montesquieu is pointing out what Orwell would indicate so vividly: terror conquers love. The degradation of the women in the harem of Montesquieu's Persian despot Usbek (in his philosophical novel the *Persian Letters*) vividly depicts how human relationships suffer under conditions of absolutism. In Montesquieu's imagined harem, there is no solidarity: there are temporary alliances as people seek to establish their place in the pecking order, and there is one thrilling act of suicidal defiance as nature rears its noble head, but there are no independent sources of power, no room for independent action, and thus no room for true affection, whether in the form of romantic love or public-spiritedness.

Fear, then, is the ultimate corruptor, just as despotism is the unambiguous *summum malum* in Montesquieu's politics. But it is not the only thing that corrupts universally. Let us now consider another corrupting influence, less destructive but nonetheless important: the desire for wealth and its attendant inequalities. If despotic regimes are based on fear, the only motivation that inspires striving in people is the desire for wealth and luxury (5.18).[7] Montesquieu articulates the standard civic-humanist view that excessive wealth leads to decadence and undermines civic freedom. This is one of the charges in his *Considerations on the Causes of the Grandeur and Decadence of the Romans*, and it is repeated in *The Spirit of the Laws* (8.2, 4). It is not merely that wealth leads to indolence and weakness—a standard trope—but that inequality undermines republican civic spirit. Montesquieu insists in particular that a democratic republic requires strict attention to equality of wealth. But immediately after making this point he qualifies it: there are such things as commercial republics. "Certainly, when democracy is founded on commerce, it may very well happen that individuals have great wealth, yet that the mores are not corrupted. This is because the spirit of commerce brings with it the spirit of frugality, economy, moderation, work, wisdom, tranquillity, order, and rule" (5.6). This is quite an encomium. However, there is a danger: "The ill comes when an excess of wealth destroys the spirit of commerce" (5.6).

Montesquieu indicates that in aristocratic republics moderation of inequality is essential for civic duty to be retained. When the aristocrats begin to enjoy privileges that are humiliating for the people, inequality begins to sting. Montesquieu writes, "This inequality will again be found if the conditions of citizens differ in relation to payments, which happen in four ways: when the nobles give themselves the privilege of not paying them; when they exempt themselves fraudulently; when they recover them for themselves on the pretext of remunerations or stipends for the tasks they do; finally, when they make the people their tributaries and divide among themselves the imposts they levy upon them" (5.8). Montesquieu admits that the last instance is rare, but he suggests in a footnote that the aristocratic use of fraud to exempt aristocrats from paying taxes is common in "some aristocracies of our time." He does not mention which, but he does indicate that "nothing so weakens the state."

Nothing weakens a state more than the absurdly low tax rates on capital gains and the ease with which the wealthy can evade and avoid taxation with foreign tax shelters (if the reader will excuse the anachronism); this is not merely because such practices deprive the state of revenue, but more because they make the state a mere avenue for the exploitation of one group by another. Such exploitation may be an objective fact of politics, but it is certainly harmful for social cohesion for exploitation to become completely transparent.[8] Such obvious subjugation is humiliating. And excessive wealth is not a problem only for republics. Monarchies' entire economies depend upon luxury (7.4), and this regime clearly requires vast inequalities of wealth to maintain the artificial divisions that honor demands. Nonetheless, it is important that such wealth be of secondary concern to the nobles. If nobles in a monarchy are given large monetary rewards for their services to the king, Montesquieu suggests, this is a sign that the principle, honor, has been corrupted (5.18). Indeed, the nobles ought to pay for their positions. Montesquieu defends the sale of public offices in monarchies, since venality, while corrupt from a republican point of view, has several advantages in monarchies: it fixes the estates, which Montesquieu thinks serves the interests of administration and hierarchy, it prevents the *secret* sale of offices (by corrupt courtiers), and it inspires industry since wealth is required in order to get station.[9] Ultimately Montesquieu thinks that those who have attained noble stations ought not to engage in commerce at all (20.21–22), as this desire for wealth is incompatible with the desire for honor and glory. The fact that English nobles engage in commerce has mixed the classes up and been responsible for the dissolution of a mediating institution (nobility) that makes monarchy function. The desire for wealth, while central to monarchical states, is corrupting when it becomes the motivation of the nobility. Avidity for gain must be encouraged in the right places, but must not be allowed to infect the realms subject to the economy of honor.

Corruption, then, entails an alteration of people's primary desires such that they no longer serve to unite disparate individuals. In the great eighteenth-century debate about the relationship between self-interest and virtue, Montesquieu does not offer a paean to selflessness; even the most public-spirited republican virtue is a product of an individual passion and of the overwhelmingly powerful legal and educational structure that channels our self-love into love of the city. In monarchies, the nobility makes a virtue out of what is traditionally considered a vice: *amour-propre* (and, in a Mandevillean manner, Montesquieu argues for the beneficial economic effects of a monarchical luxury economy). A regime's principle is that which allows it to continue to exist as a society; the things that corrupt the regime are those that undermine its principle—save in the case of despotism, where the principle itself is antisocial and would cause the regime's destruction but for some extraneous moderating elements. In all instances of corruption, the sentiments unifying people are undermined by the two powerful passions of fear and greed. Social relationships are broken apart or transformed into perversions of their natural state. But if corruption is that which weakens the sentiments at the heart of social unity, we will want to know something about Montesquieu's conception of purity. Which sentiments are natural and salutary? In the following section we will inquire into Montesquieu's conception of nature and its laws.

Nature in Its Purity:
Natural Law as a (Weak) Normative Anchor

While Montesquieu's extremely brief treatment of natural law in *The Spirit of the Laws* might appear to imply a subtle dismissal of the tradition, it is important to underline that nature remains a fundamental normative anchor in his thought. The difficulty with natural law (which, in Montesquieu's treatment, entails the basic social passions animating all human beings) is that it speaks so softly compared to history, climate, and positive laws. But this should not blind us to its centrality, and the elimination of nature as a normative basis would render Montesquieu's account of despotism and corruption void of normative force.[10] Following C. P. Courtney, I would like to insist on the importance of natural law in Montesquieu's thought, but I wish to highlight, somewhat contra Courtney, the way in which Montesquieu's natural law differs from that of most modern natural law theorists. Courtney claims that, for Montesquieu as for other modern natural law theorists, "when man's physical nature (the 'passions' and other amoral tendencies, or even instinct unguided by reason) takes over . . . the result is 'unnatural.' "[11] But Montesquieu does not treat the "laws of nature" as something to be equated with the a priori "rapports de justice" that he outlines in the book's first chapter (1.1). The laws of nature, for Montesquieu, are derived from an attempt to imagine, in a proto-Rousseauian manner, a perfectly pre-social human being. The laws of nature are not a priori rational laws of moral relationships between intelligent beings (as discussed in 1.1), but are akin to scientific laws governing physical substances: they "derive uniquely from the constitution of our being" (1.2). What is important to note here is that these laws are the results of natural *sentiments*. In the book's first chapter, when comparing human beings to animals, Montesquieu argues that animals "have natural laws because they are united by feeling; they have no positive laws because they are not united by knowledge" (1.1). In our pre-social condition, we are bestial—and we share the beasts' virtues. It is our reason that makes us err, for our reason is imperfect: "As an intelligent being, he [man] constantly violates the laws god has established and changes those he himself establishes." Passions can lead us astray, but this is largely because these passions are rendered dangerous by our *finite* intelligence, which is a source of both our freedom (or our perceived freedom) and our error. Human intelligence, because it is finite, is the source of error; passions are a surer guide.[12]

It is the complexity of society—and the tendency for people to try to turn that social union to individual advantage at the expense of social cohesion—that transforms early society into a Hobbesian state of war that can only be overcome with strong positive laws (1.3). Thomas Pangle is correct to note that "since Montesquieu holds that aggressiveness is less deeply rooted in human nature, and that affection is more deeply rooted, than Hobbes had thought, the political order which Montesquieu eventually indicated to be the solution to the human problem is much less strict or tough and much more soft and gentle than Hobbes's solution."[13] I would take this observation further than Pangle would wish and suggest that *The Spirit of the Law*'s constant refrain that despotic institutions do violence to nature is an appeal to this natural sociability that Montesquieu locates in an imagined pre-social condition. It is not that this condition represents an ideal—Montesquieu intimates that it never existed and never could. It is merely that this thought experiment allows us to see our basic, uncorrupted natural inclinations.

This is not to say that Montesquieu was offering starry-eyed optimism about human nature; on the contrary, he treated social life as if it is necessarily a source of corruption, for human intelligence, being finite, is necessarily corrupting. In his *Défense de l'Esprit des lois*, Montesquieu answered impatiently the charge that he had failed to discuss original sin (it isn't a book on theology! he spluttered).[14] But he could well have responded that the critic was simply incorrect: *De l'Esprit des lois* indicated clearly that corruption is an inevitable outcome of human beings' social nature and their limited intelligence.

If the tendency toward corruption is an essential element of political life, the duty of legislation is to mitigate it as much as possible. Montesquieu is so sparse in his treatment of an original condition not because he intends, obliquely, to denounce such speculation, but because he does not want to fill in human nature with false universal claims. But throughout the *Esprit des lois* he attacks specific institutions as unnatural, and an attentive reading of these passages gives us quite a number of rules for social life, from enjoining self-defense (and denouncing suicide) (6.13; 26.3; 10.2; 15.16; 24.6; 26.7), to defending sexual *pudeur*, the natural regulation of sexual mores, and the care for children (16.12; 26.3; 24.10; 12.14, 26.6; 23.2), to denouncing the blood-thirsty ancient republican penchant for murdering conquered peoples (10.3). Thus, for instance, Montesquieu suggested that it was a natural law for a parent to feed his child, but not to give the child an inheritance—the regulation of latter is something entirely dependent on the constitution and mores of a given state (26.6). The fundamental basis is in the four "natural laws" (which are equally natural sentiments) introduced in 1.2: the desire for peace (timidity), the desire for nourishment, the desire for sexual union, and the desire for community (born of our shared human capacity for knowledge). This is a conception of human beings as both individualistic yet born for cooperative social and sexual relations.[15] This is a very weak teleology—but a teleology nonetheless.[16]

"In the state of nature, men are born in equality, but they cannot remain so. Society makes them lose their equality, and they become equal again only through the laws" (8.3). Laws are to give people something approaching the basic goods that they would seek in an imaginary, original condition. With regard to equality, this does not entail an "extreme equality"; it entails a type of equality that threatens neither social order nor individual liberty. The laws—and the principles underpinning them—are means of mitigating the natural corruption to which human sociability tends. In different environments and different nations, different laws and psychological dispositions will be required, but there is, underlying it all, a basic conception of the good—that which does not do harm to our natural dispositions. But the "laws of nature" are too limited—they merely give us a rough outline of a natural social disposition; they say nothing about the institutions required to prevent their corruption. This is a question for the legislators of humanity: let us turn to the question of reducing corruption in the political world.

Moderate Corruption: England and the Antisocial Passions

Fear

To eliminate corruption altogether is neither possible nor, perhaps, entirely desirable. In the *Lettres persanes'* famous parable of the Troglodytes (letters

10–14), Montesquieu appears to be suggesting that a fully virtuous anarchic republic cannot possibly last; certainly we have already seen that republican severity perverts our most natural affections (just as republican self-sacrifice exceeds the demands of nature). The "principles" of the different constitutions are all both natural and unnatural: they exaggerate one passion at the expense of others. Fear is one of the most fundamental passions, but when elevated to the principle of government it entirely undermines our capacity for love and solidarity. Honor makes us vain, superficial, and decadent. Excessive virtue and public-spiritedness undermine our natural familial affections. Moderate corruption of principles appears to be the basis for humane social cohesion. The ancient Germanic tribes who conquered the Roman Empire and whose institutions resulted in the English constitution saw their own original republican constitution altered, and its principle diluted, by the changed conditions brought about by their success: "it is remarkable that the corruption of the government of a conquering people should have formed the best kind of government men have been able to devise" (11.8). Montesquieu's constant call for moderation—"The political good, like the moral good, is always found between two limits" (29.1)—is an attempt to prevent psychological imbalance. The real opposite of corruption is not virtue, but rather immoderation, that which does the most violence to human nature.

The "best type of government that men have been able to imagine" is the English government championed in book 11: this is the government that has "political liberty for its direct purpose" (11.5). And, as is well known, the main force that defends this liberty is the balance of powers, the manner in which our natural tendency to attempt to usurp the social unit for personal gain is mitigated by the institutional constraint of power checking power. Now, if Montesquieu celebrates an idealized version of the English constitution, he is much more ambivalent about England generally, and this is not merely because he thinks that the English are prone to suicidal depression (14.12).[17] Despite his enthusiasm for the English, he is of the view that fear and avarice play a central role in the commercial "republic under the guise of a monarchy." Let us consider how corruption is mitigated in that constitution.

Montesquieu's treatment of liberty is quite distinct from republican celebrations of free civic life. He famously defines political liberty for a citizen as "that tranquillity of spirit which comes from the opinion each one has of his security, and in order for him to have this liberty the government must be such that one citizen cannot fear another citizen" (11.6). Earlier Montesquieu defines political liberty as "having the power to do what one should want to do and in no way being constrained to do what one should not want to do." Or, in a different formulation, "liberty is the right to do everything the laws permit" (11.3). We are very comfortable with this last formulation—it is consistent with the Hobbesian liberty of the subject, and it fully accords with the dominant liberal conception of negative liberty. But the most striking element is the psychological claim—liberty is the *feeling* derived from the *opinion* one has of one's own security. The balance of powers that Montesquieu celebrates is there to prevent people from fearing one another.

Liberty is "the opinion one has of one's security" (12.2). Montesquieu offers an interesting hedge on the metaphysical problem of free will by merely defining "philosophical liberty" as being of the *opinion* that one's act is a product of one's will. That is, without actually dealing with the determinist challenge to voluntarism, Montesquieu nonetheless manages to sweep away the Hobbesian reconciliation of freedom and subjection to absolute power. Whatever the objective truth is, both philosophical and political liberty are matters of subjective opinion. Most important, they are states free from fear: in one's "philosophical liberty," one has the opinion of having acted freely (even if a Hobbesian could point out the appetites and aversions that determined the action); in one's "political liberty," one follows the law willingly and is under the impression of not having a sword constantly hanging over one's head. Montesquieu thought that this liberty obtained in England: "If a man in England had as many enemies as he has hairs on his head, nothing would happen to him: this is a big deal, because the health of the spirit [*l'âme*] is as necessary as that of the body." The balance of power protects the rule of law and thus helps give liberty to a people who have neither virtue nor honor.[18]

But England's constitutional structure is no panacea: the English, having undermined their intermediary institutions, are in grave danger of becoming slaves if they do not preserve their mores (2.4). Both mores and laws are essential for the minimization of corruption. Indeed, Montesquieu is quite clear that juridical and constitutional means alone will not suffice to cure people of corrupt mores, despite the intimate link between the two. We have seen that the two elements that most corrupt both individual souls and regimes are fear and avarice. England has both—indeed, England is replete with vicious passions, "hatred, envy, jealousy, and the ardor for enriching and distinguishing oneself" (19.27)—but Montesquieu thinks these passions themselves are a source of energy to England. The difficulty with England is that the very things that make it successful—its fear and avarice—are equally threats to its integrity.

First of all, Montesquieu's English citizens are not in a state free from fear—on the contrary, in a free state of an English stripe, "the people would be uneasy about their situation and would believe themselves in danger even at the safest moments" (19.27). These fears are inflamed by factionalism—party leaders in such a state would "increase even more the terrors of the people, who would never know if they were in danger" (19.27). Indeed, people become so attached to their particular party's views of reality that they lose their capacity for judgment: writers are almost as unfree as they would be in despotic regimes; "each one becomes as much the slave of the prejudices of his faction as he would be of a despot" (19.27). But Montesquieu did not condemn parties outright. Paradoxically, he thought that the partisan tendency to lie to people about the dangers of their state, throwing around groundless accusations of conspiracies and corruption, actually served to strengthen the state, since people thereby attend more to the actions of the government (19.27). The dangers of faction were moderated by the influence of the legislative body itself, which is able to calm the populace due to the respect it, as a body, commands in popular opinion.[19] Parties cannot devolve into the type of factions that so threatened ancient republics because the constitution is mixed—but if the government were to lose its balance, liberty would be in great danger. The English attempt to become a republic in the seventeenth century had failed because the English did not have sufficient civic virtue to overcome their factionalism (3.3). The danger of despotism in England is both mitigated by and derived from their passionate factionalism. It is their constitution and their spirit of liberty that protect them from their otherwise rapacious and untrusting spirit, but it is their very distrust and rapacity that prevent the destruction of their constitution.

The security that each individual feels in England is thus not total. On the contrary, people feel constantly wary; their security is rather a security from each other, and it is due to the existence of a reliable law that is enforced with punishments. Herein lies a psychological contradiction: the main object of their fear (the government) is that which protects them from fear—with threats. Montesquieu articulated the commonplace view that punishment is corrupt and counterproductive when exercised arbitrarily. But even when it is exercised in a nonarbitrary manner it ought not to be too harsh. While the state must retain a monopoly on violence, Montesquieu argued against people being overawed by fear of the sovereign's sword. Monarchies are corrupted when a prince "changes his justice into severity" (8.7), and we see in the character Usbek the complete manifestation of this corruption in his wrathful desire to purify his harem. His chief eunuch writes to him, promising to bring order and discipline to the harem: "I will punish . . . we will exterminate crime, and innocence will pale" (*Lettres persanes*, no. 160).[20] Being "tough on crime" is corrupt and corrupting. When punishments are too severe, they themselves undermine the law. "There are two kinds of corruption: one, when the people do not observe the laws, the other, when they are corrupted by the laws; the latter is an incurable ill because it lies in the remedy itself" (6.12). Fear is an essential human motivation, and it must be a part of any regime, but it deforms us and threatens the regime itself when it becomes overbearing.

The moderate and nonarbitrary manner in which punishment is exacted is a source of liberty. Montesquieu believes in the utility of punishment, but the fear that one feels must be directed toward *laws* and dependable institutions and not individuals. In England, "one fears the magistracy, not the magistrates" (11.6). This is the basis of any moderate regime. In a monarchy it is important that punishment appear to derive from the laws, of which the king is the protector, and not from the person of the king himself (12.23). Mark Hulliung has suggested that this is a step in the direction of the Weberian bureaucracy—impersonal management.[21] But if Hulliung is correct to point to the impersonal nature of Montesquieu's ideal judiciary, it is important to note that the rule of law in Montesquieu's English constitution is defended not by a bureaucratic ethos but rather by the political structure itself, which sets off against each other the competing interests of corrupted individuals wary that one group or another will undermine impersonal justice.

It is for this reason that Montesquieu is very much in accord with modern conceptions of transparency as distrust (in distinction to La Boétie's transparency as trust). English partisanship actually serves to augment transparency. The English requirement for ministers to give an account before a public body—Parliament—equally serves to keep them honest in their foreign relations (19.27). In a famous letter he wrote to an English nobleman expressing his optimism about English liberty surviving the

well-known corruption of parliamentarians, Montesquieu wrote that while
corruption would no doubt continue to affect some elections of MPs, in the
English Parliament "corruption cannot avoid being embarrassed, because it
is difficult to veil it."[22] There is a great danger in secrecy and a great merit
to openness. Montesquieu celebrated the Roman law that stated that anyone killing a night intruder must, in the act, cry out so as to draw attention
to his act (29.15) (this is the ancient equivalent of the closed-circuit video
camera). At the same time, Montesquieu offered no panopticon—the
security state ought not to shine its light on every little act of the citizens
(12.17). Indeed, Montesquieu would not have wanted transparency idolized.
Liberty, we recall, is based on subjective belief, and when authority is exercised Montesquieu does not want it to be excessively transparent. For
instance, Montesquieu preferred taxes on (nonessential) commodities to
direct taxes on persons because when the tax on merchandise is included
in the price, the payer is not made aware of the taxation (13.7–8). Transparency must work to prevent the usurpation of power by one class or branch
of government; it is not to be celebrated in itself.

The balance of power that prevents any branch of government from
becoming dominant is a product of England's mixed constitution. It is for
this reason that the main vice of the English—avarice—is so very dangerous. English parliamentarians are apt to be corrupt and to sell themselves to
royal influence. Montesquieu lamented this in his "Notes sur l'Angleterre,"
following the rhetoric of Bolingbroke's opposition to the king's placemen
in Parliament.[23] But Montesquieu ought to have seen the utility in this,
given his view that excessive purity was itself a bad thing. Isaac Kramnick
has argued that "corruption preserved the mixed constitution in the eighteenth century to such an extent that one analyst claims that this period
was indeed the only time when England enjoyed a truly balanced constitution."[24] Montesquieu celebrated this mixture: "England is currently the fre-
est country in the world . . . I call it free because the prince does not have
the power to do any imaginable harm to anyone . . . but if the lower house
became master, its power would be unlimited and dangerous . . . a good
Englishman, then, must attempt to defend liberty equally against the
encroachments of the crown and the house."[25]

The famous thesis about the balance of powers between branches of
government is a variation of this classical insistence on a balance between
the interests of different estates (royal, aristocratic, popular). The venality
of the English commons is ever a source of concern, but Montesquieu was

neither apoplectic nor sanguine about placemen.[26] In a society that places such emphasis on money, Parliament would always be in danger of being sold—it is therefore important that parliamentarians not be, as a body, sold to the same people. Montesquieu predicted the demise of English liberty "when the legislative power is more corrupt than the executive power" (11.6). Montesquieu also had a dire warning about representation: "When various legislative bodies follow each other, the people, holding a poor opinion of the current legislative body, put their hopes, reasonably enough, in the one that will follow; but if the legislative body were always the same, the people, seeing it corrupted, would expect nothing further from its laws; they would become furious or would sink into indolence" (11.6). Only regular elections combined with party antipathies could prevent such comfort on the part of parliamentarians. But the danger remains of an entrenched political class leading to widespread disaffection. Both the fury and the indolence that derive from this state of affairs can be harmful to liberty, the first leading to civil war and the second to servitude.

Desire for Wealth and Luxury

England is a kind of commercial republic (21.7), and as such is subject to the danger facing commercial republics: that its leading members abandon those mores that keep commercial societies moderate. A brief look at what Montesquieu thinks of the English should give us pause on this score. Humanity is undermined by the spirit of commerce itself: "in countries where one is affected only by the spirit of commerce, there is traffic in all human activities and all moral virtues; the smallest things, those required by humanity, are done or given for money" (20.2). This is certainly part of the English malaise—it is not just the weather that makes the English suicidal: it is their manner of interacting with each other. In contrast to the gay, sociable French subjects of a monarch, the English appear to be a dour, unfriendly, and vicious people. His early impressions of England were not laudatory: "money here is esteemed above all things; honor and virtue very little."[27] If he later altered these views somewhat (accepting that the English also value merit), he nonetheless continued to think that England's resilience and liberty largely derived from the way in which competing interests (individual interests and class interests) balance each other off in the public realm. The English regime is moderate because the English people are not;

the mixed regime and the balance of powers ensure that corruption moderates corruption. As he said with regard to the passing of an anticorruption bill in the English Parliament, "the most corrupt of parliaments is the one that has most assured public liberty."[28]

But England is more than a nation of devils. Commerce itself has a moderating influence—while it corrupts pure mores, it equally softens harsh mores (20.1). What takes the place of virtue in commercial republics is a moderating spirit of prudence, hard work, and economy; we have already seen how this ethic can be endangered by excessive wealth. English tastelessness and lack of polite manners is a sign that things are well—"the epoch of Roman politeness is the same as that of the establishment of arbitrary power" (19.27). How can the pursuit of wealth be prevented from entirely corrupting the city with luxury and undermining the necessary work ethic? "In order for the spirit of commerce to be maintained, the principal citizens must engage in commerce themselves; this spirit must reign alone and not be crossed by another; all the laws must favor it; these same laws, whose provisions divide fortunes in proportion as commerce increases them, must make each poor citizen comfortable enough to be able to work as the others do and must bring each rich citizen to a middle level such that he needs to work in order to preserve or to acquire" (5.6).[29] The establishment of a vast plutocracy and an industrial reserve army of the unemployed is the structural basis for the corruption of mores that would sap the utility of avarice and turn England down the road to despotism. The poor must have access to the labor market, and the rich must have their wealth kept within limits so that they do not begin to indulge in the useless luxuries that define consumption in a monarchy.[30]

Montesquieu was concerned that English wealth might eventually corrupt the country, but he remained optimistic that such corruption could be contained and would not follow the Roman pattern due to the vast difference between English luxury (which was a product of trade and industry) and Roman luxury (which was a product of rapine and the imposition of tributes). Montesquieu thought that wealth produced from trade is not the zero-sum wealth that the corrupted Roman officers enjoyed, and he appears to have been hopeful that this would lead to fewer extremes of inequality. This is not merely a question of violent conquest versus pacific trade—it is a question of the relationship between the bellicose, militarily successful Roman republic and avarice. The difficulty with Roman virtue was that it was entirely dependent upon the equal sharing of land. In the *Considerations on the Causes of the Grandeur and Decadence of the Romans*, Montesquieu argued that the relaxation of the laws on the ownership of land had introduced avarice, sapping the virtue of the Roman citizen-soldiers; he suggested, with some nostalgia, that this corruption described modern Europe.[31] In the same text he expressed some sympathy for the Gracchi, though suggesting that their agrarian laws came too late, at a point when civic virtue had been lost.[32] But in *The Spirit of the Laws* he appears to side with Cicero in thinking the agrarian laws unjust (26.15). The key shift is that Montesquieu had come to think that inequality in the commercial world need not entail the type of universal corruption that had been the demise of the Roman republic. But this rejection of agrarian laws is not a complete rejection of the need to moderate inequality and avarice. The key to the maintenance of English liberty, he insists, is the maintenance of a large class of "gens médiocres."[33] If Montesquieu presents a somewhat idyllic portrait of eighteenth-century English inequality, we can see his clear espousal of the classical Aristotelian teaching that a large middle class is the best support for a mixed regime.

Montesquieu believed that free states—and commercially successful states—always regulate their merchants, whereas despotisms create, if I may employ an anachronistic euphemism, business-friendly regulatory environments (20.12).[34] He did not want merchants to be overly burdened with excessive bureaucratic formalities (20.13), but he was quite clear that the purpose of commerce is to further the good of the state, and the regulation of merchants is an essential basis for freedom. Excessive taxation would harm industry, but taxation was the reason commerce was to be celebrated by governments.[35] There is a debate about the degree to which Montesquieu championed the independent, self-regulating nature of the commercial realm; certainly he thought that commerce undermined the political sovereignty of despotic countries, running counter to their tendency to want to prevent the free movement of capital outside their borders (12.14). It is also true that Montesquieu anticipated Adam Smith's worries about government-enforced monopolies (20.10). Finally, he thought it essential for a well-ordered state that private property be respected (26.15). But property right is a product of positive law, and states must be able to control matters such as inheritance in whatever manner necessary for their particular constitutions. Political interference in matters of property is not something that Montesquieu condemned, nor was he an outright enemy of high taxation (the most free countries are the most taxed, while the most despotic are the least (13.12, 10)—the key was to adjust tax policy so as not to dissuade commercial activity.

England represents a society in which the corrupt and corrupting passions of fear and greed are omnipresent but moderated. The English are avaricious and fearful, but their constitution is such that these passions serve to keep them united rather than to break them apart. Crucially, they so love the liberty they perceive in their state that they remain ready to sacrifice their wealth for its sake (19.27). But the danger remains that the English might sell their liberty—just as some English people are quite willing to abandon their country to go "seek abundance even in the countries of servitude" (19.27). The balance of corruptions is precarious; an ever-present, self-interested fear is the defense against terror, and a moderately avaricious disposition, well confined by laws, is the defense against over-reaching.[36]

Moderation and Modernity

Montesquieu stands somewhere between a civic republican warning against opulence and a full Mandevillean or Smithian embrace of commercial society. The myriad advantages of commercial republics do not negate the inherent dangers of their motivating passions—fear and the desire for private gain. Self-interested bourgeois man, whose utility and independent spirit Montesquieu so admired, is equally a potential danger—if he manages to overcome the balances in his constitution, corruption will become endemic and the state will become despotic. Commentators looking at the decline in commercial republics today might note the degree to which Montesquieu warned of precisely the institutional failures and the decline in mores that are leading to constitutional corruption.[37]

We have seen that, for Montesquieu, corruption entails the augmentation of the sentiments (fear and avarice) that undermine sociability. In this sense, it entails the abuse of public things for private gain, for the more corruption there is, the less sense there is of a public. But the complete elimination of fear is impossible in human society, and the complete elimination of greed leads to an unhealthy asceticism. His solution to the problem is one with which our liberal world is quite familiar—institutions must be designed such that public benefits derive from *moderate* private vices.

The state must neither be allowed to become too heavy-handed in its wielding of the sword nor too light in its control of commerce. Punishment must remain humane. Merchants and financiers must be encouraged but controlled: the liberty of commerce depends on merchants not being allowed to do what they want (20.12). Officeholders may be expected to want to breach the trust given to them, and watchfulness and resentment must be encouraged in order to keep them in check. Unlike ancient founders of republics, Montesquieuan legislators no longer have purity in their sights. Above all, "one must not correct everything" (19.6).

But make no mistake—this regime-craft entails soulcraft. A certain type of human personality is both the product and the defender of this balance (and in Montesquieu's more aristocratic moments he suggests that it is not a terribly admirable type). The passions of fear and avarice must not be allowed to become so dominant as to break apart natural human relationships and to turn society into zero-sum games of exploitation. However comfortable we are with this teaching, there is something decidedly uninspiring about it. Must we truly accept that societies that produce the likes of Walpole—and the attendant outcries against them—are the greatest possible political achievements? But if Montesquieu sets his sights well below civic republican heights, he nonetheless does not offer a post-moral conception of politics in which the language of corruption loses its normative force; he retains the teaching that the extreme corruption of regimes is both a product and source of the corruption of human nature. Whether Montesquieu's account of corruption could survive the philosophical evisceration of nature as a normative source is an open question.

CHAPTER 7

Kant, Robespierre,
and the Politics of Purity

Republican notions of corruption—that condition in which civic spirit is sapped, love of country compromised, martial virtue weakened, and private dependencies established—sit uneasily in liberal consciousness. We shy away from austere mores. Teenagers do not place images of Cato on their bedroom walls; one could little imagine a new city today being named after Cincinnatus. Indulgence competes with sobriety even for the mantle of civic virtue. Who did not notice the oddity in the U.S. government's response to terrorist attacks on New York and Washington in 2001, when, in an attempt to keep the country from slipping into an economic slump, the American president called on people to exercise civic virtue by spending money on luxuries for themselves? "Take your family to Disneyland," advised George W. Bush in a call to civic duty that would have made Brutus himself tremble. Even when governments facing fiscal crises speak the language of "austerity," the word is merely code for transferring wealth from the poor to the wealthy: governments continue to pursue policies aimed at increased consumption (through private and public debt) rather than true republican austerity.

We have seen that it was Montesquieu who helped usher in this world, squaring the circle between the immoderation of imperial republics and the moderation of republics for conservation. For Montesquieu gave us the ideal of a semi-monarchical commercial republic that was politically moderate so that it could be economically immoderate. *Doux commerce* was a way of acquiring without violence: fanciful as that notion was, the ideal undermined the very ferocity that was so essential to republican purity. Political moderation served economic immoderation, and mighty things were to be produced by tiny souls. We inhabit this world and have even cast off many of the virtues that Montesquieu thought concomitant with commerce. Indeed, his distinction between commerce of economy and commerce of luxury appears little applicable to our age of mass consumption. Thus, "decadent" has become a term of praise, and Mandeville reigns over the dour moralists. And thus Georges Danton, who was not in the least without blood on his hands, gets much better press than Robespierre, despite the fact that Danton's pockets were bursting with bribes. Or rather, because of that fact. For Danton wasn't so austere; or, as our contemporary, more demotic language would have it, he simply wasn't as much of a dweeb. He saw his chances and he took them. Roguery is a better sell than categorical imperatives. Drawing a parallel between Kant and Robespierre, Heinrich Heine termed Robespierre "der große Spießbürger von der Rue Saint-Honoré"[1] (Spießbürger roughly translates as "stuck-up bourgeois dweeb"), and the image has stuck; Georg Büchner's memorable picture of Danton (in Danton's Death) the bon vivant against Robespierre the stern, unbending servant of abstract principles leaves few contemporary readers unmoved by sympathy for the rogue, just as we shudder in horror before the specter of inhuman incorruptibility.

This is not merely an aesthetic preference. When one looks at the radical "incorruptibility" of Robespierre (called "the Incorruptible"), one is tempted to revert to a standard and highly sensible liberal—indeed, Montesquieuan—response: purity runs against nature. Even virtue needs limits! The stern political moralist attempted to create complete purity on earth, a radical refashioning of ancient republicanism that was doomed to failure because of the violence it did to corruptible human nature.[2] Jeremy Jennings writes, "everything indicates that the Jacobins believed that moral regeneration would be spontaneous and would be grounded upon the innate goodness of the people. . . . However, real human beings, with their earthly passions, presented the Jacobins with something of a problem."[3] Jennings's line is overstated—certainly Robespierre had no illusions about human frailty. His constant recourse to terror was largely due to his knowledge of human weakness. No doubt all authoritarians have recourse to ever-increasing violent repression when things and people don't stay where they're told; often these methods work (Napoleon, for instance, was quite good at it, proving grapeshot more effective than guillotines). But Robespierre represents more than authoritarian repression; he embodies the attempt to eliminate corruption from a fallen world. Robespierre is a sign pointing to something that will forever produce unease: holy terror. Rightly do dandyish advocates of holy terror such as Slavoj Žižek look here for inspiration: Robespierre's linking of terror and virtue has an Old Testament flavor of divine wrath.

But such observations are old hat and generally give birth to simplistic moral judgments about the dangers of radical politics or excessive idealism or fanaticism of a politico-religious nature.[4] This is not the place for such liberal pieties; the Terror was outdone by the reaction, and more innocent blood was shed by Napoleon's wars than in the Vendée. But mortuary accounting is not our purpose here either, and reactionary crimes do not excuse revolutionary ones. Nor are we concerned with psychological speculation, tempting as it is, given Robespierre's reputation for vanity, or the apocryphal stories of the wounded Robespierre obsessing over bloodstains on his white shirts. The question that animates our inquiry entails the nature of such purist politics. The Terror is not just the escalation of violence by an increasingly embattled revolution; it is a moment of supreme ideological conflict against the "English" model celebrated by Montesquieu: the model that made its peace with a limited corruption was literally at war with the National Convention. This was an ideological war of geopolitical importance. The battle was not simply between monarchy and republicanism, or between counterrevolution and revolution, and it was not simply between the carnivalesque brutality of the street and the desire for order (the choreographed brutality of war); first and foremost, it was between Montesquieuan moderation and republican virtue. "L'incorruptible" is not just a nickname: it is a political program.[5]

What does it mean to make absolute purity—ridding one's republic of corruption—a political program? How can we think purity politically? And is such an idea necessarily a prelude to the executioner's block? We noted that when Heine termed Robespierre a *Spießbürger*, he did so in the context of a comparison between Robespierre and that paragon of ethical purity Kant. There was, after all, a striking similarity between their dour, fastidious personalities. But Heine averred that Kant was in fact more radical than Robespierre (for the latter only killed a king, whereas Kant killed a god). The comparison entails more than a humorous parallelism based on their common (somewhat exaggerated) reputations for anal-retentiveness: both were grappling with the thought that the elimination of corruption was a practical program. Both sought to apply roughly Rousseauian premises, and (contra what one might be tempted to say given the contrast between their respective active and contemplative lives) both conceived of the project as a supremely practical one. The link between the two purists is not unique to Heine. Marx thought Kant offered the "German theory of the Revolution,"[6] just as Hegel had discerned in Kant something akin to the Rousseauian liberty that burst forth in revolution. But Hegel provided the following distinction:

> Rousseau had already presented freedom in the absolute: Kant had the same principle, only more on a theoretical level. The French understand it on the side of the Will; for they have an expression, "Il a la tête près du bonnet" [he has his head close to his bonnet; i.e., he loses his temper easily]. France has a sense of actuality and practicality. . . . But as much as freedom is in itself concrete, it was undeveloped in the manner that its abstraction was applied to actuality. And to make abstractions apply to actuality [*die Wirklichkeit*] is to destroy the actual. The fanaticism of freedom, put into the hands of the people, was terrible. In Germany the same principle had claimed the interest of consciousness, but it only developed in a theoretical way. We have this tumult all about us, within the head and on the head, but the German head is content to wear its nightcap, and perform its mental operations quietly under it.[7]

To some extent, this passage might be interpreted as a standard, stereotypical opposition of the German ideologist in his quietist, metaphysical profundity versus the French political activist, but it serves much more precisely to characterize the gulf between the purism of Robespierre's Terror and the philosophical purism of Kant. We should, however, take care with this portrait, accurate though it is. It is not that Kant was content merely to cogitate while others acted: the radical separation of philosophy from practice was the last thing he wished to countenance. Kant's paradoxical admiration for and rejection of the revolution is the key to understanding how Kant was able to think through the politics of purity without countenancing moral disaster. In what follows, I will attempt to show just why the Kantian version of political purity had to remain beneath his nightcap, for a time at least. The tragedy of Robespierre's purity is that it was sullied by impatience. In its revolutionary haste, it neglected the most important element of Kantian chiliasm: time.

In the first section, we will begin by outlining Robespierre's political program of purification. We will not engage in a full exploration of the political positions he took, nor will we discuss the details of the Committee of Public Safety of which Robespierre was but one member. Our purpose is to highlight the coherence of his politico-ethical rigorism and the manner in which he conceived of corruption and its cure. The second section turns to Kant and examines his political and ethical rigorism, exploring the surprisingly oft-repeated charge that his thought is terroristic in its implications. We will conclude with some remarks on Kant's solution to the problem of crooked timber.

Clean Hands: Robespierre and the Inseparability of Virtue and Terror

There is an old cliché, perhaps most famously expressed by Weber in his distinction between the "ethic of ultimate ends" and the "ethic of responsibility," arguing that one cannot achieve moral purity in politics for the political realm is full of contingencies that force one to behave in an immoral manner in order to attain moral ends. Michael Walzer has explored this difficulty in a famous essay in which he insists, against some utilitarians, that the problem is a real one and that we should not attempt to overcome it: politics requires immoral actions, but it is important for those who commit such actions not only to understand and lament that fact, but also to have available some means of public expiation (beyond the mere interior pangs of conscience that Weber thought appropriate).[8] There is much to be said about this argument: it indicates an awareness of the need for public morality and it offers a none-too-clean solution to the problem of political exception. But Robespierre had little time (literally and figuratively) for moral dilemmas of this sort. To some extent he adopted the consequentialist moral logic that Walzer wants to escape. As he wrote in his *Rapport sur les principes du gouvernement révolutionnaire*, "The revolutionary government requires extraordinary activity precisely because it is at war. It is subject to rules less uniform and less rigorous because the circumstances in which it finds itself are nebulous and shifting, and, most of all, because it is constantly forced to deploy new resources quickly for new and pressing dangers."[9] There is a necessity that justifies exceptional acts, but this necessity is not something that needs hiding; there is no need for such *pudeur*.

But his most sustained justification of terror went beyond—and, indeed, overturned—the consequentialist appeal to necessity. Of course, the Terror has a great number of meanings, not all of them confined to Robespierre's justifications. It was, among other things, an attempt to clamp down on the violence of the sans-culottes, to direct it and contain it; it was a reassertion of state monopoly on violence in the face of mob rule; terror gave violence a unified direction. This was articulated most famously by Danton when calling for the establishment of a revolutionary tribunal: "Let us be terrible in order that we may dispense the people from being so."[10] And, naturally, it had a number of consequentialist justifications by people who were keen to kill the sons of Brutus. But Danton's willingness to accept the burden of dirty hands had little to do with Robespierre's justification. And terror went beyond the matter of emergency. Terror, for the Incorruptible, was of intrinsic value, of deontological value. It was necessary even if it failed. A great number of the polemics about the Terror (and even worse, the massive crimes against the population of the Vendée) center around the consequentialist moral accounting: were these drastic actions necessary to save the revolution? Were they morally excusable given the danger in which the revolution found itself and the radical change it sought to produce?[11] Of course, such conversations are of historical importance (and, incidentally, all holy violence can be interpreted as defensive, not excluding the Levites' famous killing spree in Exodus), but the point to be made is that Robespierre did not have dirty hands, nor did he need to face the moral accounting that the dirty hands problem entails. No doubt his defense of his actions was replete with self-serving, post hoc rationalizations; no doubt there was as much hypocrisy and double-dealing in his actions as his critics allege; none of this alters the theoretical consistency of his position. Terror was not an evil; it was a constitutive part of virtue.

Indeed, Robespierre explicitly disavowed Machiavellian consequentialism.[12] There is an eternal principle that must be guarded and that will itself destroy all corruption and make sure that "every new faction meets its death in the simple thought of crime."[13] Eternal justice, engraved on the hearts of men, will see to this. The people, as general will, are always pure, but people as individuals are always corruptible. Terror and virtue are inseparable, for wherever there is government there is corruptibility, but the purity of the people was a product and guarantee of terror. The famous passage bears repeating: "the spring of popular government in revolution is at the same time *virtue and terror*: virtue, without which terror is disastrous; terror, without which virtue is impotent. Terror is nothing other than prompt, severe, inflexible justice; it is thus an emanation of virtue."[14]

If *le peuple* is always pure, how could corruption occur? Robespierre's answer to it is clearly inspired by Rousseau: insofar as citizens are not tricked or bought, their honest self-interest will be the general interest. But individuals can be corrupted or misled to see their private interests in uncivic, factional ways. Of course, Robespierre, in the thick of conspiracies and counterconspiracies was not so exacting in seeing the general will as a thing expressed/discovered though a particular institutional procedure: he preferred to spot it in the "spontaneous" expression of public vengeance (selective though he was about which riots were expressions of the general will). But the principle was consistent: as individuals with personal interests, we are all susceptible to corruption, which is nothing more or less than a lack of *civisme*. As the war and the state of revolutionary emergency continued, the command economy (with its maximum on the price of bread and laws against hoarding) multiplied the number of activities in which the clash between anticivic and civic inclinations could manifest themselves. The possibilities for corruption became nearly infinite.

Robespierre did not invent this preoccupation with corruption. The language of purity and corruption is the leitmotif of the revolution itself. The *Déclaration des droits de l'homme et du citoyen* of 1789 presents itself first and foremost as a cure for corruption, affirming in the preamble that "that the ignorance, neglect [*l'oubli*], or contempt of the rights of man are the sole cause of public calamities and of the corruption of governments."[15] At the moment this thought was expressed, these rights were mere aspirations, and the Assemblée was forging new norms. No longer bearing conservative implications (corruption is that which degrades existing norms and institutions), the language of corruption had become revolutionary (the existing norms and institutions are corrupt). But it was reaching back to a natural origin. There was a precorrupted nature that needed to be rediscovered, some fundamental facts about humanity that needed to be recovered. It is an Enlightenment doctrine: ignorance of natural rights begets oppressive government. But five years later, the language had shifted. For the Law of 22 Prairial (1794) declared criminal "those who have sought to mislead opinion and to prevent the instruction of the people, to deprave the mores, to corrupt the public conscience and to alter the energy and the purity of revolutionary and republican principles."[16] The shift might appear to be one of degree, but the types of ignorance and error are different. Corruption is not merely a product of ignorance of one's rights—not merely a question of the uninformed needing enlightenment, of a public reason needing cultivating—but a question of a public conscience that was in danger of being sullied, of mores perverted and fervor diluted. The energy and the purity of the revolution is being undermined by a moral pollution. The previous ignorance was one propounded by self-interested priests and aristocrats; its cure was a proclamation of the truth. The current ignorance, no doubt equally propounded by self-interested traitors, is not one that can be combated with information. It must be cut out with the blade. "Qu'un sang impur abreuve nos sillons" (may an impure blood water our furrows), as the "Marseillaise" has it.

Throughout—from the early revolution through the Terror—the sense of corruption as the individual abuse of a public function for private ends is equally present. The Law of 22 Prairial speaks of this, condemning those who "persecute patriotism" "by corrupting the representatives [les manda-taires] of the people,"[17] and this phenomenon grew in importance in the years of scarcity and radical change in which every ambitious person sought to better his lot and foreign influences sought to make themselves felt. Robespierre was constantly sniffing out the money of Pitt (i.e., British fund-ing of antirevolutionary movements, a policy identified with Prime Minis-ter William Pitt) and reactionary forces. But the lust for personal pecuniary advantage had become more than an individual crime; it was a symbol of private ends trumping the public good. For the money of Pitt was not merely a reality (indeed the presence of foreign money was not the fantasy of enraged revolutionaries, but has been well documented),[18] but it was also a symbol of the very Montesquieuan compromise that was to be combated. After all, it is the money of speculators and of the English crown whose very presence in England's Parliament is the sign of its degradation: its presence on French soil is a contamination of principle, the invitation to Montesquieuan moderation, to anticivic inclinations, to the unacceptable compromises with injustice.[19]

Montesquieu's desire for power to check power—the view that found itself reflected in his celebration not merely of balanced powers, but equally of parliamentary competition—was a far cry from the radical transparency that Robespierre wanted in his state. Robespierre conceived of Montes-quieu's solution as thoroughly corrupt—"a league of rival powers against the people."[20] He went on to condemn the tribunate that Machiavelli so admired for exactly the same reason: the tension within the city that it engendered was not salutary, for the tribunes themselves were corruptible. The only thing that is incorruptible is the people.[21] His vision of the world, encapsulated in the following article of his proposed declaration of the rights of man, highlighted the need for the utmost vigilence with regard to officeholders: "In every free state the law must above all defend public and individual liberty against the authority of those who govern. Every institution that does not suppose the people good and the magistrate corruptible is vicious."[22] Hence all public officeholders must be the subject of constant scrutiny and surveillance, and the slightest nonrevolutionary inclinations needed to be ferreted out. And, indeed, as the necessities of the revolution made more and more aspects of life essential to the functioning of the state, more and more individuals became the object of suspicion and the subject of accusations of *incivisme*. The utmost confidence in the people was married to the utmost suspicion of individuals.

It has often been considered fitting that Robespierre should have perished by the same weapon that did in so many of his victims. Even more fitting is the fact that the justification for it was the rumor of corruption. The Incorruptible had taken bribes and was seeking to marry the daughter of Marie Antoinette and place himself on the throne.[23] It is appropriate for the wild accusation of intrigue and corruption to have felled him, for the charge of corruption when overplayed becomes nothing but the fan that hurries the flame of violent faction. We have seen that Machiavelli knew this well—hence he celebrated public accusation that channeled public resentment, preventing the eruption of violent factions and secret plots. But we have also seen that on Robespierre's reading, this was not the Committee of Public Safety's purpose: it was not to contain and channel hatred (as Georges Danton and Camille Desmoulins saw it). It was to purify. That he himself might die in the process was not lost on Robespierre (though his oft-professed willingness to die says very little about his theory or his character).

The difficulty, of course, is the identification of the universal. Instantiating the absolute in this world is a tricky business. Hegel famously read the Terror as the contradiction of attempting to put in place a universal will that was impossibly abstract and hence wound up as a simple negativity: "this was a time of trembling and quaking and intolerance towards everything particular."[24] It is difficult to quibble with Hegel here; Robespierre's advocacy of radical mistrust for all particular officeholders was not a recipe for policy, and it became particularly unstable when the mistrust spread even to the office of electors. Dan Edelstein has argued that Robespierre's thought is not primarily a reflection of a Rousseaiuan general will, but an appeal to an objectively determinable natural right. Certainly, the institutional measures that Rousseau would have wanted to see in the determination of the general will were sorely absent from Robespierre's practice. Edelstein quotes the Incorruptible: "I adhere to the will of the majority, or to what it is assumed to be . . . but I respect justice and truth. . . . Society has a right to demand my loyalty, but not to sacrifice my reason: that is the eternal law of all reasonable beings."[25] Certainly, this would help offer a justification for Robespierre's refusal to condone a referendum on the king's execution.[26] But in Robespierre's case, it is not that the general will is expressly subordinated to natural law; it is rather that any given majority may be subject to corruption and misinformation, and hence not truly reflect the general will. The universal was at times more of a regulative ideal than a concrete reality. Of course, the distinction is arbitrary and ultimately comes down to who can affirm most forcefully their interpretation of the general will. Robespierre met the universal fate of insufficiently armed prophets.

Those attempting to come to terms with Robespierre's thought have often noted that his philosophical categories owe much more to Montesquieu than to Rousseau.[27] But Robespierre turned these very categories against Montesquieu's thought itself. The principle of republican government, Robespierre declared happily, is virtue: the love of one's *patrie* and the love of equality. But Montesquieu's urbane skepticism toward republican virtue was simply lost on the Incorruptible. In what was doubtless a direct reference to Montesquieu's comparison of ancient republics to monastic orders, Robespierre affirmed, "we do not pretend to make the French Republic in the mold of Sparta; we do not want to give it austerity, nor the corruption of cloisters."[28] But moments later he intoned, "Therefore, the representative body must begin by subordinating in its breast all the private passions to the general passion of the public good."[29] Virtue was a natural condition of people, but corruptibility was the natural tendency of governments.[30] All governments tend toward aristocracy and monarchy, for those forms are essentially corrupt; and all manifestations of extra-civic interest are essentially monarchical or aristocratic. There can be no moderation; vice must tremble, crime must be punished swiftly and fully. It is the closeness of terror and virtue that allowed Robespierre to indulge in such insignificant speech as that embodied in phrases like "the despotism of liberty against tyranny" or "punishing the oppressors of humanity is clemency."[31] One cannot blame Burke for exclaiming of France that "the foundation of their Republick is laid in moral paradoxes."[32] Nonetheless, the essence of the claim is that to deviate from harsh punishments was to commit radical injustice. In Robespierre's doing away with trials for suspects, one sees the hysterical response to a moment of crisis, but it follows the logic of his opposition to the king's trial: these are enemies undeserving of civil protection. But they do not exist in an extra-juridical space: in the space of natural justice, they merit retribution of the strictest variety.[33]

The key point is that terror was the flipside of virtue, a purifying force that was the proof of virtue's zeal and the guarantee against its corruption. Terror as a principle does not guarantee virtue by providing deterrence. Robespierre had no time for civic virtue that was merely a product of fear. Such fear itself was, indeed, a sign of corruption. As Robespierre told the Convention, "all the representatives of the people whose hearts are pure should reassume the appropriate confidence and dignity."[34] Fear need not affect the virtuous: "whoever trembles in this moment is guilty; for innocence never fears public surveillance."[35] The corrupted—the moderates, the foreigners, the *philosophes*, the atheists, the profiteers, the bribe takers, that ever widening group of individuals who showed a lack of zeal and a tendency toward personal rather than civic inclination—are in need of repression, indeed elimination. To permit their continued presence is to make the republic an accomplice in their crimes. Apologists for Robespierre can say what they will about his knowledge of and responsibility for the bloodier acts of 1794, but such acts were consistent with his principles. For there was, he thought, an impurity in the body politic that needed cutting out. Terror is not deterrence; it is excision and strict retribution.

Kant, Virtue, and Terror

It is, at first glimpse, difficult to see how Kant could be considered a philosophical expositor of political purity given his famous liberal assertion that one can concoct a political constitution that a city of rational devils could accept. This, added to his frequent praise of political obedience even in the face of injustice, makes the comparison with Robespierre seem a stretch.

"For Kant," writes Terry Eagleton, "sublime eruptions like the French Revolution could be admired as long as they were aestheticized, contemplated from a secure distance."[36] According to Jonathan Israel, Immanuel Kant belonged to the moderate Enlightenment, the Enlightenment that shrank back from revolution and, indeed, that was not merely unsympathetic to democracy but made a great crime of rebellion.[37] Not for Israel, the Kant of Heine who did in God properly and thus deserves the mantle of radicalism. But I would like to suggest that Heine was correct: in his purism, Kant was even more extreme than Robespierre, and he never abandoned the ideal of a state free from corruption.

Žižek, in one of his typically overladen rhetorical questions, writes: "Kantian ethics effectively harbors a 'terrorist' potential—a feature which points in this direction would be Kant's well-known thesis that Reason without intuition is empty, while Intuition without reason is blind: is not its political counterpart Robespierre's dictum according to which, Virtue without Terror is impotent, while Terror without Virtue is lethal, striking blindly?"[38] How might we assess this extravagant claim? It is hard to say, since the vague phrase "political counterpart" is difficult to pin down—the terrorist formula is not implied by its Kantian counterpart about intuitions and concepts ("Thoughts without content are empty, intuitions without concepts are blind"),[39] nor is there any clear relationship between the terms. Žižek appears to be playing on a superficial grammatical similarity. If Žižek's suggestion is that terror is a Kantian source of virtue, such a position is somewhat controversial. Kant, at several moments, insisted that awe is not terror: "The majesty of the moral law . . . instils awe (not dread, which repels, nor yet charm, which invites familiarity)."[40] Again, in the *Critique of Practical Reason*, Kant offered a dithyrambic praise of duty's sublimity (which we might expect to inspire terror, as sublime things are wont to do) nonetheless insisting that it "does not seek to move the will by threatening anything that would arouse natural aversion or terror in the mind but only holds forth a law that of itself finds entry into the mind and yet gains reluctant reverence."[41] We will return to sublimity and the nature of this awe or respect (*Achtung*). But for the moment we may simply note that for a person to be disposed to act a certain way only because of terror is for them to have lost their capacity for freedom: their will is entirely subordinated to empirical causality. But this is not to say that the possibility of coercion necessarily undermines the Kantian good will. The state exists in order to threaten punishment and thereby ensure external freedom, and the presence of external coercion is fully consistent with (and even an important condition for) the emergence of the good will, for in a state of nature where all property is provisional and all external liberty uncertain, inner liberty is more difficult to attain. Thus, coercion was necessary against the nation's devils to secure the possibility of its angels. But to see Kant's view as a liberal lowering of expectations is to miss the moral significance of coercion and the state itself. Because one cannot rely on everyone having good will (indeed, as Kant notes in the *Groundwork*, one can never be absolutely certain even of one's own motivations),[42] one has a duty to establish (through autonomous means) the coercive apparatus of the state because fear thereof is the only guarantee for external liberty. Virtue is not produced by terror, but we have a moral duty to establish the conditions of external coercion in order to make possible a condition of right.[43]

But the Montesquieuan goal of making peace with a mitigated corruption is not Kant's goal. Kant's argument about the possibility of establishing right for a city of devils was based on his view that while establishing the conditions of right itself is a moral duty, right entails outward compliance, not inward duty. Thus right can be attained through mere prudential considerations. Kant offers this as grounds for hope in world peace, since he perceives that conflict itself can lead to rational egoists seeing the utility of the state and of international cooperation.[44] But his constant hope is a moral improvement of humanity such that people's actions are no longer determined by external coercion.[45] The providential hope that Kant derives from the utility of rational egoism is at a great distance from the consequentialist liberalism of Hobbesian ancestry that sees the cultivation of rational egoism as the necessary condition of peace. As we shall note, everything depends upon Kant's separation of virtue and right, but that separation does not entail a liberal lowering of our ethical sights.

I do not wish to go through a systematic list of similarities and differences between Kant and Robespierre (it should go without saying that Kant found the Committee of Public Safety thoroughly despotic),[46] but the two authors do have some elements of commonality that require elaboration. Robespierre's tendency to treat the general will as if it were something he could better discern than the citizens themselves would not have troubled Kant overly given that Kant saw the general will more as an idea of reason than an empirically determinable fact, and the sovereign's duty was merely to "give his laws in such a way that they *could* have arisen from the united will of a whole people."[47] More important, like Robespierre, Kant thought sovereignty indivisible, and the very notion of a "moderate" constitution struck him as insignificant speech.[48] But his reasons for saying this were based on a rejection of Robespierre's argument for the right of revolution: Kant fully opposed such a right not merely because it entailed a contradiction of the general will with itself, but because it entailed dissolving the social contract, and one has a fundamental duty to be in a civil condition since this is the necessary condition for outer freedom. But if Kant denied that there could be a right to rebellion (and if he thought Robespierre's proposed constitutional right to insurrection self-contradictory),[49] he nonetheless shared Robespierre's assessment of the legal condition of the king leading up to his execution: Louis Capet was not a citizen being tried for a crime. He was an enemy, outside of the constitution. For Robespierre, however, his execution was not a state of exception; it was an act of natural justice.[50] His crime is a crime according to natural law; he is in a state of nature, and one may merely kill him.[51] For Kant the act cannot really be termed a punishment since, as monarch, Louis had been, in fact, exercising the general will. Given that the revolution had happened (and Kant thought he could find a way to make it acceptable by interpreting it as if the king had abdicated to the États Généraux),[52] one could kill the ex-king as a matter of necessity (an act in the same legal gray area as taking the only plank from another shipwreck victim),[53] but to clothe the act in legality would be a supreme crime, for it would entail the general will asserting the legality of rebellion. Note the contrast with Robespierre: both agree that the relationship between Louis and the people is on the order of *droits des gens* rather than civil right, and both think the execution of the king justifiable under the right of necessity, but for Robespierre to put the king on trial would mean calling into question the legal sanctity of the insurrection. He wished to treat insurrection against tyrants as of foundational justice; for Kant, putting the king on trial would be evil because it would attempt to turn insurrection—the greatest crime—into justice.[54] In this sense, it would commit the same error as the "political moralist" at the end of "Perpetual Peace," who, in contrast to the "moral politician" who attempts to correct immoral institutions, turns his immoral acts into a principle of morality.[55]

Eagleton's line about Kant admiring the revolution aesthetically from a distance is based on the conjunction of Kant's denigration of rebellion and his wild enthusiasm for the French Revolution. It is incorrect to say that Kant's attitude was "aestheticized" since he was expressing a moral judgment and not a judgment of beauty. But Kant was cheered more by the spectators than by the actors in the revolutionary drama itself. Kant thought that he could spot evidence for the teleological nature of history in the universal and disinterested sympathy that spectators felt for the French revolutionaries. "Their reaction (because of its universality) proves that mankind as a whole shares a certain character in common, and it also proves (because of its disinterestedness) that man has a moral character, or at least the makings of one."[56] Perhaps the statement was not entirely up to social scientific standards (Kant does not tell us how he determined this universal response), but it is clear that he shared the view that the struggle was between noble virtue and corruption, and that the enthusiasm for the republican ideal was surely greater than any reaction. "No pecuniary rewards could inspire the opponents of the revolutionaries with the zeal and greatness of soul which the concept of right could alone produce in them."[57] The implication is that one is either a supporter of the revolution, or one has been corrupted by some personal pecuniary advantage.

We saw that for Robespierre human nature was capable of supreme virtue and supreme corruptibility; the one derived from our adherence to the universal will (embodied in the *peuple*), the other derived from our pernicious personal inclinations. We are, as individuals, constantly inclined to corruption, to the neglecting of the universal. So too did Kant perceive human beings as torn between a moral law determined by its universal nature and private inclination that seeks to make exceptions for itself and to corrupt others: "Men . . . mutually corrupt [*verderben*] one another's moral predispositions; despite the good will of each individual, yet, because they lack a principle which unites them, they recede, through their dissensions, from the common goal of goodness and, just as though they were instruments of evil, expose one another to the risk of falling once again under the sovereignty of the evil principle."[58] In the moral realm, respect for the moral law acts as a kind of negative principle that overwhelms competing affects: "inasmuch as it moves resistance out of the way, in the judgment of reason this removal of a hindrance is esteemed equivalent to a positive furthering of its causality."[59] In the political realm, coercion (which appears on first glimpse to be a principle that would run counter to autonomy) does the same thing: "Resistance that counteracts the hindering of an effect promotes this effect," Kant writes. "If a certain use of freedom is itself a hindrance to freedom in accordance with universal laws (i.e., wrong), coercion that is opposed to this (as a hindering of a hindrance to freedom) is consistent with freedom in accordance with universal laws, that is, it is right."[60]

But if these inner and outer coercions serve the purpose of suppressing the barriers to virtue and right respectively, Kant's notorious doctrine of punishment has a striking retributivist dimension that goes well beyond the suppression of barriers to right. A murderer, Kant writes, "must *die*. Here there is no substitute that will satisfy justice. . . . Even if civil society were to be dissolved by consent of all its members (e.g., if a people inhabiting an island decided to separate and disperse throughout the world), the last murderer remaining in prison would first have to be executed, so that each has done to him what his deeds deserve and blood guilt does not cling to the people for not having insisted on this punishment; for otherwise the people can be regarded as collaborators in this public violation of justice."[61] In citing this notorious passage, I do not mean to indicate that Kant is a thoroughgoing retributivist: he has moments when his justification of punishment is future-oriented, offering an external incentive to those devils who have not sufficient inner incentive to obey the law.[62] Punishment is justifiable as a means to realizing external freedom. But the purpose of this fanciful example of the retributive islanders is clearly to offer a defense of punishment that is entirely independent of its deterrent effects. The slightest deviation from strict *lex talionis* brings "blood guilt" upon the entire people. Kant translates the maxim "Fiat iustitia, pereat mundus" as the demand that justice be done "even if all the rogues in the world perish because of it" (die Schelme in der Welt mögen auch insgesamt darüber zu Grunde gehen);[63] the perishing of the rogues is not a price one must pay for justice to be done, but a simple corollary of the injunction.

This passage has tended to inspire discomfort among Kant's admirers (and gleeful gloating among his enemies): it seems particularly perverse, a striking instance of the categorical imperative run amok. "Blood guilt" sounds like an odd, superstitious concept, as if the crime of the murderer stains the community and needs to be atoned for to appease some angry divinity. But though Kant does have things to say about the idea of divine punishment, that is not the principle at work here. The corruption that the community would take on by failing to kill murderers is born of the fact that their omission in punishing is akin to accepting and even ratifying the crime. They are corrupted by their clemency.

The reason that Kant so emphasized the retributive dimension of punishment is linked to the categorical imperative not to use another human being as a means only. If punishment is thought of as a deterrent and if it only has a consequentialist, eudaemonist grounding, one has left the purity of justice and entered into the wavering, uncertain realm of happiness. It is worth noting the manner in which Kant's mind slips immediately from eudaemonism to corruption. Considering the possibility of lessening a punishment in order to procure a great benefit to society—say, permitting a criminal to live if he allows himself to be a guinea pig for medical experiments—Kant scoffs: "A court would reject with contempt such a proposal from a medical college, for justice ceases to be justice if it can be bought for any price whatsoever."[64] To base one's actions on empirical consequences rather than the unshifting ground of a priori practical reason is akin to the bribe-taking judge who allows the extraneous pecuniary consideration to cloud his devotion to the law. When Kant describes the categorical imperative in terms of a Kingdom of Ends, he is engaging in a classic separation of that which is tradable (which has a price; i.e., inclinations and needs) from that which is not (dignity).[65] The corrupt have their price.

This same stern purity was on display when Kant wrote his famous rebuttal to Benjamin Constant, "On a Supposed Right to Lie from Philanthropy." The locus classicus for anti-Kantians in search of perverse purism, the text was written in response to a pamphlet in which Benjamin Constant had charged the "philosophe allemand" with absurdity. I do not wish to enter into the details of this article—it is very well known and the bulk of Kant scholarship on it entails attempts to save Kant from himself and to mitigate the implausibility of his advice. In the text, we recall, Kant argues against lying in any instance, even if it is well intentioned. He goes so far as to argue that one has a duty not to lie to a murderer seeking his victim. Honesty is an absolute duty. One might emphasize that the exchange took place during the Directorate, when the subject of political purity was a clear subtext (and in the case of Constant, surface text); Kant's rigorism here might be thought to be a reaction to Constant's famous pliancy.[66] Be that as it may, this rigorist posture is present throughout his works, the result of seeing corruption in any concession to empirical matters. In matters of external freedom (right) and matters of internal freedom (virtue) there are universal, a priori principles, and to deviate from them based upon some conception of good consequences is to be fatally corrupted in both. For if someone lies, not only does he violate an ethical duty to himself and "annihilate his dignity as a human being," turning himself into "a thing,"[67] but he equally harms the condition of right.[68] This is not because lying entails undermining someone's right to truth (that was an error that Constant had made), and it certainly has nothing to do with the lie's effect (for Kant's reconstruction of the murderer-at-the-door scenario is meant to show the unreliability of consequentialist moral judgment).[69] Rather, it is because lying does harm "to humanity generally" for it "makes the source of right unusable."[70] Clearly no individual lie will have such an effect of destroying all contracts; rather, Kant is making a corruption argument, and the corruption is not primarily from the immediate act of lying, but from the pretense that the mendacity can in some instances be treated as a universal maxim.

We have seen that in the realm of right, Kant adopts a strict, unbending purism that seeks to cut out corrupting elements from the body politic lest corruption spread. What prevents this from taking on "terroristic" overtones is both Kant's strict separation of right from virtue and his determined stance against a politics aimed at happiness. For even if Robespierre's Committee of Public Safety had succeeded in applying strict, bloody justice without arbitrariness (a possibility that is difficult to imagine historically, no doubt), it would still have sinned against Kantian principles for its eudaemonism.

It is in this anti-eudaemonism that lies Kant's greater philosophical purity. It is sometimes averred that Kant's rejection of the right of rebellion indicated a pulling back from the radicalism of his republicanism, as if there were a contradiction between his enthusiasm for the revolution and his rejection of rebellion. But the principles were fully consistent and born of his more thoroughgoing conception of what constituted universality. Robespierre's head was so close to his bonnet because he sullied his notion of the general will with considerations that were less than noumenal: his constant affirmation of the state's goal to promote happiness and virtue was precisely what Kant termed anti-republican: "no one can coerce me to be happy in his way (as he thinks of the welfare of other human beings)." A government that does this is "the greatest *despotism* thinkable."[71] Similarly, it is not possible to legislate virtue, since legislation can only affect external action, not inner dispositions.[72] Robespierre's desire to craft convinced revolutionaries was despotic not primarily for the Hobbesian reason that one cannot legislate thoughts, but for the moral reason that to do so is to undermine persons' autonomy and to fail to treat them as ends in themselves. Duties of virtue, Kant explains, "have to do with an end which (or the having of which) is also a duty. No external lawgiving can bring about someone's setting an end for himself (because this is an internal act of the mind), although it may prescribe external actions that lead to an end without the subject making it his end."[73] To attempt to break into the soul is to make war on our moral disposition itself: "Woe to the legislator who wishes to establish through force a polity directed to ethical ends! For in so doing he would not merely achieve the very opposite of an ethical polity but also undermine his political state and make it insecure."[74]

To the anti-perfectionist liberal, this distinction between justice and virtue can appear most comforting: no one will force us to be angels. But if Kant thinks rational self-interest can produce a situation of justice, he equally thinks that there are strong moral imperatives to civic union and a strong moral purpose to our political life. The goal of moral improvement is displaced, but it is not rendered extra-political. It simply cannot be legislated.

Rigorous as Kant's doctrine of right was, his doctrine of virtue was even more so. Is this a case of displacing terror into the inner realm, a kind of fear and trembling of the God who is nothing but a regulative idea? Do we become our own terrorists making war on our phenomenal selves? This accusation needs to be rejected. The moral feeling of respect for the moral law—a feeling that is rather an anti-feeling—is sublime. We touched on this difficulty above. The mere notion of a divinity that scares one into acting properly is thoroughly anti-Kantian: if I act from fear of punishment, I am acting out of pathological motives.[75] The sublime feeling of respect, which acts as a kind of muting of our other feelings, is akin to a fear that is not a fear. In the *Critique of Judgment*, Kant insists that actual fear is not sublimity. Rather, sublimity is a feeling that is aroused when we are aware of the vastness of natural causes that overwhelm us, but we equally recognize our own moral freedom: we judge an object fearsome, but we are not afraid.[76] That which is sublime is the moral law within, but we attribute it falsely to the vast object without. Humility, "voluntary subjection of ourselves to the pain of self-reprimand so as gradually to eradicate the cause of [our] defects" is sublime.[77] There is no space to enter here into the textual difficulties concerning the nature of the sublime and its relationship to the moral feeling of respect. Nor is there room to explore the various Nietzschean and neo-Nietzschean accusations of inner despotism; let it suffice to note that it is precisely Kant's greater purism that renders terror an inadequate means of virtue. He who trembles is already guilty.

Conclusion: Kantian Patience and the Politics of Virtue

Critics of the Enlightenment project have tended to find in Kant's moral purism an object of disdain. For some it demonstrates the prime example of abstract, universalizing reason denuding itself of ethical content.[78] The dialectically inclined happily link Kant to that which seems to be his radical opposite (Sade, the Holocaust, radical cruelties of all sorts), either because Kant's rigorism harbors unavowed sadistic desires (it is Tartuffery, or worse yet, straightforward authoritarian personality), or because of a structural similarity between Sade's pure injunction to cruelty without even pleasure and Kant's injunction to pure ethical acts that withstand all inclinations.[79] I do not wish to decide here whether the purity of the a priori overreaches—elsewhere I have indicated my sympathy for the objection that Kant's a priori simply does not have the purity to which it pretends. But for the purposes of this chapter, I merely wish to indicate that Kantian purism, while it follows the radical cleansing path that was taken by the Terror in its rigid conception of justice, ultimately breaks with the Terror because the Terror exhibits insufficient moral purity. But the Kantian separation of virtue and justice is not the basis of liberal anti-perfectionism, for politics has a moral purpose. By way of conclusion, I mean to suggest briefly the manner in which Kant sought to bridge the two poles in his thought.

Kant's mixture of enthusiasm and disapproval for the French Revolution is based on his view that republicanism is in keeping with right and morality and his judgment that rebellion could be justified by neither.[80] Revolution is not permissible, but constitutions arising from successful republican revolutions are sacrosanct, and the emergence of republican constitutions is a thing worthy of admiration.[81] That unjust means could provide just ends was a simple fact of history; Kant's historical optimism was due to his view that reform could come—even reform based on pathological self-interest—due to injustices. In the first supplement to "Perpetual Peace," Kant treats nature as if it has purposes for humanity, noting how the crimes by which humans render one another's lives miserable are the very things that push them toward an ever-increasing condition of right. "What we here neglect to do eventually comes about of its own accord."[82] The very facts of history offer a ground for hope. So too do matters like the widespread enthusiasm about the French Revolution, which indicate the presence of a moral feeling.

But it is not enough merely to hope passively. Hope is possible—it is even required—as a stimulus to action. For mere right is insufficient. The inevitable tension between our duty to obey (as the fundamental basis of a condition of right) and our ethical duty to the categorical imperative can only be overcome through the gradual reform of the state toward ever greater political morality.[83] To fail to hope and work for this is to reconcile oneself to the perpetual corruption of humanity (and it is simply histori-cally unjustified given the tangible moral progress that Kant believed he could observe).[84]

Kant's injunction to obey is not a call to leave ethical concerns at the door. He offers some possibilities for passive resistance (he terms it "nega-tive resistance") of a parliament to its executive authority, and he even goes so far as to indicate (with an implicit reference to English placemen) that a parliament's excessively punctual obedience to the crown and minister is a sign of corruption.[85] But it remains the case that reforms must come from above; the citizen's duty is above all one of publicity: "*freedom of the pen* . . . is the sole palladium of the people's rights"[86]

Both Kant and Robespierre spoke of publicity as the greatest defense against oppression and corruption.[87] But there is an immense difference between the two doctrines. Kantian publicity serves two ends. First, it serves as a test for the rightfulness of an action. Thus a revolution is ruled out because one could not openly proclaim one's intention to launch a revolu-tion without thereby contradicting one's purpose.[88] But the second, more important aspect of Kantian publicity is its capacity to serve as a refinement of truth and a means of gradual reform. For this reason, while a degree of control is reasonable for speech that is attached to one's official responsibil-ities, one must always be able to communicate freely in the public realm.[89] Robespierre's publicity is entirely in the service of surveillance (what we typically term "transparency," as Chapter 4 has indicated): with millions of spectators watching every move of the government, "neither corruption, nor intrigue, nor yet perfidy would dare show their face."[90] Robespierre's critics rightly deride him for his later use of censorship, but one can see how he might have convinced himself that his shift to censorship was not a complete reversal of principle. If late Robespierre fulminated against the tendency of corrupt journalists "to mislead public opinion,"[91] his avowed purpose was ever the same: to make certain that the honest *peuple* had possession of the truth so that it could cast its thunderbolts in the right direction. Since his justification for press freedom was always the discovery and punishment of perfidy and corruption, it was no difficult leap to turn on the writers when they themselves became (in his estimation) the mercenary fomenters of that very corruption.

Whether Kant's defense of press freedom would ultimately forbid Robespierre's attacks on (possibly) foreign-funded counterrevolutionary propaganda is an open question. Kant's defense of freedom of the pen was expressly aimed at the scholarly community, and Kant thought it was precisely their lack of participation in political propaganda that made scholars' works a source of dispassionate critique to which sovereigns should attend (even if sovereigns do not admit they are doing so).[92] Perhaps it is because French philosophers' heads are so close to their bonnets that Robespierre was unable to see the distinction between philosophy and propaganda. Whatever the case, the more thoroughgoing Kantian defense of liberty of expression was a means of gradually improving the moral condition of humanity; Kant's philosophical chiliasm calls on philosophers to move things along through public expression, but it ultimately sees purification as something that does not come with thunderbolts and fire. He speaks of "gradual" enlightenment and "distant epochs," far in the future.[93] There is a philosophical duty to further moral progress through rational public expression, but one cannot expect, nor should one hope, to be able to overturn corrupt constitutions overnight. Kant was able to adopt a politics of radical purity without a call for the guillotine, but he could only do so because he had time on his side. Isaiah Berlin liked to quote Kant, taking comfort from the thought that even this rational idealist knew where to draw the line: "out of the crooked timber of humanity no straight thing was ever made."[94] But in making Kant an ally of liberal pluralism, Berlin left out the rest of the quotation: "Only the approximation to this idea is laid upon us by nature." Kant proceeded to point out the obstacles and to conclude that if a perfectly just constitution occurs, "it will only be very late, after many fruitless attempts."[95] However unattractive Kantian purity might appear to us, it is not a monstrous ideal; its radicalism is rendered humane by the existence of a quiet, rarely noticed virtue that Kant described as the companion of courage and hope: patience.[96]

CHAPTER 8

Purity and the Public Official

Max Weber on Bureaucratic Integrity

We have seen that the language of civic virtue is particularly appealing to people trying to escape the confines of the dominant understanding of corruption today. We have also seen that it can serve radically different purposes, despite a certain "republican" origin. But talk of civic virtue sounds rather odd when we are discussing contemporary corruption in large bureaucratic states. This is not due to the fact that Aristotelians and Machiavellians have no conception of a distinction between the interests of the individual officeholder and the city. As we have noted, the Aristotelian division of regimes into healthy and corrupt forms relies entirely on the possibility of public office being abused for private gain. But deploying civic republican language (in either ancient or modern variants) somehow jars when one is attempting to describe "good governance practices" in modern states. This goes beyond the mere aesthetic clash between the jargon of administration and that of classical political philosophy. Modern bureaucracy resists the language of civic virtue.

The gulf is one we began to perceive in Bolingbroke's adoption of civic republican language to denigrate the new financial-bureaucratic state that seemed to be undermining the influence of traditional rural elites. Bolingbroke saw the growth of central administration as the source of a new ruling class that served and buttressed the crown, and he chose to interpret the influence of this class as corrupt. Bolingbroke was not arguing for civil service reform—rather, he was harking back to an era in which offices had been fewer and controlled by solid landed gentry (rather than liquid urban financiers). That is, he was not offering a principled opposition to patronage, but rather a reaction to the rise of a new social class. In this sense, he was decrying as corrupt an excluded group's intrusion upon the protected turf of an historical elite.[1] The explosion of corruption talk in the eighteenth century is the product of older practices being taken over by a new class of people combined with the very tangible rise of the centralized state. The manner in which offices had been purchased, perquisites paid, and so on, increasingly looked corrupt both to the rising bourgeoisie and to falling country elites, and as the century wore on with no diminishment to the administrative needs of Britain's wars and its empire, administrative reforms became more and more the order of the day. A new set of strict divisions arose, including the specifically modern inflection of the distinction between public and private—the strict differentiation between public authority and subjective rights, depersonalized office and the household or private sphere, and between state and economy. This is a central element of what Weber termed "rationalization," and it remains ubiquitous.

I have argued that it is incorrect to affirm that the private-public split is entirely modern, but there *is*, in the official's strict separation of work life from private life, an opposition with distinctive modern overtones. Modern officials have acquired a strong consciousness of this separation, and the casuistry of keeping the two separate is a growth industry in the ethics of administration. But there is more to the rational state than this. This strict separation is only one of a series of separations that structure the modern state, not the least of which is the distinction between politics and administration.

The emergence of this mode of thinking about corruption is a story of civil-service reform in the long nineteenth and early twentieth centuries. It is a story with many protagonists, from largely forgotten officials to famous reformers (Woodrow Wilson comes to mind).[2] But the most important theorist of modern administrative integrity is surely Max Weber. Weber is doubly informative on this subject, for he was not only a perceptive student of the modern state form, but also a writer whose descriptions have had a powerful determinative effect on modern consciousness. The ideal-type Weberian bureaucracy has an important normative force in the modern political imaginary. Indeed, his description of bureaucracy is often treated in administrative studies not as an ideal type, but rather as an ideal.[3] This might seem lamentable. Serious students of Weber often express indignation that his description of bureaucracy is sometimes reduced to a template in textbooks on management. One writer asks, polemically, whether we are to understand Weber as "management consultant or political theorist?"[4]

But the fact that Weber is sometimes treated as a management consultant is due to the very normative power of Weberian bureaucracy in modern administration. Bureaucracy, as he described it, was a type of domination whose basic outlines were the central components of a modern industrial state. Weber's ideal type was certainly no ideal in the sense of a higher mode of life to be pursued, for the very bureaucratic tendencies of industrial society were what most worried him. But Weber never for one moment doubted how essential it was to have a functioning bureaucracy, and he provided arguments for how it should be kept pure. His culturally pessimistic worries about bureaucratization (which have found themselves echoed loudly throughout the twentieth century by Frankfurt School theorists, Foucauldians, civic republicans, and virtue ethicists) did not undermine his admiration for its efficiency or his interest in seeing it kept uncorrupted. Keeping bureaucracy pure meant keeping it from invading—and from being invaded by—other domains. His political writings contain a number of proposals for keeping bureaucracy in its place, and keeping it in its place equally buttressed its ideal-type structure. Thus, despite Weber's attempt to distance his political utterances from his sociological expertise, the ideal-type model and the prescriptive mode come together, for the pure form of bureaucracy outlined in Weber's sociology cannot exist without the very separations that Weber advocated in his political writing.

In this chapter I will indicate, through the study of Max Weber's views on corruption and ideal-type bureaucracy, the manner in which the separations required for the bureaucratic form of integrity differ significantly from the virtues that are supposed to keep impurity off the medieval throne and out of the classical citizen. The Weberian model, with its technocratic overtones, does not renounce that activity of soulcraft that characterized those two models of integrity. On the contrary, Weberian bureaucracy entails a novel form of social and ethical pedagogy suitable to a modern administrative state. Uncorrupted bureaucrats do not feel the pull of anticivic passions, but this is not because they have tamed their personal inclinations (like Erasmus's virtuous prince), nor yet had a lust for glory channeled (like Machiavelli's ambitious, virtuous citizen). Weberian bureaucracy reinforces integrity in government insofar as it creates bureaucratic subjects in whom there is no gap between the natural person of the official and the office. The separations necessary for pure, uncorrupted bureaucracy are part of a new, functionally differentiated state. They make sense in an ethically plural universe, and they depend not merely on the distinction between public and private, but, even more important, on the distinction between politics and administration. Bureaucracy's purity entails social division; its integrity is based on the crafting of a bureaucratic soul.

I will suggest that the Weberian ideal type is often held as an ideal for modern administration, but that its hegemonic place is under threat. Elements of the model live on in "best practices," but a number of current trends in management and the provision of public services have the effect of blurring the boundaries that are at the root of the Weberian ideal type. Weberian bureaucracy is a product of differentiations that are increasingly being treated as harmful or meaningless. Whether the conception of corruption and integrity operative in the Weberian model of bureaucratic integrity will survive such a shift remains an open question.

Corruption and the Bureaucrat

Weber's ambivalence toward bureaucracy is mirrored in modern treatments of the subject. No one loves the lowly bureaucrat; no one celebrates red tape, procedure, or the cold, impersonal, calculating nature of bureaucratic control. Who does not nod in agreement with the now-clichéd lamentations about the "iron cage" (*stahlharte Gehäuse*, or steel-hard shell)? Yet who would like the administration of public service to be amateurish, inefficient, partial, or arbitrary? We might, if we profited from the arrangement (if, say, the most important officials were friends of ours), but those who did not enjoy such privilege would be less impressed. That which strikes us as "living," human, and personal is, in administrative matters, precisely that which is termed corrupt.

The characteristics of ideal-type Weberian bureaucracy are well known: clear hierarchy; strict adherence to rules and procedures (knowledge of which is part of the bureaucrat's expertise); a fixed, functional division of labor; management through documentation; full-time, salaried, and tenured professional staff; appointment and advancement based upon meritocratic principles (assured through the process of examinations that both ensure meritocracy and develop the officeholders' personalities). Officeholders do not simply see their work as temporary, mercenary salary work, but as a full-time calling. What is particularly important is that their work be *impersonal*. Indeed, many of the characteristics (particularly the rule-boundedness and the meritocracy) exist in order to prevent the intrusion of "irrational, and emotional elements which escape calculation."[5] Nothing is to enter into consideration save the efficient accomplishment of the ends concerned. The status system and psychological conditioning of the bureaucratic system reinforce the impersonal. This is, of course, what makes bureaucracy so alienating, for its systems of rules and regulations are intended to prevent the exercise of subjectivity or discretion. Anything that appears to bear the stamp of individuality has the taint of arbitrariness. The separation of individual economic interest from official duty is simply part of this depersonalization process. So, for example, tax farming such as that well known in the ancien régime, is not a pure bureaucratic institution. Apologists for irregular gifts to officials, "grease money," and the like, often suggest that at base these things are no different from fixed salaries, arguing, in a somewhat relativistic (and, frankly, sophistic) manner, that these are simply two different ways of achieving the same end of securing administrative services. But regardless of the (dubious) merits of "grease money" systems, to confound them with pure bureaucracy is to fall into analytical confusion. There are essential distinctions to be made between patrimonialism and rational-legalistic models of administration, just as there are essential differences between traditional gift economies and modern capitalism—differences that cannot be reduced to their common denominator of entailing reciprocal exchange.

The key to the rationalization of the modern state has been the separations that made bureaucratization possible. "Traditional" domination, for Weber, entails different manners in which personal ties to the patrimonial leader are forged—they can be through fiefs (in a feudal pattern) or through benefices accorded to dependents of the king (prebendalism).[6] The rational-modern method of administration is much more depersonalized. "In today's 'state' (and this is fundamental to the concept), the 'separation' of the material means of administration from the administrative staff, the officials and employees of the administration, has been rigorously implemented."[7] When prebendal and feudal vestiges intrude upon administration they undermine its pure bureaucratic character and make the official's relationship to his office one that is largely motivated by a quest for personal enrichment. The official "can assume the character of an 'entrepreneur,' like the *condottiere* or the holder of a leased or purchased office in the past, or like the American 'boss' who regards his expenses as a capital investment from which he will derive a yield by exploiting his influence. Or he can draw a fixed wage, as does . . . [a] political official."[8] In *Politics as a*

Vocation, Weber presents a list of instances in which the administration of the state is fought over as a means of self-enrichment. He describes the then-existing American "spoils system," in which even the most minor offices are patronage appointments distributed as booty to loyal troops in election campaigns. The key division between private business and public office is a late development of rationalization that Weber thought the Americans had yet to achieve (but were beginning to seek).[9] Against these systems in which public office is primarily sought as a source of profit, Weber offers the modern ideal of the professional bureaucrats, who conceive of administration as a realm for expertise and who are socialized such that they think of themselves as servants of the state: "Modern bureaucracy in the interest of integrity has developed a high sense of status honor; without this sense the danger of an awful corruption and a vulgar Philistinism threatens fatally. And without such integrity, even the purely technical functions of the state apparatus would be endangered. The significance of the state apparatus for the economy has been steadily rising, especially with increasing socialization, and its significance will be further augmented."[10] The problem of corruption is thus dealt with by handing over power over technical matters, and accompanying honor, to an administrative class. Much in the same way that militaries are rendered loyal through the formalized granting of status (pageantry, flashy costumes) and socialization (training in obedience to authority, invocation of honor), public servants are granted high social status (and the incomes necessary to sustain this) and have their personalities formed through their "long years of preparatory training" and the manner in which their hopes and ambitions are tied to a strictly meritocratic system of advancement. Unlike the political actors who struggle for power, the civil servants must be above—or rather sink below—the fray; they must be impartial and dispassionate.[11]

What this socialization accomplishes is to render the state's apparatus subservient to the state's will. The need for expert administration in large states has always raised the difficulty of the administrators (or soldiers) usurping power due to their greater expertise (or force). (The danger of the clerk/cleric is manifest in his access to a hidden realm—there is an important etymological link between grammar and glamour, or magic.) Keeping the officials in line had, to some extent, been accomplished in the past through other means. Clerical celibacy made clerics useful public administrators, as Weber points out, because they were both literate (had expertise), but did not pose any dynastic challenge. Hence they could be employed in the central state's struggle against aristocracy. Another method (even more effective than celibacy) is simply to cut off the testicles of men destined for civil service (a long-lived phenomenon that finds surprisingly little traction in contemporary civil-service reform). In addition to reducing the possibility of cuckoldry and insuring that any cuckolding that might occur would produce no offspring, this cuts the civil servant off from a powerful source of political corruption, parental love. The modern state achieves the same ends with strict separations.

On this view, the reduction of corruption in public administration is a result of separating the source of decision from the instrumental reasoning required for implementation. The splitting of the state into functional units extends to the manner of reasoning, with bureaucrats excelling in instrumental reason (which Weber distinguishes not only from "value rationality," but also from traditionalism and emotional concerns).[12] The bureaucrat's ethical and emotional abstemiousness mirrors Weber's own reluctance to allow his political positions to inform his university lectures. (Weber thought the classroom was not the place for him to expound his political "values.") It would be pointlessly polemical to call the modern bureaucrat a court eunuch, but we might give a Freudian alteration to the analogy by pointing out that he or she practices a form of repression. As Weber writes, the civil servant's "honor" is tied to the capacity to obey the orders of government regardless of his judgment or passion: "This holds even if the order appears wrong to him. . . . Without this moral discipline and self-denial, in the highest sense, the whole apparatus would fall to pieces."[13] Weber never says that bureaucrats *only* exercise instrumental rationality (for one thing, absolutely pure *Zweckrationalität* is but an ideal type, never encountered empirically), but it is a central value they hold. Their "value rationality" is highly attuned to the importance of means-ends calculations, order, and rule following.

The flip side of this impersonality for Weber is the "leveling" of social orders subject to bureaucracy. This is what makes bureaucratic administration, which is not in itself particularly democratic, appropriate to mass democracies with formal equality. Our feelings about the impersonality of administration are akin to our feelings about impersonality before the law—to have separate law for particular people (based on bribes, birth, caste, friendship, kinship) offends against our formal egalitarian sensibilities, and we extend the same norms to other government offices. We might hate red tape, but we would hate even more the thought of partiality in administration. The very dehumanization that allows bureaucratic organization to devour its victims (see Zygmunt Bauman's interpretation of the Holocaust)[14] is the same that, in less pathological political contexts, frees the subject of government from humiliating interpersonal relations. For when one is seeking justice, or applying for social assistance, or drawing unemployment insurance, one is often pleased to be "just a number."

For this reason, Weber's ideal-type bureaucracy, in all its monstrous impersonality, nonetheless describes something that strikes many modern readers as the minimum conditions of public service integrity. And, indeed, if we look at many anticorruption efforts today, we see this ideal held up as the goal of civil-service reform. Consider the World Bank's "Administrative and Civil Service Assessment Tool," a series of questions designed to assess the integrity of countries' civil services: it touches on all the basic Weberian elements—professionalism, meritocratic appointment and promotion, independence from patronage, objective criteria for evaluation, rule following, and so on. One study, partially funded by the World Bank, finds a significant correlation between high growth in developing economies and the "Weberianness" of their administrative apparatuses.[15] Weber himself presented ideal-type bureaucracy as the opposite of corruption. In his discussion of civil-service reform in the United States, he praised the shift away from treating offices as a form of booty toward the meritocratic establishment of tenured, pension-meriting officialdom: "The reform works out in such a way that university-trained officials, just as incorruptible and quite as capable as our officials, get into office."[16]

The Bureaucrat's One Body

Samuel Johnson's definitions of corruption in his dictionary begin with the concrete, corporeal meaning: "Corruption: 1. the principle by which bodies tend to the separation of their parts."[17] The very nature of Weberian rationalization, however, is to separate into parts. Holists like Alasdair MacIntyre tend to regret this tendency to compartmentalize moral life, but it is hard to conceive of modernity in its absence. The separations that Weber cites appear to be a mere extension of the life of the city. "This conceptual separation of private and public was first conceived and realized in urban communities; for as soon as their officeholders were secured by periodic

elections, the individual power-holder, even if he was in the highest position, was obviously no longer identical with the man who possessed authority 'in his own right.' Yet it was left to the complete depersonalization of
administrative management by bureaucracy and the rational systematiza-
tion of law to realize the separation of public and private fully and in principle."[18] In this sense, there is a certain continuity between the distinction
between holder of office and office itself and the bureaucratic distinction
between public and private. But the separation that he described in the fully
rationalized system is qualitatively different.

The distinction between interest of the governed and the governors has
been drawn in different manners in different ages. As we noted in Chapter
1, the late medieval manner of dividing the king's natural person from the
office itself is outlined in Ernst Kantorowicz's classic study of medieval
political theology, *The King's Two Bodies,* which details the manner in
which the metaphor of the body politic served to mediate the two separate
realities of the sovereign's natural person and his eternal office, his concrete
and abstract self. The duality posits an eternally uncorrupted body politic
being inhabited by a corruptible, temporal human being. Much like the
Eucharist (in which a transitory object is at the same time an eternal one),
and anticipating fictional corporate personhood, this "political theology"
was a means of dealing with the gulf between the pure and the corruptible,
between being and becoming. In Kantorowicz's treatment, the doctrine of
the king's two bodies is an important element in the emergence of the
modern state, the abstract collectivity institutionally embodied in the
crown. Writers treating the subject of corruption have sometimes placed
this dualism at the origin of the modern distinction between public and
private. Peter Bratsis writes, "The two bodies principle is evident in the
rules that distinguish between the person as a public servant and as a private
citizen."[19] For Bratsis, this heritage is a sign of the distinction's relative
historical novelty (and of its metaphysical absurdity). As we have seen, he
calls for us simply to reject these dualisms as "bourgeois fantasies designed
to support the fiction of the polity."[20]

I do not think it a fantasy (though it is certainly a product of the
imagination), nor do I think Bratsis correct to draw in this manner the
connection between the two-bodies doctrine and the modern public-
private distinction. The distinctions at the heart of the legal-rational state
(among which is the distinction between public and private) entail a different mental structure and call for a different set of dispositions on the

part of officeholders. Just as republican civic virtue appears out of place in the modern bureaucracy, so too does the mirror-of-princes tract—that late medieval and Renaissance manner of crafting royal selves so that their corruptible body is truly an image of their eternal one—read awkwardly when applied to bureaucracy.

The rational-legal division between private and public is both different from and a continuation of more traditional attempts to make offices subject to a rule more permanent than that of fallible, fickle, self-interested human beings. Weberian bureaucracy does not solve the problem of rule in the interests of rulers, but it circumscribes the realm in which such abuse is possible. In the realm of administration, the issue is resolved through the crafting of bureaucratic personality, a crafting entirely due to the structure of bureaucratic office, with its professional training, exams, and lifelong attachment to the hierarchy and the files. The bureaucrat might experience this as a division between personal will and the needs of office, but the socialization of the bureaucrat and the rule-bound nature of office are meant to ensure that this split rarely manifests itself. The Renaissance king faced, with his two bodies, a fundamental difficulty in the fact that "his body politic contains his body natural":[21] the body natural can be corrupted, while the body politic is incorruptible. Reconciling the two required some delicate thinking, especially in cases in which the body natural seemed, in all its dirtiness, to be in the ascendant. Consider the odd consequences when the rebellious English Parliament in 1642 claimed to be fighting for the king (that is, for his body politic against his body natural). Given this possible split between the two bodies, the utmost effort must be expended on the care for the king's character (and hence the control of his counselors). The possible split between the office and the man (or woman) is the reason the Renaissance humanist constantly seeks to motivate the man to live up to the office. Weberian bureaucracy, too, engages in the crafting of character, for bureaucracy requires a particular type of character. It "promotes a 'rationalist' way of life," furthering "the personality type of the professional expert."[22] But insofar as their discretion is hemmed in by the rules and the files, and their motivation is crafted by the system of advancement and status honor, professional experts are less inclined to see themselves as divided: "The individual bureaucrat cannot squirm out of the apparatus in which he is harnessed. In contrast to the honorific or avocational 'notable,' the professional bureaucrat is chained to his activity by his entire material and ideal existence."[23]

As we noted above, Weber was not holding this up as an ideal for human existence. Its very necessity in modern industrial states was a source of major ethical concern. Insofar as it represents an ideal, it is, in Weber's word, an extremely "dehumanized" (*entmenschlicht*) ideal:[24] the proper bureaucrat does nothing but what he or she believes is the most efficient means to the established end; the bureaucrat is not committed to particular human beings but to an abstract office. Weber's ambivalence toward the nihilistic world of bureaucrats—the "specialists without spirit"[25] who make the disenchanted world so dreary—is so well known as to require little elucidation. But given the necessity of bureaucracy, the real political challenge for Weber was to imagine an order in which bureaucracy did not choke out individuality and liberty throughout the society. He did not wish to undermine the purity of the bureaucratic realm, which promotes integrity and prevents corruption. The bureaucrat's integrity is ensured not by moral training (which humanistic literary education had attempted to provide officials in certain stages of early modernity), but by aligning individual self-interest and self-esteem to the conscientious attendance to his or her duties. When Weber speaks of the bureaucrat's self-restraint as heroic, he is acknowledging the difficulty of such self-overcoming. But when he denigrates bureaucrats as lifeless and prescribes the socialization techniques that ensure bureaucratic mores, he largely takes their actions out of the realm of heroic, stoic self-denial and into the realm of behavioral conditioning. The fundamental division Weber makes is less between private and public interests than between administration, with its fully formed administrative psychology, and politics, with its emphasis on struggle, charisma, and ambition.

The political theology that Kantorowicz thought had granted, in the late medieval period, symbolic eternity to corruptible human beings fades in the disenchanted world, and corporate temporal continuity is conferred simply through the constant application of the rules and the creation of artificial memory in the files. Pure bureaucracy contains this element of seeking universality and permanence—that which is beyond corruption—by finding an institutional arrangement that keeps it working though its parts are replaced. What was, theologically, located in a transcendent, eternal realm is translated to an immanent world—it is no longer eternal, but is merely perpetual (the conceptual distinction being that the eternal is beyond time, while the perpetual is something within time that simply continues without stopping).[26] The bureaucracy is not an immortal *corpus mysticum*, but rather a kind of perpetual-motion machine.

Whatever the moral demands they make upon the bureaucrat, these divisions exist in order to separate office from officeholder's human idiosyncrasies. This might appear to be a psychologically untenable situation. J. P. Olivier de Sardan has suggested that Weberian bureaucracy is a product of European culture and its transplantation in Africa causes a "schizophrenic" disposition in those societies.[27] But the same schizophrenia is an ever-present possibility in European contexts, where the official has had to learn to differentiate strictly between roles. This whole manner of viewing one's moral life as divided between one's human ("value"-driven, emotional, or traditional) motivations and one's official duty to perform one's function according to the rules and the dictates of efficiency is a product (among other things) of the modern bureaucratic state. We can see an earlier version in Kant, that master of divisions, who delights in the Frederickian call to public officials, "Argue as much as you want [in the realm of publication, in your nonofficial capacity], but obey!" One is a rational being who follows the categorical imperative, but one is also an official who is duty bound to set aside one's own judgment when it comes to official work.[28] In an apparently more trivial example, we can see these same divisions at play in the bureaucrat's desire not to "talk shop" during leisure hours. (Though with the advent of the iPhone and other such weapons of management, this prohibition is undermined somewhat; the colonization of the lifeworld is advanced considerably with every innovation of Apple Inc.) But the Weberian bureaucrat is not really a Kantian official, writing thoughtful public critique on his own time; he is not so bifurcated. Of course, the perfect creature of the bureau is never to be found in experience: in every corner of the globe, officials have been known to set aside regulations in the name of emotional, traditional, or moral commitments (sometimes termed "common sense"). The stereotypical figure of the bureaucrat is such a source of derision because his commitment to rules and procedures overrides the elements that define normal social life. Anyone who has ever worked in a large bureaucratic organization recognizes that nothing would ever get done without regular transgressions of procedural rules. But in "rational-legal" bureaucracies these little safety valves are usually recognized as such and the general structure of rule following is never openly questioned.

Politics as a Barrier to Bureaucratic Corruption

While the person whose vocation is politics famously experiences the full weight of the clash between the "ethic of ultimate ends" (*Gesinnungsethik*, better translated as "ethics of conviction") and the "ethic of responsibility," the problem is somewhat mitigated for the official, reduced as it is to a division of labor. "We are placed into various life-spheres, each of which is governed by different laws."[29] Insofar as Weber was offering a normative ideal, it was one premised on the necessary divisions—and even tensions—between the political and the administrative. Without this division, the championing of ideal-type Weberian bureaucracy becomes the defense of technocracy. Weber was wary of this fate—indeed, technocracy was in many respects the pinnacle of corruption. Weberian bureaucracy cannot exist in its pure form unless it is accompanied by an autonomous political realm that delimits it: ideal-type bureaucracy requires, *for its very purity*, the existence of parliamentary politics to oppose it.

Weber himself made this point with regard to the Wilhelmine constitution. It was the very weakness of parliamentary politics that led to the rule by bureaucrats. This is the great danger of this type of office. It is often assumed that because Weber drew his model of the bureaucrat from German experience that he somehow held up Wilhelmine bureaucracy as exemplary. But though he thought that Germany had developed an efficient administration, it suffered from this very success. The difficulty was that the constitution—and Bismarck—had reduced the Germans to depoliticized subjects and had made the Reichstag essentially powerless (and the Bundesrat was unparliamentary); the upshot was that the bureaucracy was largely uncontrolled. Weber wrote, "this form of rule put people with the *minds of officials* into leading positions which ought to have been filled by *politicians*, in other words by men who had learned, through political struggle, to weigh the potential significance of *public statements* and who, above all, would have had the *leading politician's* sense of responsibility, rather than the official's feeling that his duty lies in subordination, something which is quite proper in its place but which was very damaging here."[30] Bureaucrats make bad leaders because they have not been formed in parliamentary battle and cannot take political responsibility before electors.[31] Neither politics nor administration were well served by this mixing. Both at the central level and at the state level, bureaucracies had arrogated to themselves unchecked power. "Very soon after the foundation of the Reich the bureaucracy of the individual states proceeded to eliminate as far as possible the scrutiny of their work by the parliaments of the individual states."[32] The bureaucratic tendency to secrecy and discretion became, unopposed, a kind of cabal. Only in parliamentary regimes, where administrations "must give an account of themselves, exhaustively and subject to verification by parliament and its committees,"[33] could this tendency be checked (the English parliamentary committee was the model he had in mind). When parliament was rendered powerless, parliamentarians' highest goals became the securing of personal profit through patronage positions. "Officialdom benefits from the arrangement by being free to operate *without* personal *control*, in return for which it pays gratuities to the parties which count in the form of patronage of *minor* prebends."[34] The powerless politicians gave up on their vocation and sought a benefice;[35] functionaries became place-seekers first. As Weber wrote in a 1917 letter outlining his disgust with Wilhelm II's government, "I see now no other way than ruthless parliamentarization . . . to freeze out these people [dilettantes]. The civil servants must be subordinated to parliament. Altogether and without exception. They are technicians."[36]

When Weber accused the Wilhelmine constitution of being insufficiently political, he was striking a civic republican note—German parliament and parties were weak because the people had been educated to passivity by Bismarck.[37] But he did not entertain any heady appeal to the ancients—politics would be representative politics in the context of mass democracy. And bureaucracy would not be purified through civic virtue: on the contrary, the bureaucrat's impersonality denies him or her the recourse to republican virtue. It is, after all, surely the furthest thing from a classical republican view to see office holding as dehumanizing, but Weber described it that way. Bureaucrats are public servants, but their service is not heroic, born of patriotism and burning desire for glory or the charms of leadership. Bureaucrats are, indeed, temperamentally ill-disposed to thinking in this manner: they must write the briefing notes. *Sine ira et studio* means precisely without the zeal that animates the citizen (it does not mean stoic virtue). No doubt bureaucrats may think of themselves as devoted to a greater good, but they are not called on to demonstrate civic virtue; they are not called on to rule in any political sense. *Techne* rather than *phronesis* is their glory.[38] Their ambition is channeled toward a rising rank within the hierarchy, and they most of all must not think of themselves as possessing political responsibility. In the same way as a professor is not to behave like a politician or prophet (as Weber argues in *Science as a Vocation*), so too is the expert not to be anything but an expert. And the nonofficial for the most part cedes to this expert authority.

The clearest example of this shift is the development of professional armies—to the republican, civic freedom meant that the state's monopoly on violence was prevented from infringing the liberty of the citizen because the citizen was the very agent of that violence and held out the perpetual threat of either omitting to act, or worse applying violence as he sees fit. For Weber, the notion of citizens playing a large role in any significant public office had become laughable in the modern world. Public functions require expertise. The key organization to think of in this respect is the military: one can speak with republican nostalgia of the citizen-soldier, but it remains the case that even in heavily militarized societies in which there is universal compulsory military service today, the military is run by a body of technically proficient professional experts. No doubt, the martial virtues continue to play a role in the lives of soldiers carrying out their duties, but success or failure in any major combat is predominantly due to the technological and logistical organization. We might, for effect, juxtapose the image of the Roman farmer-soldier with that of the CIA employee who spends his day remotely piloting an attack drone half a world away, before going home at five o'clock to his house in a Nevada suburb. The one supplied his own arms; the other, the specialist without spirit, is part of a massive technostructure. The point is, while some civic republican ideals can continue to inform modern life, there is an element of the participatory mantra that is difficult to reconcile with technological modernity.

The elitism that this entails creates tension between bureaucratization and democracy. Bureaucratization, Weber argued, is tied to the phenomenon of *mass democracy*. In mass democracies, there is a great deal of formal equality and rule-boundedness, and ad hoc decisions or status privileges are rejected. Such democracy has little to do with popular rule: "the *demos* itself, in the sense of an inarticulate mass, never 'governs' larger associations; rather, it is governed."[39] Mass democracy is defined by formal legal equality, which overrides any other personal or patrimonial relationships of power and authority. Rational administration both provides this formal equality but also, by setting up an administrative elite of experts, engenders opposition. "Thereby democracy inevitably comes into conflict with the bureaucratic tendencies which, by its fight against notable rule, democracy has produced."[40] The very elitism of meritocratic examinations makes the bureaucracy a source of popular resentment.[41] This is why Weber thought the Americans were sanguine about corruption: "Despite the resultant corruption, this system was popular because it prevented the emergence of a bureaucratic *caste*."[42] This well-known phenomenon is particularly evident today in the cynical strategy of populists to deride expertise as a form of snobbery and public service as inherently self-seeking. Mass democracy thus experiences a tension between the competing imperatives of bureaucratic management (which requires not merely expertise, but the development of an elitist, bureaucratic class-consciousness) and the antielitist rhetoric, which, while entailing subordination to the charismatic authority of party leaders, balks at the establishment of expert elites (and hence tends to see office as a reward for allegiance).

But it is not primarily its elitism that makes bureaucracy anticivic. Rather, it is the fact that bureaucratic office is not an extension of civic personality. The pure bureaucrat is not primarily a classical citizen, but a functionary. He or she has neither the universal excellence to which aspired the Aristotelian gentleman, nor the civic *virtù* that channeled the energies of the Machiavellian citizen. Weberian rationalization of state administration seeks to establish a separate estate of public administrators who are subservient to the will of political masters, but who are repaid for their selflessness in the esteem and social comfort granted to their class.

This speaks to the division between public and private in the polis. The Aristotelian division between the household and the city is not in the least a strict separation: rather, the household belongs to the city.[43] The citizen sees the city as primary, and his individual family, health, pleasures, possessions, and ambitions belong to it and in it. To elevate one's household over the city is to reverse the classical moral order, to stand the world on its head. The modern liberal typically sees the relationship the other way around, and this is often decried as reducing politics to mere instrumental significance. But the Weberian distinction is not that between two aspects of one's existence that are weighed in different manners, but between different forms of life, that of the administrator, the capitalist, the laborer, the party politician. The "value pluralism" that Weber thinks defining of modern existence can be a source of anxiety or despair, but Weber thinks there is something useful in the bureaucrats following their specific calling and sacrificing exclusively to the gods of the office.

Weber had no nostalgia for active civic virtue—the time for the polis was over. But he was arguing that corruption was a result of insufficient politics. The Wilhelmine constitution abandoned politics to administration. In this, we might note, it was akin to the imperial governance over distant subject peoples: it was all administration and no politics. (And, we might equally note, it had certain similarities to the postcolonial so-called prebendalist state in which no institutions—parties, unions—are sufficiently strong to balance the rent-seeking tendencies of the bureaucracy.)[44] Such an overstepping of bounds corrupts both politics and administration. Thus, when anticorruption reformers seek to implement Weberian bureaucracy in countries with weak parliamentarism, they are missing a key piece of the Weberian puzzle. The key is to oppose holism: the purity and integrity of the bureaucrat is dependent on his compartmentalization and containment—by politics itself.

Weberian Bureaucracy Under Attack

We have noted that much modern discussion of corruption contains implicit (and often explicit) appeals to the ideal-type Weberian bureaucracy. But an ideal-type bureaucracy is no proof against other attempts to steer public goods to private ends. It purifies administration, leaving politics to sort itself out, and Weber certainly had no illusions about the civic-minded purity of party struggle in mass democracy or the importance of the generally clandestine party financing of elections (though he naturally thought that the decrease of "spoils systems" would greatly reduce the extent of the electoral prize).[45] But most reformers have been content to think this a good place to start.

That said, Weberian bureaucracy finds itself under attack from several directions today. The increasingly common turn away from professional bureaucracy to forms of "outsourcing" or "public-private partnerships" threatens the separations that kept administration bureaucratically "pure." The capitalist chasing after piecework or contracts is a far cry from the vocational, wage-earning functionary. If Weberian bureaucracy partially solved the problem of the abuse of public office for private gain by making the office into a fixed, separate body operating according to its particular logic and cultivating its distinctive form of personality, the turn to private delivery of government functions risks bringing an entrepreneurial spirit to public office. Naturally, it also risks politicizing administration, since the companies vying for contracts will seek to court parties in order to secure the booty distributed after elections.

The theoretical justification for this turn comes from a movement that in principle refuses to accept the basic Weberian claim that different life spheres are governed by different laws.[46] The distinctive morality and personality crafted by public service is treated as a fiction by a theory that perceives *homo economicus* in every realm. Hence, there is something alien to the mentality of public choice theory in Jacob van Klaveren's definition of corruption: "we will conceive of corruption in terms of a civil servant who regards public office as a business, the income of which he will, in the extreme case, seek to maximize."[47] After all, for public choice theory and for the new management, public office is a business, and officials are entrepreneurs.[48] The best way to ensure administrative integrity, therefore, is to make administration follow the rules of entrepreneurs. The result of these considerations is the attempt either to subvert the structure of bureaucracies by imposing market-style measures internally (contract work, greater job insecurity, competition) or to "outsource." One can find no better example of the evisceration of the Weberian bureaucracy than in the American town of Sandy Springs, Georgia (a suburb of Atlanta). The town has contracted almost all of its administration except firemen and policemen (who by law must be public) to private corporations. Employees of these corporations are paid lower wages than public officials would be and do not have the pensions or job security traditionally associated with the public service.[49] While there is plenty of room for case-by-case debate about provision of government services, the general shift entails a deliberate attack on pure Weberian bureaucracy and threatens a return to modes of indirect taxation that are reminiscent of the patrimonial state. Civic republicans typically decry this type of move because it turns citizens into mere consumers. For the Weberian, however, it is a sign of a reversion to a pre-rationalized world, and this bleeding of one sphere into another is corruption.

The Weberian model is also under attack for the very reason that Weber thought it unpopular in the United States of his day: there is resentment against perceived *caste* difference. In a paradox of our economic order, the richer societies become, the less they appear to be able to afford paying for government services. The perpetual financial crisis of the modern bureaucratic state finds itself expressed in popular resentment of the very factors that maintain the purity of the bureaucratic order: the stability of income and tenure, the reception of a pension. The things that "formed the person-ality" of the bureaucrat—the sense of belonging to a distinct order, having a predictable career ladder, or being insulated from the vagaries of the market—are commonly looked upon with bitter jealousy, and year after year champions of reform seek to bring market motivations to administra-tion. Insofar as this shift gains public support, I would suggest that the dominant political motivation is less the quest for savings than the opposi-tion to perceived privilege.

Finally, the Weberian separation faces a grave threat from those who would turn administration into politics. Based on the suspicion that emerges in hyperpartisan environments toward independent expertise, numerous political actors attempting to consolidate executive authority have sought to attack the so-called "deep state" (which is a euphemism for both the independence of administration and the rule of law), replacing career bureaucrats with loyalists. In turn, opposition figures have been known to encourage oppositional bureaucrats in the hope that they can serve the role of political check that Weber thought belonged to the parlia-mentary realm. The response is another symptom of the same disease—the politicization of bureaucracy is the death knell of Weberian purity. The norms that undergird administrative independence depend upon a wide-spread acceptance of the division between the ethical realms of politics and administration.

The appeal to the Weberian model, then, faces some significant opposi-tion today. I do not propose here to hold it up as an unambivalent ideal, though I think, following Paul du Gay, that those who wish to see it back need to give serious consideration to its benefits. What I have attempted to demonstrate, rather, is that Weberian bureaucracy depends on a system that cultivates the personality of the bureaucrat by ensuring, via institutional mechanisms, the relative purity of administration. That such a system con-stitutes a fail-proof check against the abuse of office is not in the least clear—certainly there is much more to be said on this front. But it is impor-tant to note that when writers both endorse the Weberian ideal type as a model to be followed and urge the privatization of government services they are simultaneously affirming two positions that are in great tension.[50]

If the new public management proposed to undermine bureaucratic purity in the interest of an ethical holism or participatory civic life, it would perhaps be a worthy, if quixotic, ethical pursuit. But this is not its purpose; rather, it seeks to replace the mores of Weberian bureaucracy with those of private, profit-making organizations. In this sense, it is the opposite of what Weber worried about in the socialization of the economy: Weber thought the abolition of private property would simply swallow up the market bureaucracies in the public with dire results for individual liberty. The new public management seeks, in effect, to swallow the public functions in wealth-seeking institutions. I have indicated that the Weberian model cannot be understood as a return to the polis, and the very participatory nature of ancient citizenship is no longer truly accessible in modern administration. But pure administration of a Weberian sort calls for the existence of politics—indeed, the longing for administrative purity was part and parcel of Weber's heartfelt cry for political leaders who could take *responsibility* for decisions and exercise that careful balance between convictions and consequences (with ultimate accountability to mass electors) that was the ultimate proof of a person's political calling. The greater question is what type of politics can exist in the modern, mass-population administrative state. In many respects, Max Weber, with his insistence on the plebiscitary, party-machine mass democracy, may be accused of lacking sufficient political imagination to envisage modern versions of rule that resurrect ancient participatory ideals.[51] But it is a serious challenge for the civically inclined to craft a political imaginary fit for a modern administrative state without sacrificing the dull, reliable integrity of the Weberian bureaucrat.

CONCLUSION

The Abuse of Public Things

We left off the last chapter with an argument about the dangers of neglecting the Weberian separation between value spheres. The contamination of bureaucracy (and, indeed, of the judiciary) with "political" and/or entrepreneurial mores is widely thought today to be the soul of corruption, but the cost of maintaining bureaucratic (or even judicial) purity sometimes inspires wariness. We have noted, for instance, that Weber's separations run up against republican participatory ideals. The Weberian divisions are also troubling for other reasons, for though we sometimes assume such distinctions in political practice, we equally are beset with a universalist mind-set that questions them, either methodologically (as is done in the theories that see state bureaucracies as simply following the same impulses as capitalist organizations), politically (as in the inchoate resentment of bureaucrats' special status, or, in the case of legal bureaucracies, in the populist disavowal of undemocratic court constitutionalism) or yet morally (as in rational universalist disavowals of ethical separations). Weber's separation between bureaucracy and politics is part of a wider vision of the healthy regime, but in Weber and in the work of corruption reformers employing Weberian notions of uncorrupted administration as an ideal, one does not encounter the type of regime analysis that fully justifies the inclusions, exclusions, and lines of demarcation that are essential to this mode of purity. Weber's value-free science—and his conception of "values" more generally—render such a normative reflection on regimes ultimately problematic as a scientific project.[1] In this sense, it is exemplary of the modern experience of corruption discourse: crafting careful separations and insisting on a kind of ethical pedagogy, Weberian science nonetheless eschews larger foundational arguments about the political good.

This study began with a defense of corruption discourse against the suspicion that it is moralism at best and ideological mystification at worst. I suggested that the worry about corruption is perennial and morally indispensable—indeed, even if a blessed day comes when the state as we know it withers away, the need for a discourse of corruption will remain. For there will always be public things—institutions tending to common concerns—and they will always be liable to abuse: the integrity of institutions and officeholders will ever need guarding.

We have seen the same term—corruption—exploited by the reactionary, the revolutionary and the moderate; we have seen it deployed by the soulless crafters of souls and the transparent dreamers of brotherhood, the defenders of bureaucrats and the pedagogues of princes. And in all these modes, we have seen that the question of corruption entails both a notion of boundaries and a notion of civic character. Corruption is always the reverse side of the tapestry that is the good regime. But in modernity, the perfectionist dimensions of the question—the crafting of city and soul, the right ordering of passions and persons—have often been difficult to articulate. I have presented the modern predicament of corruption discourse as a tension between its teleological presuppositions and our inarticulacy about the human good.

Part of this inarticulacy manifests itself in our skepticism about strict distinctions between ethical realms. The intellectual historian Conal Condren argues that we have lost a capacity to think of ethics in terms of particular duties of one's station; early modern society was conceived as a series of *offices* in which everyone had a role, and in which each office had its ethical duties and its particular casuistry. Our difficulty understanding this way of thinking, he argues, accounts for much anachronistic reading of early modern political theory.[2] Condren lays a great deal of blame for this incomprehension at the feet of ethical universalists like Kant.[3] In a world of universal, abstract, a priori ethical imperatives, the particularistic ethics of office come to look strangely pluralistic, and the Weberian argument about the personality attached to specific callings looks like a radical innovation.[4] Condren is of the view that we are so little attuned to thinking of ethics in terms of offices (and so used to thinking of office only as government posts rather than a wider series of social roles) that we have little capacity to understand such ethical divisions when they appear in early modern political thought. (Hence, for instance, Machiavelli's arguments about the ethical distinctiveness of rule struck someone like Isaiah Berlin as revolutionary ethical pluralism rather than merely an extreme version of the casuistry of office.)[5]

This is an important thesis that I would like to echo, but I would qualify it. First, the particularistic ethics of office never entirely went away even in moments of universalist enthusiasm. Kant's *What Is Enlightenment* is, after all, a text that offers two radically different ethical imperatives to people in their official capacity (as servants of their sovereign who must obey) and in their capacity as public intellectuals (as people who must be permitted to think and write freely). The second manner in which I would like to modify Condren's thesis is as follows: what he presents as a historically distant mode of thought is, in my view, a way of thinking that continues to live on, albeit in modified and sometimes inchoate forms. (Perhaps Condren would not disagree with this, for he has suggested that contemporary virtue ethics is a partial—if insufficient—rediscovery of this mode of thought.)[6] If an office-based ethics seems odd to us it is perhaps not because we tend toward ethical universalism, but because this type of ethical system functions best in a world with a more or less coherent—and holist—view of social roles and social health. An ethics of office entails, if the reader will excuse the ponderous phrase, an ontology of office: to have a duty means to *be* a sort of person, it means to have one's personality develop to fit the *persona* of the office, and this multiplicity of personae makes sense when we have a unified view of the whole in which each has his or her role. That view of the world has indeed grown rare, and not merely because the notion of conforming oneself to the character of an office seems in tension with romantic moral ideals of individual self-creation or ideals of individual autonomy. It suggests fixities and social distinctions that are difficult to countenance. When Montesquieu argued that in monarchical regimes nobles should not engage in commerce, he was insisting that monarchy's continued existence would require the fixing of boundaries between orders and ethical-political roles that seemed to be slipping. In England, where they had, he thought, slipped drastically, Montesquieu thought a different solution was required.

A great deal of political thought depends upon the crafting of dispositions fit for citizens, sovereigns, bureaucrats, and bourgeois denizens of commercial republics, and the opposition between different ways of slicing up the ethical universe is the stuff of political philosophy more generally. This can entail divisions of a Weberian sort; it can entail other forms of ethical separation. The difficulty of seeing ethics in terms of the particularistic and differentiated norms of office, then, is only one element of the wider difficulty of thinking of any given political regime as a healthy and integral form in which humans flourish.[7]

Thinking about how we should divide the political world, preventing the public thing from being colonized or contaminated by its other is the goal of ambitious political philosophy that dares to think about the human good.[8] Political theorists today tend to eschew this type of grand theory for a number of very good reasons. The baffling variety of political forms and regimes around the world and throughout history makes such teleological notions appear parochial at best; on a philosophical level, such claims also seem to bear little force in our post-metaphysical condition; and a number of very important liberal political commitments have led us to be wary of perfectionism in all its forms.[9] But corruption discourse travels on the back of perfectionist ideas. To be sure, to deploy the language of corruption coherently is not necessarily to insist that there is *one single* right political regime in which human beings flourish best (Montesquieu, again, shows us how one can speak at once in both the plural and singular mode), but it is to insist that there is a wrong relationship between officeholders and the public; it is to insist that there is such a thing as an unhealthy political order. Pluralism need not entirely block the path of universalist theory: we can, after all, affirm that human bodies come in myriad shapes and configurations without entirely abandoning the distinction between health and illness (however blurry and contestable the boundaries might be).[10] To deploy the language of corruption meaningfully requires one to be able to refute the Thrasymachean argument of old Peachum. When used in the absence of a conception of civic integrity or purity, the discourse of corruption comes to look incoherent, a metaphor that has lost all connection with its concrete meaning.

I am not merely arguing that the student of corruption would do well to attend to the wider notions of civic health or integrity underlying the term. It is also important to insist that those articulating political ideals not neglect the study of corruption. For corruption is not merely the *absence* of integrity, justice, or civic good—it is the breach that depends on the rule. It is the breach that derives from the tension between an ethical order and the imperfect beings who inhabit it. To attempt to derive ideals by bracketing corruption is to neglect something that is central to political life itself. One of the great drawbacks of so-called "ideal theory" as it sometimes manifests itself is its tendency to wish away the difficulties of human corruptibility. This is—we should note—not the case of serious utopian writing:

writers like Plato and Thomas More do not assume away corruption and corruptibility in their imagined regimes; on the contrary, their ideal cities are, among other things, studies of corruption and corruptibility.

This study has led us to distant historical contexts, but it has throughout been a description of ourselves. Each of the conceptions of corruption that we have examined is alive and well in contemporary reflection on the subject. Leadership ethics, the republicanism of mistrust, ideals of transparency, nostalgic denigrations of the bureaucratic state, liberal moderation, revolutionary purism, and bureaucratic separation all rear their heads in contemporary anticorruption talk, but they all point to very different notions of the healthy polity or the officeholder of integrity. Each of the variants of corruption discourse we have examined—and it is certainly not an exhaustive list—is, in some way, an ambivalent one. The minimalist Montesquieuan creed seems insufficiently appalled at the Walpoles of the world; Kantian purism seems—in light of our argument—not excessive, but perhaps excessively patient. Weberian purity offers an officeholder's ethics, which we admire, with an officeholder's prestige and authority, with whose inegalitarian and somewhat antidemocratic implications we feel distinct discomfort. The republican commitment to active virtue seems inadequate to the needs of office in the modern bureaucratic state. The Machiavellian republicanism of distrust thrills with the grandeur of its civism and dismays with its glory-seeking, rapacious purpose. The call for a pure, mutual transparency of trust seems to come at the expense of plurality. The ethics of leadership appear least effective in the political contexts where they are needed most. Yet all these visions of corruption have something to recommend them. Even the least attractive—because most transparently hypocritical—of our corruption theorists, Bolingbroke, was quite insightful about the role of property in determining constitutional balances. Imbalances in property relations are a source of corruption. The egalitarians among us would differ from Bolingbroke in viewing the correct balance differently—and appealing to remedies that he would have thought part of the problem.[11]

The practical-minded reformer might reasonably ask, where are we left if we are presented with so many divergent conceptions of political corruption and its cures? Are we to pay our dime and take our pick? Are we to despair at the ethical morass into which such a series of ambivalent ethical ideals has left us? Do we leave the book with the feeling with which we leave the theater after a performance of the *Threepenny Opera*? I hope the reader will not feel this way. The primary argument of this work has been an apology for the activity of normative political theory on the classical model of seeking an account of the healthy constitution in which rule is in the interests of the ruled. The normative core of corruption discourse is as essential, and as intuitively appealing, as it ever was. I have been at pains to indicate that there are profound differences between the modes of thinking about corruption that we have canvassed and important ambivalences at the heart of each. The ambivalences and paradoxes of the various conceptions of corruption we have explored are not to be taken as signs of the word's irredeemable confusion; they are invitations to the activity of political philosophy. Far from offering a counsel of despair, I am offering a challenge to recapture the enormous moral and political force of the term by reinvesting it with the perfectionist content it so demands. The definitional debates besetting the studies of corruption will not and should not cease, for they are at heart debates about the nature of the public good itself and the possibilities of realizing it.

We have noted that corruption worries rise in moments of blurred boundaries. We live in just one of those moments. And though I am loath to draw false hope from such dire circumstances, it is perhaps to be observed that the disquieting trends in political practice are leading to a heartening trend in political science: might we be witnessing a reawakening to the importance of corruption as a category of analysis concerned with institutions, mores, and the character of officeholders?[12] When one sees levels of nepotism, collusion, and straightforward kleptocracy unheard of in our lifetime in the most powerful and wealthy nation on the planet—when one sees the spirit (not to mention the letter) of the laws so flagrantly abused, one is inclined to revisit these long-neglected ethical themes. And the accusation of corruption itself is a central part of this very unsettling political moment: across the democratic world, so-called 'populist' parties are denigrating the most important institutions of their countries as a "swamp," mixing racially and confessionally charged rhetoric of pollution with constant denunciations of the corruption of previously respected institutions. Talk of corruption is on the rise, and with it the clash of competing conceptions of purity and competing hopes for civic integrity. While this is not the place to delve into the details of the current era's depredations, the attentive reader will have noticed that each of the views we have examined has something important to offer to the analysis of the current civic disease in apparently consolidated democracies— just as each has its own unique deficiencies.

The question of political corruption is fundamentally a moral question about the healthiest and most integral manners for human beings to structure their shared lives. That even the most positivistic social scientists have recourse to metaphors of corruption and purity is revelatory of an underlying but unacknowledged acceptance of political morality. As certain understandings of corruption are turned into global standards, visions of the good regime—however confusedly or implicitly expressed and however replete with internal contradictions—are reproduced and disseminated. There is no global consensus on the nature of the good regime, but almost everyone is against corruption. Those who win the game of definition stand to clean up, in both senses of the phrase. But beyond the power implications of the problem is the need for clarity. The questions concerning how we divide up the public world, ordering its passions, places, people, power, and profits and how we determine illegitimate deviations from such norms are fundamentally philosophical questions. And inarticulacy is the corruption of thought.

NOTES

Preface

1. David Redlawsk and James McCann, for instance, note quite different interpretations of corruption among the American electorate (differences that align with income); see their "Popular Interpretations of 'Corruption' and Their Partisan Consequences," *Political Behavior* 27, no. 3 (2005): 261–283.

2. Transparency International, for instance, regularly surveys public opinion with its "Corruption Barometer." People in societies where bribes are regularly solicited tend to cite as a reason for not reporting it the dangers of retaliation. In a 2015 survey in sub-Saharan Africa, only 7 percent of those respondents agreed with the statement "Corruption is normal"; in North Africa in 2016 and the Middle East, the number was just 8 percent. See *People and Corruption: Africa Survey 2015*, 23; and *People and Corruption: Middle-East and North Africa Survey 2016*, 25. Both reports are available at http://www.transparency.org/.

3. Mark Warren, "Political Corruption as Duplicitous Exclusion," *PS: Political Science & Politics* 39, no. 4 (2006): 803–807. There have been several attempts to give philosophical precision to the concept of corruption. Mark Philp has offered several important papers on the subject, as well as some interesting reflections on the behavior of political actors in *Political Conduct* (Cambridge, Mass.: Harvard University Press, 2007). A recent paper that offers a "realist" theory of the term and gives a useful overview of recent work on the subject is Mark Philp and Elizabeth Dávid-Barrett, "Realism About Political Corruption," *Annual Review of Political Science* 18 (2015): 387–402. See also Bo Rothstein and Jan Teorell, "What Is Quality of Government? A Theory of Impartial Government Institutions," *Governance* 21, no. 2 (2008): 165–190; Bo Rothstein, "What Is the Opposite of Corruption?" *Third World Quarterly* 35, no. 5 (2014): 745–746; Oskar Kurer, "Corruption: An Alternative Approach to Its Definition and Measurement," *Political Studies* 53, no. 1 (2005): 222–239. Joseph Nye's famous definition, tied to formal duties and existing rules, would make it impossible to indict existing laws as corrupt: "Corruption is behavior which deviates from the formal duties of a public role because of private-regarding (personal, close family, private clique) pecuniary or status gains; or violates rules against the exercise of certain types of private regarding influence." See Joseph Nye, "Corruption and Political Development: A Cost-Benefit Analysis," *American Political Science Review* 61, no. 2 (1967): 419.

4. Philp and Dávid-Barrett, "Realism About Political Corruption," 389. See also Lawrence Lessig, *Republic, Lost* (New York: Hachette, 2011); Seumas Miller, Peter Roberts, and Edward Spence, *Corruption and Anti-Corruption: An Applied Philosophical Approach* (Upper Saddle River, N.J.: Pearson/Prentice Hall, 2005). On the impartiality definition, we noted Rothstein,

but we might also note Emanuela Ceva and Maria Paola Ferretti, "Liberal Democratic Institutions and the Damages of Political Corruption," *Les ateliers de l'éthique/The Ethics Forum* 9, no. 1 (2014): 126–145. There is an important response to the impartiality definition in Marcus Agnafors, "Quality of Government: Toward a More Complex Definition," *American Political Science Review* 107, no. 3 (2013): 433–445. Some interesting work, including recent interventions by Philp, Warren, and Kurer, can be found in Paul Heywood, ed., *The Routledge Handbook of Political Corruption* (London: Routledge, 2015).

5. E.g., J. Peter Euben, Arlene Saxonhouse, Peter Bratsis, Lisa Hill, Adrian Blau, Bruce Buchan.

6. J. G. A. Pocock, *Virtue, Commerce and History* (Cambridge: Cambridge University Press, 1986), 48.

7. Arvind Jain, "Corruption: A Review," *Journal of Economic Surveys* 15, no. 1 (2001): 73.

8. Dennis Thompson popularized this phrase in his *Ethics in Congress: From Individual to Institutional Corruption* (Washington, D.C.: Brookings Institution, 1995). He differentiated institutional from individual corruption. Much subsequent writing has explored the gray areas in which legitimate private-interest competition appears to slide over into institutionalized forms of influence. Thompson spoke of "political gain" as opposed to "private gain." The phrase "institutional corruption" is used by the school surrounding Lawrence Lessig's project at Harvard University's Safra Center to mean any form of established influence that perverts an institution from its avowed ends or undermines public trust in that institution.

9. See, for instance, *Helping Countries Combat Corruption: The Role of the World Bank* (Washington, D.C.: World Bank, Poverty Reduction and Economic Management, 1997), chap. 2, http://www1.worldbank.org/publicsector/anticorrupt/corruptn/cor02.htm.

10. Susan Rose-Ackerman, ed., *International Handbook on the Economics of Corruption* (Cheltenham: Elgar, 2006), xiv. Joseph Nye, trying to come up with a clear, parsimonious definition of corruption wrote something in a similar vein: "we might describe the revolutionary student who returns from Paris to a former French African country and accepts a (perfectly legal) overpaid civil service post as 'corrupted.' But used this broadly the term is more relevant to moral evaluation than political analysis"; he goes on to define the concept in terms of breaches of existing public norms ("Corruption and Political Development," 419). I think we need to reject thoroughly the notion that moral evaluation and political analysis are separate things.

11. Mark Philp, "Defining Political Corruption," *Political Studies* 45, no. 3 (1997): 446.

12. John A. Gardiner, "Defining Corruption," in *Coping with Corruption in a Borderless World*, ed. Maurice Punch et al. (Boston: Kluwer, 1993), 21–38, reprinted in Arnold J. Heidenheimer and Michael Johnston, eds., *Political Corruption: Concepts and Contexts*, 3rd ed. (London: Transaction, 2002), chap. 2; Carl J. Friedrich, "Political Pathology," *Political Quarterly* 37, no. 1 (1966): 70–85; Michael Johnston, "The Search for Definitions: The Vitality of Politics and the Issue of Corruption," *International Social Science Journal* 149 (1996): 321–335.

13. Many books on corruption begin with the problem of definitions, but quickly settle on one and move on. See Raymond Fisman and Miriam A. Golden, *Corruption: What Everyone Needs to Know* (Oxford: Oxford University Press, 2017). Leslie Holmes similarly begins *Corruption* (Oxford: Oxford University Press, 2015) with a first chapter asking straightforwardly "What is corruption?" The chapter is an excellent introduction to some of the definitional difficulties, but it settles quickly on a set of workable criteria. Holmes's piece is

exemplary, but the sensible desire to settle on a definition and move on is that against which I am pushing here. In the secondary literature, I can count upwards of fifteen sources that employ Justice Potter Stewart's famous phrase "I know it when I see it."

14. One recent work by Bo Rothstein and Aiysha Varraich, *Making Sense of Corruption* (Cambridge: Cambridge University Press, 2017), examines the numerous phenomena that can be understood under that "umbrella concept." An invaluable mapping of the conceptual terrain in the social sciences, Rothstein and Varraich's book rightly affirms the normative core of the concept. Their foray into the history of the concept has a number of assertions that I think untenable, but the conceptual ground-clearing in its treatment of contemporary debates is praiseworthy as is its direct engagement with the Philpian challenge. But though they are intent on understanding corruption as a breach of *justice*, they ultimately return to an argument Rothstein has been making for some time: that the opposite of corruption is impartiality. I have argued elsewhere that this definition is ultimately antipolitical. Robert Alan Sparling, "Impartiality and the Definition of Corruption," *Political Studies* 66, no.2 (2018): 376–391.

15. Judith Shklar, *Ordinary Vices* (Cambridge, Mass.: Harvard University Press, 1984), 1.

16. One recent, interesting historical survey is Bruce Buchan and Lisa Hill, *An Intellectual History of Political Corruption* (New York: Palgrave Macmillan, 2014). Buchan and Hill organize their fine work around the distinction between classical views of corruption as moral degradation of the entire society and modern, individualistic views of corruption as particular abuses of public office for pecuniary gain. While they are aware that these two dimensions can go together, they nonetheless insist upon the importance of this distinction. In my view, even the typically modern individualist definitions trade upon the metaphor of sickness and decay and point to a particular type of soulcraft.

17. For a thorough discussion of Pocock's use of the term, see my "The Concept of Corruption in J. G. A. Pocock's *The Machiavellian Moment*," *History of European Ideas* 43, no. 2 (2016): 156–170.

18. Linda Levy Peck, *Court Patronage and Corruption in Early Stuart England* (London: Routledge, 1993).

19. A very interesting, brief history of corruption and reform can be found in Alina Mungiu-Pippidi, *The Quest for Good Governance* (Cambridge: Cambridge University Press, 2015), chap. 3.

Chapter 1

1. John Gay, *The Beggar's Opera* (London: W. Strahan et al., 1777), 17.

2. *Fressen* refers to the manner in which animals eat.

3. Hannah Arendt, *Totalitarianism*, part 3 of *The Origins of Totalitarianism* (New York: Harvest, 1968), 33.

4. The *Threepenny Opera* was not intended as a Marxist piece and it was criticized in the communist press for its lack of social analysis. Peter Thomson and Glendyr Sacks, eds., *The Cambridge Companion to Brecht* (Cambridge: Cambridge University Press, 2006), 235. Not all viewers of Brecht embrace the play's pessimism. Eric Uslaner, who frames a fine study of corruption with epigraphs from the *Threepenny Opera*, suggests that one can escape the logic of inequality and predation that Brecht painted as universal; see Uslaner, *Corruption, Inequality, and the Rule of Law* (Cambridge: Cambridge University Press, 2008), 22.

5. Augustine, *City of God Against the Pagans*, ed. and trans. R. W. Dyson (Cambridge: Cambridge University Press, 1998), book 4, chap. 4, p. 148. The example serves to illustrate the point that in the absence of justice, rule is but robbery.

6. Stephen Kotkin and András Sajó, eds., *Political Corruption in Transition: A Skeptic's Handbook* (Budapest: Central European University Press, 2002).

7. Jean Elshtain, in *Public Man, Private Woman* (Princeton, N.J.: Princeton University Press, 1981), dates this distinction back to the Greek distinction between *oikos* and *polis*. I differ with her reading of this distinction in Aristotle and Plato, but I appreciate her attempt to define capaciously the distinction between public and private.

8. Marcel Mauss, "Essai sur le don, " in *Sociologie et anthropologie* (Paris: Presses Universitaires de France, 1966), 206.

9. Bo Rothstein, "The Three Worlds of Governance: Arguments for a Parsimonius Theory of the Quality of Government" (QoG Working Paper Series 2013:12, Quality of Government Institute, University of Gothenburg, Gothenburg, Sweden, August 2013); see also Rothstein and Varraich, *Making Sense of Corruption*, 55ff.

10. Ibn Khaldun, *Muqaddimah*, trans. Franz Rosenthal (Princeton, N.J.: Princeton University Press, 1967). In *Making Sense of Corruption*, Rothstein and Varraich cite Ibn Khaldun's understanding of corruption as proof of the universality of their definition of corruption as a breach of impartiality (55–57). They rightly note a number of elements in Ibn Khaldun's view that seem remarkably modern. But they neglect the most important concept of the *Muqaddimah*, group feeling. Impartiality, for Ibn Khaldun, has a place in justice, but the loss of group partiality is a sign of a vitiated and corrupted society (a view, incidentally, that can be seen in a number of civic republican champions of Gemeinschaft in modern European political thought). Ibn Khaldun's thought is a complex reflection on where and when group feeling should reign; to assimilate it to contemporary visions of impartiality such as that of Brian Barry is unconvincing.

11. There are two different Greek terms are usually translated as "corrupt." The first is *phthora*, which is literally "rotting," and is the term employed by Plato in his discussion of regime corruption. It is also the term employed in Aristotle's *On Generation and Corruption*. The word employed in the context of his schema of correct and deviant regimes is *parekbasis*. See Richard Mulgan, "Aristotle on Legality and Corruption," in *Corruption: Expanding the Focus*, ed. Manuhuia Barcham, Barry Hindess, and Peter Larmour (Canberra: ANU Press, 2013).

12. Quentin Skinner, "The State," in *Political Innovation and Conceptual Change*, ed. Terence Ball, James Farr, and Russell L. Hanson (Cambridge: Cambridge University Press, 1989), 118.

13. Jacques Bénigne Bossuet, *Oeuvres choisies de Bossuet* (Paris: Hachette, 1865), 2:113 (book 5, art. 4); my translation.

14. Ibid., 2:13 (1.3). Kantorowicz, in the context of discussing the doctrine that the "king never dies," quotes a sermon of Bossuet: "Vous êtes des dieux . . . mais ô dieux de chair et de sang, ô dieux de terre et de poussière, 'vous mourrez comme des hommes.' N'importe, vous êtes des dieux, encore que vous mouriez, et votre autorité ne meurt pas." Ernst H. Kantorowicz, *The King's Two Bodies: A Study in Mediaeval Political Theology* (Princeton, N.J.: Princeton University Press, 1997), 409.

15. Bossuet, *Oeuvres*, 2:14 (1.4).

16. John of Salisbury, *Policraticus*, trans. Cary Nederman (Cambridge: Cambridge University Press, 1990), 40.

17. Mogens Hermann Hansen, "Was the *Polis* a State or a Stateless Society," in *Even More Studies in the Ancient Greek* Polis, ed. Thomas Heine Nielsen (Stuttgart: Steiner, 2002), 22.

18. In discussing the development of *the* modern concept of the state, Michael Oakeshott objected to Skinner, "there was no 'shift,' nothing disappeared beyond recall and nothing was established beyond peradventure—not even the requirement that the authority of the government of a state should be 'sovereign.' And, of course, the states of modern Europe have themselves remained as various and as ramshackle as those of the sixteenth century and as the realms, principalities and republics which preceded them." Oakeshott, review of *The Foundations of Political Thought*, by Quentin Skinner, *Historical Journal* 23, no. 2 (1980): 453.

19. Peter Bratsis, "The Construction of Corruption, or Rules of Separation and Illusions of Purity in Bourgeois Societies," *Social Text* 21, no. 4 (2003): 12. See the same passage in his *Everyday Life and the State* (Boulder, Colo.: Paradigm Publishers, 2006), 56. Bratsis also discusses the two-bodies doctrine, but he reads Kantorowicz in an idiosyncratic manner.

20. Lisa Hill makes this point forcefully, rejecting Bratsis and others who would draw a strict distinction between ancient and modern: "Conceptions of Political Corruption in Ancient Athens and Rome," *History of Political Thought* 24, no. 44 (2013): 555–587. She revisits this article in her work with Bruce Buchan, *An Intellectual History of Political Corruption*, though there they nonetheless wish to insist upon a historical shift that took place in modernity privileging the "public office corruption" over the view of corruption as a kind of moral degeneration, which was more prominent in the classical world.

21. See Zephyr Teachout, *Corruption in America: From Benjamin Franklin's Snuff Box to Citizens United* (Cambridge, Mass.: Harvard University Press, 2014).

22. Isaac Kramnick, "Corruption in Eighteenth-Century English and American Political Discourse," in *Virtue, Corruption, and Self-Interest: Political Values in the Eighteenth Century*, ed. Richard K. Matthews (Bethlehem, Pa.: Lehigh University Press, 1994), 74.

23. Dennis Thompson speaks about "the modern" and "the traditional" conception of corruption in *Ethics in Congress*, 29; Mark Warren divides corruption between the moralistic/cosmological versions and "modern" conceptions (taking as "the modern" version that dominant in the economics literature). Thus the Greeks and the early modern civic republicans (from Machiavelli to Rousseau) are out. See Warren, "What Does Corruption Mean in a Democracy?" *American Journal of Political Science* 48, no. 2 (2004): 328–343. Warren draws on Peter Euben's discussion about the gulf between the manner that corruption is understood in civic republican political theory and the way it is conceived in individualistic, Hobbesian thought, a distinction with which I have sympathy. Sara Shumer offers a helpful account of Machiavelli's conception of corruption, highlighting, like Euben, its distance from the individualistic conception dominant in late twentieth-century American political discourse; see S. M. Shumer, "Machiavelli: Republican Politics and Its Corruption," *Political Theory* 7, no. 1 (1979): 5–34. But Shumer is not making historicist declarations; rather, she is making an argument for the reinvigoration of republican language. Michael Johnston separates "modern" from "ancient" definitions, but he does not do so in a historicist fashion. Indeed, he rightly insists that in the search for definitions, one must pay heed to the "vitality of politics." See Johnston, "The Search for Definitions," 321–335. This is a position that Bratsis largely shares, in spite of his problematic historical essentialism: the question that corruption discourse seeks to examine is largely a political one. The simple distinction between *the* ancient

and *the* modern meanings is widespread even among great historians of ideas. In Albert O. Hirschman's classic *The Passions and the Interests* (Princeton, N.J.: Princeton University Press, 1977), 40, one finds the misleading view that there is a clear separation between an ancient "Polybian" use of "corruption" as deterioration of government and the modern use of "corruption" as referring to bribes. The lines are much more blurred than this account would suggest.

24. John T. Noonan Jr., *Bribes* (New York: Macmillan, 1984), 14ff.

25. Cicero, *On Duties*, trans. Walter Miller, Loeb Classical Library 30 (Cambridge, Mass.: Harvard University Press, 1913), 3.10.

26. Many accounts paint Bacon's conviction as largely political. E.g., Perez Zagorin, *Francis Bacon* (Princeton, N.J.: Princeton University Press, 1998).

27. See Gary Stansell, "The Gift in Ancient Israel," *Semeia* 87 (1999): 82. Stansell cites the passage in 1 Samuel 10:26–27 where people dishonor Saul by not bringing him presents. The word employed in this passage is *minchah*, a word typically employed with reference to offerings and tributes. http://www.blueletterbible.org/lang/Lexicon/Lexicon.cfm?strongs = H7810& t = KJV. Noonan indicates instances in which sacrifice becomes forbidden because it looks like a bribe. God certainly does not take *shachad*. It might be noted that Martin Luther's animadversions against indulgences were partly based on the perception that such practices gave the impression that God would be swayed by such gifts.

28. *Lord Chesterfield's Letters*, ed. David Roberts (Oxford: Oxford University Press, 1992), no. 133, pp. 381–382.

29. Samuel Shellabarger, *Lord Chesterfield and His World* (New York: Biblo & Tannen, 1971), 177, 251.

30. Conal Condren, *Argument and Authority in Early Modern England* (Cambridge: Cambridge University Press, 2006), 26.

31. World Bank, *Anticorruption in Transition: A Contribution to the Policy Debate* (Washington, D.C.: World Bank, 2000), xiii.

32. Mary Douglas, *Purity and Danger: An Analysis of Concepts of Pollution and Taboo* (London: Routledge, 1966).

33. Bratsis, "The Construction of Corruption," 29.

34. Ibid.

35. Douglas, *Purity and Danger*, 104.

36. Ancient Israelite worries about people marrying worshippers of Baal are part of this story, but one need not go so far. Multicultural societies, in spite of their inclusiveness, can have similar anxieties, building walls to protect the body politic from human matter out of place. Note, however, that the figure of the foreigner can often also serve as a king of cleansing or renewing force. See Bonnie Honig, *Democracy and the Foreigner* (Princeton, N.J.: Princeton University Press, 2001), 1–4.

37. Michael Walzer, "Liberalism and the Art of Separation," *Political Theory* 12, no. 3 (1984): 315–330. That said, I question Walzer's juxtaposition of liberal modernity with premodern holism: "The old, preliberal map showed a largely undifferentiated land mass, with rivers and mountains, cities and towns, but no borders" (315). One understands the conceptual shift Walzer wishes to evoke, but the presentation is misleading: borders are always there, even when they are internalized in the person of the king.

38. Gaspard Koenig, *Les discrètes vertus de la corruption* (Paris: Grasset, 2009).

39. See his *Hind Swaraj* in *The Penguin Gandhi Reader*, ed. Rudrangshu Mukherjee (London: Penguin, 1993), 3–66. His views on the mores of English administration are more complex than one would think from *Hind Swaraj*, but the point is that he saw in legalism and abstract administration a corruption of the close-knit rule of mores in village life.

40. For a wonderful ethnographic study of corruption discourse, see Akhil Gupta, "Blurred Boundaries: The Discourse of Corruption, the Culture of Politics, and the Imagined State," *American Ethnologist* 22, no. 2 (1995): 375–402.

Chapter 2

1. Sheldon Wolin, *Politics and Vision* (Boston: Little, Brown, 1960), 92. The most sustained case for the importance of Seneca to Renaissance mirrors of princes is Peter Stacey, *Roman Monarchy and the Renaissance Prince* (Cambridge: Cambridge University Press, 2007).

2. See "The Federalist No. 51 [Madison]," in Alexander Hamilton, James Madison, and John Jay, *"The Federalist" with "Letters of 'Brutus,'"* ed. Terence Ball (Cambridge: Cambridge University Press, 2003), 252; also David Hume, *Essays: Moral, Political, and Literary*, ed. Eugene F. Miller (Indianapolis: Liberty Fund, 1985), 42. Liberal virtue theorists such as William Galston and Stephen Macedo distance themselves from the claim. Kant himself, who celebrated liberal structural design, was not rejecting the importance of virtuous politicians.

3. Cited in Noonan, *Bribes*, 549.

4. William L. Richter and Frances Burke's edited volume *Combating Corruption, Encouraging Ethics: A Practical Guide to Management Ethics*, 2nd ed. (Lanham, Md.: Rowman & Littlefield, 2007), begins with an excerpt from the *Nicomachean Ethics*. More directly, a 2001 book from the Club of Rome argues, "The idea that elected politicians and appointed senior officials must be superior in virtues and moral character should become a central tenet of democracy." Yehezkel Dror, *The Capacity to Govern: A Report of the Club of Rome* (London: Fran Cass, 2001), 101.

5. Robert Klitgaard, *Controlling Corruption* (Berkeley: University of California Press, 1988), 75.

6. James Tracy, *Erasmus of the Low Countries* (Berkeley: University of California Press, 1996), 116–119. All parenthetical citations are to Erasmus, *The Education of a Christian Prince*, ed. Lisa Jardine, trans. Neil M. Cheshire and Michael J. Heath; with the *Panegyric for Archduke Philip of Austria*, ed. and trans. Lisa Jardine (Cambridge: Cambridge University Press, 1997).

7. David Staines, "Havelok the Dane: A Thirteenth-Century Handbook for Princes," *Speculum* 51, no. 4 (1976): 602–623.

8. Davide Canfora has found in the Vatican library nine different treatises published in Venice from 1539 to 1560 alone. "Su Erasmo 'Politico': Modelli umanistici e ricezione cinquecentesca," in *Erasmo da Rotterdam e la cultura europea*, ed. Enrico Pasini and Pietro B. Rossi (Florence: Galluzzo, 2008), 251.

9. James VI and I, in his own *Basilikon Doron*, declared Kings to be the best mirror of princes that exists.

10. The standard work emphasizing continuity is Allan H. Gilbert, *Machiavelli's "Prince" and Its Forerunners: "The Prince" as a Typical Book* de Regimine Principum (1938; repr. New York: Barnes & Noble, 1968). I need not enumerate the texts arguing for discontinuity.

11. See the dedicatory epistle to his *Apophthegmata*, vols. 37 and 38 of *Collected Works of Erasmus* (Toronto: University of Toronto Press, 2014), 37:3: "Aristotle had much to say on the subject of ethics, but he wrote for philosophers, not for a prince."

12. For Quentin Skinner, this is a defining characteristic of Renaissance mirrors of princes. See Skinner, *The Foundations of Modern Political Thought*, vol. 1, *The Renaissance* (Cambridge: Cambridge University Press, 1978), 118ff. Felix Gilbert argues that this insistence on worldly fame separates the Renaissance texts from their medieval counterparts in "The Humanist Concept of the Prince and *The Prince* of Machiavelli," *Journal of Modern History* 11, no. 4 (1939): 461.

13. The editor of volume 27 of the *Collected Works of Erasmus* (Toronto: University of Toronto Press, 1986) is typical in his assertion that "Erasmus . . . at this date takes so little account of drives for power, political realities, and patterns of human behaviour as to read more like the euphoric projection of a dream than a serious programme for political education" (xxvi). See Canfora, "Su Erasmo 'Politico,'" 274. Fred Dallmayr defends Erasmus from this charge of "idealism," leveled by Norberto Bobbio; see Dallmayr, *Peace Talks: Who Will Listen?* (Notre Dame, Ind.: University of Notre Dame Press, 2004), 183–184.

14. Elsewhere, Erasmus argues that the martial virtues are human vices: "the less good a man is, the better suited he is to war" (*Panegyric for Archduke Philip*, 134). There is an implicit recognition here that power and Christian virtue might be in tension.

15. *Praise of Folly*, in *Collected Works of Erasmus*, 27:100.

16. Richard F. Hardin, "The Literary Conventions of Erasmus' *Education of a Christian Prince*: Advice and Aphorism," *Renaissance Quarterly* 35, no. 2 (1982): 160.

17. Consider also the following: "Admittedly, the prince is not a priest . . . nor is he a bishop, and so he does not preach to the people on the mysteries of Christianity. . . . But more than all this, he is a Christian" (19).

18. Resonances of this are not absent in modern corruption literature. See Susan Rose-Ackerman, *Corruption and Government: Causes, Consequences, and Reform* (Cambridge: Cambridge University Press, 1999), 120: "Corruption at the top creates expectations among bureaucrats that they should share in the wealth and reduces the moral and psychological constraints on lower-level officials." See also Robert I. Rotberg, "Leadership Alters Corruption," in his edited volume *Corruption, Global Security, and World Order* (Washington, D.C.: Brookings Institution Press, 2009), 343. Erasmus might have cited Xenophon's *Cyropaedia* 8.1.30: "[Cyrus's] own temperance and the knowledge of it made others more temperate" (*The Education of Cyrus*, trans. Henry Graham Dakyns [London: Dent, 1914], 257).

19. Note, in passing, that the appearance of these themes—luxury, inequality, and large standing armies as the sources of popular corruption—in a thoroughly monarchical text should remind us that they are not the unique possession of civic republicans, as readers of Pocock might be inclined to think.

20. See, for instance, Sören Holmberg and Bo Rothstein, eds., *Good Government: The Relevance of Political Science* (Cheltenham: Elgar, 2012), 191.

21. *Collected Works of Erasmus*, 37:3.

22. The line is also cited at the very beginning of Erasmus's text (9). For Xenophon's claim (*Oeconomicus* 4.19), see Xenophon, *Oeconomicus*, trans. Sarah B. Pomeroy (Oxford: Clarendon, 1994), 127; one can also see this in Xenophon's *Education of Cyrus*, 253. Elsewhere, Erasmus repeats the claim (made most distinctively by Xenophon in the *Oeconomicus*) that slaves may be made willing servants through humane treatment; see *Collected Works of Erasmus*, vol. 26 (Toronto: University of Toronto Press, 1985), 327. It should be noted that Erasmus expressed revulsion at the institution of slavery (ibid., 328).

23. Socrates in the *Oeconomicus* makes this point about willing obedience with reference to Cyrus at 4.19, p. 127 and with reference to the farmer's treatment of his slaves at 5.15, p. 133.

24. That said, we should equally note his powerful attack on laws against lèse-majesté and his endorsement of the statement "in a free state, tongues should be free" (88).

25. Seneca writes, in *On Clemency* 1.11, "what is the difference between the tyrant and the king—for all their outward symbols of authority and their powers are the same—except it be that tyrants take delight in cruelty, whereas Kings are only cruel for good reasons and because they cannot help it." L. Annaeus Seneca, *Minor Dialogues Together with the Dialogue "On Clemency,"* trans. Aubrey Stewart (London: George Bell & Sons, 1889), 396. For Seneca in this passage, the distinction is one of character rather than deeds. There appears in Seneca to be a greater concession to the problem of "dirty hands." One is reminded of Lewis Carroll's Walrus, who commiserates with the oysters he is about to consume: " 'I weep for you,' the Walrus said: 'I deeply sympathize' " (*Through the Looking-Glass: And What Alice Found There* [London: Macmillan, 1872], 78).

26. The precise passage is the following: "The honour he [the tyrant] should distribute himself, but the punishment should be inflicted by officers of the court of law" (*Politics* 1315a6). Aristotle, *"The Politics" and "The Constitution of Athens,"* ed. Stephen Everson, trans. Benjamin Jowett, rev. Jonathan Barnes (Cambridge: Cambridge University Press, 1996), p. 149. All subsequent citations of the *Politics* are drawn from this edition.

27. This is a commonplace of *specula* literature. See Xenophon, *Cyropaedia* 8.22 (*The Education of Cyrus*, 256): "the good ruler is a living law." The same spirit animates Seneca's *On Clemency*; consider the inner colloquy (380–381) recommended to Nero in which he proclaims to himself that he is the author of law and a god on earth.

28. Similarly, when discussing his translation of Xenophon, Erasmus wrote, "The ancients recognized no distinction between a 'king' and a 'tyrant'; later, however, the word 'tyrant' and the word 'king' came to be abominated by everyone, at least in those states where democracy was well established." *The Correspondence of Erasmus: Letters 2204–2356 (1529–1530)*, vol. 16 of *Collected Works* (Toronto: University of Toronto Press, 2015), 189.

29. *The Correspondence of Erasmus: Letters 1356 to 1534 (1523–1524)*, vol. 10 of *Collected Works* (Toronto: University of Toronto Press, 1974), 113–126.

30. Fritz Caspari, "Erasmus on the Social Functions of Christian Humanism," *Journal of the History of Ideas* 8, no. 1 (1947): 102, quotes one reader of Erasmus who declares him to be democratic in theory, aristocratic in inclination, and monarchic in his realism.

31. Erasmus was aware that intermediate powers can undermine monarchical power, writing in one of his adages that princes often foment war so that they can exploit the emergency to overcome any opposition of senates, laws, or magistrates. Cited in Pierre Mesnard, *L'essor de la philosophie politique au XVIe siècle* (Paris: Vrin, 1969), 111–112.

32. The analogy of the ship (5) is employed to recommend knowledge as the criterion for ruling, as is the analogy of the physician (51), kings are urged to be philosophers (2, 15), the masses are argued to be in the cave (13), princes should be taught that death is not to be feared (14), laws are to be few (80), the king's rule over his subjects is akin to reason's rule over the appetites (39), philosophy is described as an escape from erroneous popular opinion, and so on.

33. This is outlined well in Stacey, *Roman Monarchy and the Renaissance Prince*, 196–204.

34. This is also the basis for his insistence on educating the prince from a young age, before he has come to realize that he is superior to all others (6). Or again, in his panegyric

to Philip, when he asks "how much care ought to be expended on educating those who nobody will dare to reprimand once they have grown up a little" (143).

35. Isocrates, "To Nicocles," in *The Orations and Epistles of Isocrates*, trans. Joshua Dinsdale (London: T. Waller, 1752), 17.

36. This letter is reprinted in the Cambridge edition of *The Education of a Christian Prince*, 115. Educators may be encouraged to test the utility of this method on their students. Whether it tends more to create complacency than endeavor is surely a question amenable to empirical inquiry.

37. Ibid.

38. David Wootton, "Friendship Portrayed: A New Account of Utopia," *History Workshop Journal* 45 (Spring 1998): 28–47.

39. Erasmus, *The Adages of Erasmus*, ed. William Barker (Toronto: University of Toronto Press, 2001), 29.

40. See his *Paraphrase on the Acts of the Apostles*, vol. 50 of *Collected Works of Erasmus* (Toronto: University of Toronto Press, 1995), 37. For Anabaptist defense of the community of goods, see James Stayer, *The German Peasants' War and Anabaptist Community of Goods* (Montreal: McGill-Queens, 1991).

41. *Collected Works of Erasmus*, 50:37–38.

42. Erasmus, adage no. 30, "Intus canere," in *Collected Works of Erasmus*, vol. 33 (Toronto: University of Toronto Press, 1991), 33–34.

43. Hanan Yoran, *Between Utopia and Dystopia: Erasmus, Thomas More, and the Humanist Republic of Letters* (Lanham, Md.: Lexington Books, 2010), 102.

44. Plato, *Republic*, trans. G. M. A. Grube, rev. C. D. C. Reeve (Indianapolis: Hackett, 1992), 107.

45. Erasmus (46) cites Plato, who makes this claim at *Republic* 539a–b. Aristotle equally argues that political philosophy is not for the young (*Nicomachean Ethics* 1095a).

46. *Collected Works of Erasmus*, 37:3. See also Hardin, "Literary Conventions," 157.

47. Aristotle, *Nicomachean Ethics*, 2nd ed., trans. Terrence Irwin (Indianapolis: Hackett, 1999); all subsequent citations of the *Nichomachean Ethics* are to this edition.

48. In the panegyric, he recounts the old fable of a king who is mistaken by his hosts for a normal traveler and succeeds in hearing people express true criticism of his rule. The king expresses gratitude for having learned these things (130). Erasmus proceeds to say that Phillip is the type of wise prince who encourages truth telling, can take criticism, and despises flattery. The panegyric is a ripe field for performative contradiction.

49. Of course, it would be difficult to ascertain precisely the effect of these texts, but we should be wary of denouncing them as dross. This type of document has a history of several millennia, with some of the finest intellects in all parts of the world engaging in it. While such texts probably never directly made people virtuous, I suspect they have greater utility than is commonly believed—they represent but a literary pinnacle of ritualistic and casual moral discourse that takes place with regularity in all walks of life.

50. Caspari, "Erasmus on the Social Functions of Christian Humanism," 92.

51. Whether he harbored philosophic-political views at odds with the emerging absolutist principalities is difficult to determine. H. R. Trevor-Roper, writing about the eclipse of the medieval city, seems a bit uncharitable but perhaps correct with his pronouncement that Erasmus, a "figure of the city Renaissance," "is swept up in the princely embrace and made a

mascot of royal courts, until he flees to die in a free city on the Rhine" ("The General Crisis of the 17th Century," *Past & Present* 16 [November 1959]: 41).

52. The products of such ethicists range from the serious to the amusing, and they are legion. One example is Lindsay J. Thompson, *The Moral Compass: Leadership for a Free World* (Charlotte, N.C.: Information Age Publishing, 2009), which conceives of itself as an extension and application of Aristotelian ethics. More scholarly attempts have proliferated in the world of business ethics, and a cursory review of the *Journal of Business Ethics* turns up much more Aristotelianism than one might have expected.

53. Daniel Terris, *Ethics at Work: Creating Virtue at an American Corporation* (Waltham, Mass.: Brandeis University Press, 2005), 8. I do not know whether the game remains part of their ethics training.

54. William D. Hartung, *Prophets of War: Lockheed Martin and the Making of the American Military-Industrial Complex* (New York: Nation Books, 2010).

55. Jonathan Hopkin, "States, Markets and Corruption: A Review of Some Recent Literature," *Review of International Political Economy* 9, no. 3 (2002): 584–585.

56. Martha C. Nussbaum provides such an argument in *Not for Profit: Why Democracy Needs the Humanities* (Princeton, N.J.: Princeton University Press, 2010). She lauds liberal education for expanding imaginative sympathies, and she correctly denounces the fact that the good of humanistic education is unlikely to palliate economic inequalities if it is merely the preserve of a "wealthy elite" (11). But she goes on to celebrate America's "private-endowment structure of funding" (132) because "rich people remember with pleasure the time when they read books they loved" (122), and they contribute money to their alma mater. Whether private or public patrons best foster humanistic education is an important question, but there is something about the system that Nussbaum is describing that is decidedly troubling for the ideals she celebrates. Whether a humanistic education funded by (and largely serving the children of) oligarchs can serve to undermine oligarchy itself is a question worth posing.

Chapter 3

1. See J. G. A. Pocock's *The Machiavellian Moment* (Princeton, N.J.: Princeton University Press, 1975). See also Alfredo Bonadeo, *Corruption, Conflict and Power in the Works and Times of Niccolo Machiavelli* (Berkeley: University of California Press, 1973).

2. J. Peter Euben, "Pure Corruption," in *Private and Public Corruption*, ed. William C. Heffernan and John Kleinig (Lanham, Md.: Rowman & Littlefield, 2004), 62.

3. Unless otherwise noted, all references to Machiavelli's works are to the following editions: *Discourses on Livy*, trans. Harvey C. Mansfield and Nathan Tarcov (Chicago: University of Chicago Press, 1995), cited parenthetically as *D* with book and chapter numbers; *The Prince*, trans. Harvey C. Mansfield (Chicago: University of Chicago Press, 1985), cited parenthetically as *P* with chapter number; *Florentine Histories*, trans. Laura F. Banfield and Harvey C. Mansfield Jr. (Princeton, N.J.: Princeton University Press, 1990), cited parenthetically as *FH* with book and chapter numbers. When referring to the original, I cite Machiavelli, *Opere*, ed. Corrado Vivanti, 2 vols. (Torino: Einaudi-Gallimard, 1997). Machiavelli rarely employs the term "purity," but in addition to using the language of corruption, debasement, and sickness, he speaks of a republic whose mores are *maculati*, "stained" or "soiled" (*D* 2.3, 3.1), the opposite of "immaculate."

4. Shumer, "Machiavelli," 12.

5. Maurizio Viroli, *The Liberty of Servants: Berlusconi's Italy* (Princeton, N.J.: Princeton University Press, 2012).

6. This is certainly the case with Viroli. Some separate the wheat from the chaff. Hanna Fenichel Pitkin, *Fortune Is a Woman: Gender and Politics in the Thought of Niccolò Machiavelli* (Chicago: University of Chicago Press, 1984), 324, referring to Machiavelli "at his best," gives us an Arendtian and quasi-Aristotelian figure grappling with the problems of political judgment and the reconciliation of our desire for independence with the needs of a historical world of particulars, conflict, and interdependence. This is in notable contrast to Machiavelli at his worst.

7. See Jean-Jacques Rousseau, *The Basic Political Writings*, trans. and ed. Donald A. Cress (Indianapolis: Hackett, 1987); this is clearest in *On the Social Contract* 4.8, on civil religion.

8. Michael Walzer articulates a liberal rebuttal of these republican tropes, pointing out the trade-off between republican civic virtue and liberal civility and refusing to accept that the decline of the first is in any way a corruption; see Walzer, "Civility and Civic Virtue in Contemporary America," *Social Research* 41, no. 4 (1974): 606. It was Hume who first defended civility against classical virtue.

9. J. Patrick Dobel, "The Corruption of a State," *American Political Science Review* 72, no. 3 (1978): 958–973, runs together Machiavelli, Plato, Rousseau, Thucydides, and Aristotle. See also Johnston, "The Search for Definitions," 322. That said, Johnston goes well beyond this dichotomy, making the essential point that the definition of corruption is fundamentally political. S. M. Shumer writes, "For him [Machiavelli], as for previous political theorists, the concepts of political corruption and health were tools for critical understanding, for understanding the personality of whole political systems." ("Machiavelli," 8; see also 13–14). This point is of fundamental importance, but it risks assimilating Machiavelli to those previous theorists.

10. On the breach, see Paul Rahe, "Situating Machiavelli," in *Renaissance Civic Humanism*, ed. James Hankins (Cambridge: Cambridge University Press, 2000), 270–308. Vickie Sullivan also effectively refutes the continuity thesis in *Machiavelli, Hobbes, and the Formation of a Liberal Republicanism in England* (Cambridge: Cambridge University Press, 2004). In her otherwise excellent discussion, S. M. Shumer slips into the erroneous continuity thesis ("Machiavelli," 13). Machiavelli's consequentialism is uncontroversial. The one exception is a recent esoteric reading arguing that Machiavelli was actually a deontological ethicist: Erica Benner, *Machiavelli's Ethics* (Princeton, N.J.: Princeton University Press, 2009); a photo negative of Strauss, Benner's argument is highly speculative.

11. Polybius, *The Histories*, trans. Robin Waterfield (Oxford: Oxford University Press, 2010), book 5, chap. 9, p. 377.

12. Machiavelli, *Art of War*, trans. Christopher Lynch (Chicago: University of Chicago Press, 2003), chap. 2, p. 305.

13. That said, perpetual terror is no recipe for longevity. The population must feel a degree of security; it is the ambitious who should be periodically shocked back to virtue. Bertrand Dejardin links terror to corruption itself. Dejardin, *Terreur et corruption: Essai sur l'incivilité chez Machiavel* (Paris: L'Harmattan, 2004).

14. Pocock, *Machiavellian Moment*, 333.

15. Leo Strauss, *What Is Political Philosophy? And Other Studies* (Chicago: University of Chicago Press, 1959), 49. Samuel Bowles understands it this way in "Niccolò Machiavelli and

the Origins of Mechanism Design," *Journal of Economic Issues* 48, no. 2 (2014): 1–11. Bowles has announced a wish to correct "Machiavelli's mistake" by insisting that "good laws are no substitute for good citizens." Unfortunately, this was exactly what Machiavelli was arguing. Others have seen Machiavelli as the author of *homo economicus*. Hirschman suggested, for instance, that Machiavelli was responsible for popularizing "the assumption of a uniform human nature" (*Passions and the Interests*, 49). This is not wrong, but it is misleading if we take it to mean that people are interchangeable cogs in a machine of state.

16. It is misleading to say, with Sheldon Wolin, that Machiavelli's civic virtue "symbolized an end to the old alliance between statecraft and soul-craft" (*Politics and Vision*, 213).

17. Vickie Sullivan correctly insists on this point (*Machiavelli, Hobbes*, 58ff.).

18. Thus, we cannot accept the formulation of Maurizio Viroli, *Machiavelli* (Oxford: Oxford University Press, 1998), 131, that corruption entails citizens' "unwillingness to put the common good above private or factional interest." While this captures an element of Machiavelli's thought, it suggests that in a noncorrupt republic people place the common good above self-interest, rather than having self-interest channeled by artificial necessity to correspond with the common interest.

19. Paul Rahe, *Against Throne and Altar* (Cambridge: Cambridge University Press, 2009), 45. Rahe is, however, correct in his assessment of Machiavelli's distance from humanist moral philosophy.

20. This argument undermines the interpretation that longevity is the ultimate marker of a good regime. See Louis Althusser, *Machiavelli and Us* (London: Verso, 1999), 40.

21. Claude Lefort, *Le travail de l'oeuvre Machiavel* (Paris: Gallimard, 1986), end of chap. 7.

22. Would we be correct to say, with Nikola Regent ("Machiavelli: Empire, *Virtù* and the Final Downfall," *History of Political Thought* 32, no. 5 [2011]: 753), that freedom is of mere instrumental value to expansion? Machiavelli never fully fleshed out which is means and which end. John McCormick, "Tempering the *Grandi*'s Appetite to Oppress: The Dedication and Intention of Machiavelli's *Discourses*," in *Politics and the Passions, 1500–1850*, ed. Victoria Kahn, Neil Saccamano, and Daniela Coli (Princeton, N.J.: Princeton University Press, 2006), reads Machiavelli's argument as a veiled claim that Venice and Sparta are not truly free (they are free of external domination, but not internally free). Whatever the case, Sheldon Wolin's memorable phrase "the economy of violence" (*Politics and Vision*, chap. 7) ill describes Machiavelli's political thought; Venice was much more economical with its violence than Rome.

23. Buchan and Hill, in *An Intellectual History of Political Corruption*, 85, quote the line from the *Florentine Histories* that "the avarice of citizens is much more harmful to peoples than the rapacity of enemies," which they take at face value, even though they indicate an awareness in their endnote that the line was reported speech (from a speech of a faction leader trying to convince a foreign prince to invade his own country). Machiavelli certainly thought that avarice could contribute to a city's corruption, but the matter is more complex than this line would suggest.

24. As with everything in Machiavelli, there are grounds for myriad interpretations. He claims to be denigrating a misuse of Christianity, and Maurizio Viroli thinks that he was neither anti-Christian nor pagan, but a fierce republican Christian; see Viroli, *Machiavelli's God* (Princeton, N.J.: Princeton University Press, 2010).

25. Pocock, *Machiavellian Moment*, 316.

26. Even glory has an uncertain status as the ultimate end of political life, since Machiavelli advises abandoning honor and glory when survival is at stake (*D* 3.41).

27. Pocock points this out well in *Machiavellian Moment* (209) but is left puzzled by Machiavelli's subsequent inattention to fixing property relations (211), the natural solution to such dependencies (and the conclusion to which the English political theorist James Harrington would come).

28. J. G. A. Pocock, *Politics, Language, and Time: Essays on Political Thought and History* (Chicago: University of Chicago Press, 1989), 89.

29. Machiavelli suggests that Venetian gentlemen are not really a problem because their wealth is not in land but in movable goods. Still, it is hard to see the Venetians as models of civic virtue, since they purchase their military defense from mercenaries, but Machiavelli does not spell that out. (Pocock fills it in for him, however, in *Machiavellian Moment*, 211.)

30. Machiavelli repeated the same claim about German frugality in his report on German affairs, written after his diplomatic mission to the imperial court; Erica Benner assures us that Machiavelli didn't mean it literally (*Machiavelli's Ethics*, 273).

31. Machiavelli, "Rapporto di cose della Magna," in *Opere*, 1:75.

32. Pocock, *Machiavellian Moment*, 209, correctly notes that "the term [inequality] connotes neither inequality of wealth nor inequality of political authority—there is no reason to suppose that Machiavelli objected to either—but a state of affairs in which some individuals look to others . . . when they should be looking to the public good and public authority." But Pocock has no explanation for why Machiavelli did not support agrarian laws, merely declaring it "curious" (211).

33. For a fine presentation of the debates around the agrarian laws, see Eric Nelson, *The Greek Tradition in Republican Thought* (Cambridge: Cambridge University Press, 2004).

34. Edward Andrew, *Imperial Republics: Revolution, War, and Territorial Expansion from the English Civil War to the French Revolution* (Toronto: University of Toronto Press, 2011), 23.

35. Lefort, *Le travail de l'oeuvre Machiavel*, 518.

36. Leo Strauss (*Thoughts on Machiavelli* [Chicago: University of Chicago Press, 1958], 149–150) indicates that Cincinnatus's poverty was not actually voluntary. Edward Andrew, Harvey Mansfield, and Patrick Coby all point out that there are important omissions in Machiavelli's version of the story of Cincinnatus's poverty: notably, Cincinnatus was not poor voluntarily.

37. Machiavelli notes that the Roman nobility were always happy to give plebeians honor but fought tooth and nail for their property, suggesting that they saw it as a fair exchange (*D* 1.37).

38. Eric Nelson argues that there are two competing traditions in modern republican theory—a Greek tradition, concerned with making the distribution of property serve justice and human excellence, and a Roman tradition, which was convinced in the Ciceronian dictum that the central purpose of the state is the maintenance of property. Machiavelli, he writes, was both inside and outside the Greek tradition, aware of the economic basis of corruption, yet unconcerned with the articulation of equality as a kind of justice; Machiavelli's "willingness to empty *virtù* of its conventional content and to endorse reprehensible actions for the sake of *grandezza* places him outside the debate" between Greek and Roman views of justice (Nelson, *Greek Tradition*, 85). I suggest that this curious ambivalence toward the agrarian law is the product of adopting the teleological language of corruption without anything approaching the classical telos it was meant to protect.

39. See Aristotle, *Nicomachean Ethics* 1167b.

40. In addition to the figures we have just cited, see Machiavelli's discussion of the decemvirs' liberality at the end of *D* 1.40, or his discussion of Cosimo de' Medici, who, he claims, displayed "greater zeal and more liberality toward his friends than his father had done" (*FH* 4.26).

41. It is worth noting that the type of personal dependencies that Machiavelli thought noxious were equally the soul of republican Rome. Nowhere in the *Discourses* does Machiavelli discuss the centrality of patron-client relationships to the success of Roman institutions.

42. Hence Machiavelli laments, at one point, a popular revolt that brought the great low: "The ruin of the nobles was so great . . . that they never again dared to take up arms against the people; indeed, they became continually more humane and abject. This was the cause by which Florence was stripped not only of its arms but of all its generosity" (*FH* 2.42). The nobles are an important part of the republican puzzle.

43. In the *Florentine Histories*, a would-be tyrant promises to rid the city of "sects, ambition and enmities," arguing that only a unified state is truly free (*FH* 2.35).

44. For an interesting discussion of this, see Julia Hairston, "Skirting the Issue: Machiavelli's Caterina Sforza," *Renaissance Quarterly* 53, no. 3 (2000): 687–712.

45. It is not convincing to assert, with Viroli, that Machiavelli is "in full agreement" with the civic tradition in which a city "must be just, if liberty has to be effectively preserved" (*Machiavelli*, 121); Viroli rightly stresses the importance of law, but overstates the degree to which laws should be just.

46. Viroli convincingly claims that "Machiavelli regards the rule of law as the basic feature of civil and political life," but he is less convincing to insist that "when he speaks of rule of law, Machiavelli always means the rule of just laws—that is, laws . . . that aim at the common good" (*Machiavelli*, 122–123). Injustice and the common good are often compatible. Miguel Vatter is correct to challenge this interpretation, though he offers a much more antinomian Machiavelli than is consistent with the text's constant invocation of law; see Vatter, *Between Form and Event* (Kluwer: Dortrecht, 2000), 11. For another example of lawful injustice, see Machiavelli's advocacy of decimation, *D* 3.49, or his argument in *D* 2.2 that the common good is attained in republics because "although [that which is done] may turn out to harm this or that private individual, those for whom the aforesaid does good are so many that they can go ahead with it against the disposition of the few crushed by it."

47. Note, in passing, that the very calumnies Machiavelli discusses in his call for public over private accusations are charges of official corruption (*D* 1:8).

48. Danielle Allen, "Anonymous: On Silence and the Public Sphere," in *Speech and Silence in American Law*, ed. Austin Sarat (Cambridge: Cambridge University Press, 2010), 129.

49. Livy, *History of Rome* 6.19, in *Livy*, trans. George Baker (New York: Harper & Bros., 1836), 1:394.

50. See *D* 1.26. Guicciardini thought Machiavelli somewhat excessive on this score.

51. Andrew, *Imperial Republics*, 178.

52. Some have suggested that it fundamentally upends the Machiavellian call for a redeemer. See John M. Najemy, "Society, Class, and State in Machiavelli's *Discourses on Livy*," in *Cambridge Companion to Machiavelli*, ed. John M. Najemy (Cambridge: Cambridge University Press, 2010), 101–102. Hans Baron made a similar claim in "Machiavelli: The Republican Citizen and the Author of 'The Prince,'" *English Historical Review* 76, no. 299 (1961): 230.

53. Harvey Mansfield celebrates this in *Machiavelli's Virtue* (Chicago: University of Chicago Press, 1966), 314.

54. John McCormick, "Machiavelli's Greek Tyrant as Republican Reformer," in *The Radical Machiavelli*, ed. Filippo del Lucchese (Leiden: Brill, 2015), 306–336.

55. Mary Dietz, "Trapping the Prince: Machiavelli and the Politics of Deception," *American Political Science Review* 80, no. 3 (1986): 785–786.

56. Consider Robert Putnam's brief appeal to Machiavelli as the source of civic engagement, solidarity, trust, and tolerance in *Making Democracy Work: Civic Traditions in Modern Italy* (Princeton, N.J.: Princeton University Press, 1993), 86ff.

57. Chantal Mouffe, *The Return of the Political* (London: Verso, 2006), 38.

58. "But to construct a 'we' it must be distinguished from a 'them,' and that means establishing a frontier, defining an 'enemy'" (ibid., 69; see also 114).

59. Vatter, *Between Form and Event*, 305.

60. Pitkin, *Fortune Is a Woman*, 308ff.

61. Iseult Honohan, *Civic Republicanism* (London: Routledge 2002), 166.

62. Mouffe, *Return of the Political*, 112.

Chapter 4

1. Machiavelli, quoted in John P. McCormick, *Machiavellian Democracy* (Cambridge: Cambridge University Press, 2011), 106.

2. Louis D. Brandeis, "What Publicity Can Do," in *Other People's Money: And How the Bankers Use It* (1914; repr., Mansfield Centre, Conn.: Martino, 2009), 92. Brandeis's essay was concerned here with collusion among bankers.

3. One Foucauldian treatment (more complex than the caricature I offer here) is Jacqueline Best, *The Limits of Transparency* (Ithaca, N.Y.: Cornell University Press, 2005). On her reading, transparency means control, and it equally entails the elimination of room for *phronesis*, though Best does not use the term.

4. Koenig, *Les discrètes vertus de la corruption*, 265. Trans. mine.

5. Jean-Jacques Rousseau, "Discourse on the Origin of Inequality," in *Basic Political Writings*, 26.

6. Mlada Bukovanski rightly thinks anticorruption discourse has too long been deaf to this central tradition; see "The Hollowness of Anti-Corruption Discourse," *Review of International Political Economy* 13, no. 2 (2006): 183.

7. There is a sizable literature in French (particularly in the work of Pierre Clastres, Miguel Abensour, and Claude Lefort), but fairly little in English. A good introductory essay is Nannerl O. Keohane, "The Radical Humanism of Etienne de La Boetie," *Journal of the History of Ideas* 38, no. 1 (1977): 119–130; see also the small collection of essays edited by David Lewis Schaefer, *Freedom over Servitude: Montaigne, La Boétie, and "On Voluntary Servitude"* (Westport, Conn.: Greenwood, 1998); an excellent work by Marc D. Schachter, *Voluntary Servitude and the Erotics of Friendship: From Classical Antiquity to Early Modern France* (Aldershot: Ashgate, 2008); and the theory is key to Michael Rosen's *On Voluntary Servitude: False Consciousness and the Theory of Ideology* (Cambridge: Polity Press, 1996).

8. Estienne de La Boétie, *Oeuvres complètes*, ed. Paul Bonnefon (Geneva: Slatkine Reprints, 1967), 5. Hereafter, cited in text as *OC*. Translations of all French texts, unless otherwise stated, are mine.

9. In an aside, he assumes a pious tone with regard to his own monarchy's superstitions, indicating that traditions of divinizing the king have served the French well, since their kings have always been so beneficent. Also, he notes, eliminating such things would take away some wonderful material for the poets!

10. Pierre Clastres, "Liberté, malencontre, innommable," in Étienne de La Boétie, *Le discours de la servitude volontaire*, ed. P. Léonard, with *La Boétie et la question du politique*, texts by Pierre Clastres, Claude Lefort, et al. (Paris: Payot, 1976), 233. Clastres's argument might be strengthened if we consider the similarity of Montaigne's reflections on "cannibals": asked what they found striking in Europe, visitors from the New World declared that they were surprised to see many well-armed men obeying a child (Charles IX). This echoes the surprise that La Boétie sought to elicit at the strange fact of obedience to a little *hommeau*. But there is no textual evidence in La Boétie's text suggesting that indigenous people are the reference; there is much pointing directly to the ancient polis, as I shall argue.

11. In his life he never gave any signs of disobedience. Montaigne emphasizes this point, while noting that his friend would nonetheless have preferred to live in Venice than in France. See Michel de Montaigne, *Les Essais*, ed. Jean Balsamo, Michel Magnien, and Catherine Magnien-Simonin (Paris: Gallimard, 2007). "De l'amitié," 201.

12. In an aside, he declares that he will not discuss the best regime, but at the same time he intimates clearly that monarchy is illegitimate (*OC*, 2). There is an interesting contrast to be made with Xenophon's *Oeconomicus*, a text that La Boétie translated into French. Here we learn that the art of governing slaves in a household is akin to a general's art in governing free men: both need to make the governed *serve willingly*. Xenophon, through the mouth of Isomachus, suggests that good government of slaves (government based on the cultivation of their love of honors and praise) can almost make the master-slave relationship monarchical rather than despotic. In the *Contr'un*, such voluntary servitude is treated as essentially slavish. It is as if he has learned from Xenophon that servitude can be voluntary, but that this is precisely what makes it so worthy of contempt. For an excellent discussion of La Boétie's translation of Xenophon, see Schachter, *Voluntary Servitude*.

13. "The Grand Turk recognizes that books and teaching, more than anything, give men the sense and understanding to know themselves and to hate tyranny" (*OC*, 30).

14. See Thomas Hobbes, *Leviathan* (London: Penguin, 1985), chap. 21: "I think I may truly say, there was never any thing so deerly bought, as these Western parts have bought the learning of the Greek and Latine tongues" (267–268).

15. The reference is to a story told in Lucian's *Hermotimus*.

16. Hobbes, *De Cive: The English Version*, ed. Howard Warrender (Oxford: Clarendon Press, 1983), 13.7, p. 159. In the preface, he points out the need for perpetual suspicion of others, and he calls on his readers to denounce those who believe regicide is justifiable (36).

17. Claude Lefort, "Le nom d'un," in La Boétie, *Le discours de la servitude volontaire* (1976), 256–257.

18. Eric Voegelin, *The Collected Works of Eric Voegelin*, vol. 23, *History of Political Ideas (Volume V): Religion and the Rise of Modernity*, ed. James L. Wiser (Columbia: University of Missouri Press, 1998), 39; Miguel Abensour and Marcel Gauchet, "Présentation: Les leçons de la servitude et leur destin," in La Boétie, *Le discours de la servitude volontaire* (1976), p. xxix.

19. Lefort, "Le nom d'un," 257–258.

20. Ibid., 265–267.

21. Ibid., 268–269.

22. Ibid., 271.

23. Ibid.

24. Much hangs on how one translates the plural *uns*. Miguel Abensour, in *Democracy Against the State: Marx and the Machiavellian Moment* (Cambridge: Polity, 2011), xxxvi, suggests, following Lefort, that La Boétie is opposing "all ones" against "all one." I do not think, however, that the plural *uns* here is meant to be a term of art to indicate diversity. Some modernized French translations read "pas seulement unis, mais tel un seul être"; other modernized French versions read "tous un." Harry Kurz translated the passage, "not so much to associate us as to make us one organic whole." Étienne de La Boétie, *Politics and Obedience: The Discourse of Voluntary Servitude*, trans. Harry Kurz (Auburn, Ala.: Mises Institute, 2008), 50. Schaefer, *Freedom over Servitude*, 198, translates it "all one[s]," thereby avoiding taking a stand on the issue (though on p. 24, n. 65, he agrees with Lefort). I do not think, however, that the *s* in *uns* ought to be taken to indicate plurality. La Boétie, in his translation of Plutarch's writing on marriage, gives the following line: "Les philosophes disent que les unes choses sont faittes de pieces diverses & separees, comme une armee de mer & un camp; les autres sont de parties assemblees & unies, comme une maison . . . les unes toutes unies & d'un naturel, comme chasque animal en soy mesmes est conforme à soy. Quasi de mesme sorte le mariage: si c'est de personnes qu s'entrayment il est lors du ranc de choses qui *sont unes & conformes*; si c'est de gents qui sont mariez pour le bien . . . il est de parties assemblees & unies" (*OC*, 175). Here, being *unis* means being separate people united together for an instrumental purpose, artificially assembled, whereas being *uns* means being *one* because of mutual love. The *s* in *uns* is a grammatical variant in sixteenth-century French, not a claim about individualism. The grammatical construction "ils sont uns," meaning "they are one" (not "they are separate ones"), is not novel to La Boétie. His contemporary Jacques Amyot would later translate a passage in the same essay from Plutarch as follows: "Or fault il, que comme les physiciens disent que les corps liquides sont ceulx qui se meslent du tout en tout l'un avec l'autre, aussi que de ceulx qui sont mariez ensemble, et les corps et les biens, et les amis, et les parents soient *tous uns et communs*" (*Oeuvres morales de Plutarque, traduites du grec par Amyot* [Paris: De Cussac, 1802], 3:20). Consider the following passage from Jean Godard's *La Langue françoise* (1620), which equally speaks of language as a unifying force: "Nature ayant fait les hommes pour habiter et vivre tous ansamble leur a aussi baillé à tous ansamble la faculté de parler, comme une chose requise et necessaire à la societé humaine. . . . C'êt par là que la hantise qui se forme de plusieurs, fait comme un seul cors de plusieurs, ou plutôt comme une seule ame qui se communique à tous ces divers cors, qui leur donne même intellijance, même pansee, même desir, et qui les rand *tous uns* d'affection." Text included in Peter Rickard, *The French Language in the Seventeenth Century: Contemporary Opinion in France* (Cambridge: Brewer, 1992), 227. A seventeenth-century dictionary, defining *commun*, reads, "le mari & la femme sont uns & communs en biens" (Antoine Furetiere, ed., *Dictionaire universel* [La Haye: Arnout & Reinier Leers, 1690], vol. 1). I could go on citing random examples, but I might just finish by suggesting that if La Boétie had intended to point to the difference between "ones" and "one" as Abensour would have it, he would have been clearer to have written "qu'elle ne vouloit pas tant nous faire tous *un* que tous *uns*."

25. This contrasts interestingly with Rousseau's view that the general will can only be arrived at if people refrain from communicating with each other at voting time.

26. Hannah Arendt, *The Human Condition*, 2nd ed. (Chicago: University of Chicago Press, 1998), 243.

27. Montaigne, *Essais*, 190; Aristotle, *Nicomachean Ethics* 1155a.

28. Montaigne, *Essais*, 194–195. Montaigne faults Cicero for having denigrated someone who had put obedience to his friend above civic duty. His response is that a true friendship of virtue entails such complete knowledge of the other that one could no more doubt his (always his) civic piety than one could doubt one's own—the friend is *known*. But this raises a further question—can one truly know oneself?

29. La Boétie does not specify exactly what type of equality this would entail in a free city.

30. Estienne de La Boétie, *Mémoire sur la pacification des troubles*, ed. Malcolm Smith (Geneva: Droz, 1983), 63. Hereafter, cited in text as *Mémoire*.

31. The argument was first made at the turn of the twentieth century by Arthur Armaingaud, *Montaigne pamphlétaire: L'énigme du "Contr'un"* (Paris: Hachette, 1910), engendering a heated polemical exchange with Paul Bonnefon. See Schaefer, *Freedom over Servitude*; though Schaefer, Daniel Martin, and Régine Reynolds-Cornell dispute some of Armaingaud's arguments, they basically agree with him. Their argument has not undermined the widespread consensus that the attribution to Montaigne is, as Simone Goyard-Fabre asserted in 1983, "definitively" refuted; see Étienne de La Boétie, *Discours de la servitude volontaire*, ed. Simone Goyard-Fabre (Paris: Flammariom, 1983), introduction, 40; see also Schachter, *Voluntary Servitude*, 52, which rejects Schaefer and his associates' claim, albeit somewhat dismissively. One motivation for the attribution to Montaigne is the apparent distance between the *Discours* and the *Mémoire*; I argue, however, that the two texts are actually closer than they might at first appear. I do not think it correct to say that they are "at opposite ends of the political spectrum," as does Reynolds-Cornell, in "Smoke and Mirrors," in Schaefer, *Freedom over Servitude*, 123. The *Mémoire* calls for enforced religious uniformity, but that is certainly not something that necessarily clashes with republican liberty—particularly when the religious doctrine championed is specifically crafted to be so elastic as to comprehend various competing interpretations. Tensions still exist between the two texts, as I shall show, but it is misleading to characterize the political spectrum as does Reynolds-Cornell.

32. Xavier Bouscasse de Satin-Aignan, "Parler sous le masque: Les difficultés de l'écoute dans le *Discours de la servitude volontaire* d'Étienne de La Boétie," in *"Parler librement": La liberté de parole au tournant du XVIe et du XVIIe siècle*, ed. Isabelle Moreau and Grégoire Holtz (Lyon: ENS Éditions, 2005): "Aujourd'hui, seul D. Martin continue de soutenir que Montaigne est le véritable auteur du *Discours*, avec des arguments ésotériques assez peu convaincants" (21). (He was perhaps unaware of Schaefer's English-language collaboration with Martin et al.) I have not the space here to enter into the details of the Schaefer/Martin/ Reynold-Cornell thesis. Some of their arguments (Martin's) are highly speculative; others (notably Schaefer's) draw on interesting textual affinities between La Boétie and Montaigne (but these could be explained in a way consistent with Montaigne's characterization of events). Prior to the publication of Schaefer and Martin's books (for Martin makes the same argument in his *Montaigne et son cheval, ou les sept couleurs du discours de la servitude volontaire* [Tours: Nizet, 1998]), the thesis of Montaigne's authorship was widely rejected, and Schaefer and Martin have not (yet) succeeded in reviving it, though they do cause one interpreter to hedge her bets: Biancamaria Fontana writes that "in the absence of new evidence it

seems impossible to establish" the amount Montaigne contributed (*Montaigne's Politics: Authority and Governance in the "Essais"* [Princeton, N.J.: Princeton University Press, 2008], 34). But if there is no "smoking gun" evidence of any of these positions, one is justified in leaning toward the majority opinion that La Boétie was indeed the author of his most famous book. The bulk of the argument for Montaigne's authorship rests on Schaefer's previous reading of Montaigne as a closet political radical. Sarah Bakewell thinks Schaefer's theory implausible; see Bakewell, *How to Live; or, A Life of Montaigne in One Question and Twenty Attempts at an Answer* (London: Chatto & Windus, 2010), 99–100. Nonetheless, Schaefer's work on the political thought of Montaigne is insightful and provocative; see Schaefer, *The Political Philosophy of Montaigne* (Ithaca, N.Y.: Cornell University Press, 1990).

33. *Mémoire*, 36; see also Smith's introduction, p. 13. Smith elaborates upon this argument (somewhat overstating his case) in *Montaigne and Religious Freedom: The Dawn of Pluralism* (Geneva: Droz, 1991), chap. 3. I don't think the text can be made into a defense of political freedom, but it is worth noting that the distinction between calling for enforced uniformity of action and calling for enforced uniformity of belief is a real one.

34. On this we might merely note that Montaigne did not embark on his solitary life of study and reflections on skepticism until well after La Boétie's death.

35. In particular, as the editor to the *Mémoire* notes (47, n. 17), Philip II of Spain was being encouraged by Rome to threaten invasion in order to preserve Catholicism in France.

36. In response to a possible rejoinder that Christians live in apparent peace with Muslims in the Ottoman Empire, he argues that this is because they are completely subject to the sultan. The multiplicity of confessions contributes to their servitude (*Mémoire*, 60). He also suggests that Islam and Christianity can live side by side because they are so different and live entirely separately, and hence are not in competition with each other. Heresy, he thinks, is a greater source of strife than "paganism" (as he describes the Turks' faith).

37. In Lefort's interpretation of the *Discours*, the phantasmagoric reference to the many eyes that spy on one, and so on, is a repudiation of the image of the body politic. Here we see La Boétie employing this imagery in a univocal manner.

38. Virginia Reinburg, "Liturgy and the Laity in Late Medieval and Reformation France," *Sixteenth Century Journal* 23, no. 3 (1992): 541; emphasis mine.

39. Cicero, *Laelius, on Friendship; and The Dream of Scipio*, ed. and trans. J. G. F. Powell (Warminster: Aris & Phillips, 1990), 37–39.

40. La Boétie's civil religion should not be understood as overtly Erastian. He insisted on the clergy's rights and the unity of the universal church. But he nonetheless argued that the king should intervene directly and make decisions on church organization by fiat. He felt the need to defend this policy at length and tried to make clear that this did not involve the crown overstepping its bounds.

41. To mention just one author in the burgeoning 'trust' literature, Eric Uslaner has done some useful empirical work on trust, following and qualifying the views of Robert Putnam. See *The Moral Foundations of Trust* (Cambridge: Cambridge University Press, 2002); see also *Corruption, Inequality, and the Rule of Law* (Cambridge: Cambridge University Press, 2008), 48–53, where the relationship between trust and equality is discussed. For an interesting discussion of diversity and trust, see Patti Lenard, *Trust, Democracy, and Multicultural Challenges* (University Park: Pennsylvania State University Press, 2012). One study arguing for the ineffectiveness of placing all one's efforts in scrutiny of officials is Frank Anechiarico and James

Jacobs, *The Pursuit of Absolute Integrity: How Corruption Control Makes Government Ineffective* (Chicago: University of Chicago Press, 1996).

42. One of the more powerful reinvigorations of classical *philia politikē* in recent political thought is Danielle Allen's *Talking to Strangers* (Chicago: University of Chicago Press, 2004). Allen attempts to find a balance between intimacy and strangeness, encouraging a trusting relationship among citizens without proposing that they attain radical unity (chaps. 9 and 10).

43. "L'amitié . . . a son vrai gibier en l'equalité, qui ne veut iamais clocher, ainsi est toujours egale."

44. This raises a fundamental question that preoccupied Rousseau, as Jean Starobinski argued in *Jean-Jacques Rousseau: La transparence et l'obstacle* (Paris: Gallimard, 1957).

Chapter 5

1. "The Idea of a Patriot King," in Bolingbroke, *Political Writings*, ed. David Armitage (Cambridge: Cambridge University Press, 1997), 251. All parenthetical citations of Bolingbroke are to this edition.

2. Alexander Charles Ewald, *Robert Walpole* (London: Chapman & Hall, 1878), 458–459. Walpole's son Horace wrote, "I never heard him say, that all men have their prices; and I believe no such expression ever came from his mouth." Horace Walpole, *Walpoliana* (London: Burnett et al., 1800), 62.

3. Isaac Kramnick, *Bolingbroke and His Circle: The Politics of Nostalgia in the Age of Walpole* (1968; repr., Ithaca, N.Y.: Cornell University Press, 1992). Pocock denies the claim, arguing that he couldn't have been nostalgic because Aristotelian-Machiavellian champions of the *vita activa* believed the few needed to be controlled and tempered by the many, so he couldn't have been an old-fashioned aristocratic elitist (*Machiavellian Moment*, 485). Pocock's argument is both circular (*was* Bolingbroke a Machiavelian-Aristotelian? Does such a marriage even make sense?) and elliptical (as in proceeding by ellipsis; much development is left out of the claim). I will not attempt to square the circle of this misshapen argument. None of this is meant, however, to diminish Pocock's enormous contribution in spelling out the difficult relationship between virtue and commerce in eighteenth-century thought.

4. John Brewer, *The Sinews of Power* (London: Unwin Hyman, 1989), 91.

5. This burgeoning professionalism is discussed by Geoffrey Holmes, *Augustan England: Professions, State and Society, 1680–1730* (London: Unwin & Allen, 1982), 245.

6. Bolingbroke, in his 1717 "Letter to Sir William Windham," describes English politics in this way, admitting that when he and his Tory friends gained office they set about redistributing offices in a partisan spirit. "A Letter to Sir William Windham," in *The Works of Lord Bolingbroke* (Philadelphia: Carey and Hart, 1841), 1:114–115; hereafter cited as *Works*.

7. Oliver Goldsmith wrote that the young Bolingbroke was a fierce drinker, libertine, and rake. His deism would emerge later. "Life of Bolingbroke," in *The Miscellaneous Works of Oliver Goldsmith* (London: John Murray, 1837), 385.

8. George Wingrove Cooke, *Memoirs of Lord Bolingbroke* (London: Richard Bentley, 1836), 2:57.

9. H. T. Dickinson, *Bolingbroke* (London: Constable, 1970), 240.

10. Walpole held on until 1742, and subsequently faced no consequences for corruption; he received an earldom (a higher rank than a viscount). Edward Pearce, *The Great Man: Sir*

Robert Walpole; Scoundrel, Genius and Britain's First Prime Minister (London: Random House, 2007), 417–420.

11. J. H. Plumb, *Sir Robert Walpole: The Making of a Statesman* (London: Cresset, 1956), 60.

12. Ibid., 59–60.

13. This was a contested claim, however, as Whig champions of the act argued that triennial elections were more ruinous and prone to corruption.

14. Kramnick, *Bolingbroke and His Circle*, 117–118. Of course, the most important opinion was that of the court, not the public, and Walpole was as assiduous as any in using public funds to this end. Shortly after the death of George I, Walpole helped to double the amount of money granted to the new queen Caroline. This placated her annoyance at the rumor that Walpole had called her a "fat bitch." With his gift of an extra £50,000, she was more than satisfied, writing him a sweet note saying that the "fat bitch had forgiven him." Horace Walpole, *Walpoliana*, 61–62. Caroline would prove to be an important source of political support.

15. Walpole exclaimed at one point, "A patriot! Why, 'tis but to refuse an unreasonable or an impertinent demand, and up starts a patriot! I could raise fifty of them within the four-and-twenty hours!" Ewald, *Walpole*, 460.

16. See *A Full and True Account of the Strange and Miraculous Conversion of all the Tories in Great Britain: By the Preaching of Caleb D'Anvers, Prophet and Apostle to these Nations* (London: J. Roberts 1734).

17. This is important to note given Pocock's tendency to present the country opposition as opposed in principle to political patronage (*Machiavellian Moment*, 407).

18. Cited in Edward Andrew, "The Senecan Moment: Patronage and Philosophy in the Eighteenth Century," *Journal of the History of Ideas* 65, no. 2 (2004): 284. Andrew's monograph on the role of patrons in making possible the Enlightenment, *Patrons of Enlightenment* (Toronto: University of Toronto Press, 2006), is a judicious exploration of the relationship between philosophy and its material requirements.

19. Francis Fukuyama, *Political Order and Political Decay* (New York: Farrar, Strauss & Giroux, 2014), chap. 5. He derives this usage from some of James C. Scott's writings on corruption. Naturally the usage is not universal. Other languages do not have two separate words for the phenomena. A work in Italian seeking to come to terms with the concept of "clientelismo" translates English-language articles discussing "patronage." That said, the author is keen to distinguish between the two phenomena I have described. See Luigi Graziano, *Clientelismo e sistema politico: Il caso dell'Italia* (Milano: Franco Angeli, 1980), 16.

20. Just to show the muddiness of the terms "Whig" and "Tory," Bolingbroke is standardly seen as a Tory, Pulteney was an important Whig who found himself on the wrong end of things when Walpole came into power, and so, banished to the political wilderness, he found himself a leader of the "country" opposition. Bolingbroke's ideological work entailed an extended attempt to craft ideological solidarity among opponents of Walpole.

21. *Works*, 1:236–239; see Kramnick, *Bolingbroke and His Circle*, 22.

22. *Works*, 1:238.

23. *Works*, 1:492–493.

24. *Works*, 1:475. All of which is rather rich from someone famous "for keeping Miss Gumley, the most expensive prostitute in the kingdom." Goldsmith, *Life of Henry, Lord Bolingbroke* (London: Davies, 1770), 8–9.

25. Hume, "Of the Parties of Great Britain," in *Essays*, 72.

26. Shelley Burtt, " Ideas of Corruption in Eighteenth-Century England," in Heffernan and Kleinig, *Private and Public Corruption*, 112.

27. James Boswell, *The Life of Samuel Johnson*, ed. Herbert Askwith (New York: Modern Library, 1950), A.D. 1783, p. 1022. The conversation was with General James Oglethorpe. Elsewhere, however, Johnson suggested that the Parliament was not corrupt, largely because it almost never had any business worth bribing for (1777, p. 750).

28. *Cobbett's Parliamentary History of England* (London: Hansard, 1806–1820), 9:473.

29. Kramnick, in *Bolingbroke and His Circle*, 121, writes that this speech contained a defense of corruption, but no such defense is in evidence there. The line in question is doubtless "When no incroachments are made upon the rights of the people, when the people do not think themselves in any danger, there may be many of the electors, who by a bribe of ten guineas, might be induced to vote for one candidate rather than another; but if the court were making any encroachments upon the rights of the people, a proper spirit would, without doubt, arise in the nation, and in such a case I am persuaded, that none . . . even of such electors could be induced to vote for a court-candidate, no not for ten times the sum." He is saying that bribery might take place in instances where there is no other motivation on the part of people, but this is not to argue, as Kramnick paraphrases it, "that corruption marked a healthy political system." That is Kramnick's inference.

30. Hume, "Of the Independency of Parliament," in *Essays*, 45; Kramnick, *Bolingbroke and His Circle*, 123–124, cites this essay as a continuation of Walpole's position.

31. Kramnick, *Bolingbroke and His Circle*, 16, rightly points to the influence of the *thèse nobiliaire* of Boulainvilliers to the intellectual circles Bolingbroke frequented in France.

32. Bolingbroke, "Remarks on the History of England," in *Works*, 1:360ff.

33. "Letters on the Study and Use of History," in *Works*, 2:188.

34. Walpole's personal enrichment had some secret sources, but this type of personal malfeasance was not the most dangerous thing.

35. Jeremy Black, *Eighteenth-Century Britain, 1688–1783*, 2nd ed. (New York: Palgrave Macmillan, 2008), 211.

36. Linda Colley, *In Defiance of Oligarchy: The Tory Party, 1714–60* (Cambridge: Cambridge University Press, 1982), 95.

37. Recall that when Bolingbroke speaks for frequent elections and the frequent change of MPs, he is aware that many boroughs will remain in the pockets of important families. His first election, to Wootton Bassett, was in his traditional family borough, and Bolingbroke won it without effort. His call for frequent elections was a call to *return* to the classic order where men from well-established families were always returned. One of the things complained of by the enemies of the Septennial Act was that strangers were parachuted into a given borough. Bolingbroke wanted to reestablish the local links.

38. As usual, the most scandalous thing about the South Sea Company was the part that was the least controversial.

39. Kramnick, *Bolingbroke and His Circle*, 67.

40. H. T. Dickinson, *Walpole and the Whig Supremacy* (London: English Universities Press, 1973), 38; see also *Cobbett's Parliamentary History of England*, 6:1362.

41. Kramnick's assessment is entirely accurate, *Bolingbroke and His Circle*, 65–70.

42. Bolingbroke, *Works*, 2:458. In his "Letter to Sir William Windham," he lamented "the prodigious inequality between the condition of the moneyed men and the rest of the nation.

The proprietor of the land, and the merchant who brought the riches home by the returns of foreign trade, had during two wars bore the whole immense load of the national expense; whilst the lender of money, who added nothing to the common stock, throve by public calamity, and contributed not a mite to the public charge" (*Works*, 1:116).

43. Brewer, *Sinews of Power*, 98.

44. Philip Harling, *The Waning of "Old Corruption": The Politics of Economical Reform in Britain, 1779–1846* (Oxford: Clarendon, 1996).

45. Brewer, *Sinews of Power*, 110ff.

46. Bolingbroke, *A Collection of Political Tracts* (London: Cadell, 1788), 259.

Chapter 6

1. All parenthetical citations are to book and chapter. The translation used is *The Spirit of the Laws*, trans. and ed. Anne M. Cohler, Basia C. Miller, and Harold S. Stone (Cambridge: Cambridge University Press, 1989). All other translations are mine.

2. One can hear echoes of Machiavelli's *Prince*, chap. 4.

3. Sharon Krause emphasizes this passage in her attempt to rehabilitate honor in liberal democratic societies. See Krause, "Politics of Distinction and Disobedience: Honor and the Defense of Liberty in Montesquieu," *Polity* 31, no. 3 (1999): 476; also Krause, *Liberalism with Honor* (Cambridge, Mass.: Harvard University Press, 2002).

4. Voltaire, *L'ABC* (London: Robert Freeman, 1762), 21. Voltaire's charge has recently been taken up by Corey Robin, who thinks Montesquieu's account of despotism in *The Spirit of the Laws* lacks the thoughtful detail that is found in the *Lettres persanes*. Corey Robin, "Reflections on Fear: Montesquieu in Retrieval," *American Political Science Review* 94, no. 2 (2000): 347–360.

5. This observation is at the heart of Judith Shklar's justly celebrated "liberalism of fear" (Shklar, "The Liberalism of Fear," in *Liberalism and the Moral Life*, ed. Nancy L. Rosenblum [Cambridge, Mass.: Harvard University Press, 1989], 21–38).

6. In this sense, Montesquieu represents an inversion of Hobbes, who saw social unity as a product of artifice, kept together with a dominant fear; Montesquieu sees sociability as natural and undermined by the *Leviathan*'s sword. Despotism *creates* atomistic Hobbesian individuals.

7. That is, they seek wealth from state benefices; people rarely seek wealth in commercial activity under despotism, since property is so tenuous. For a detailed discussion of Montesquieu's concerns about wealth and luxury, see Roger Boesche, "Fearing Monarchs and Merchants: Montesquieu's Two Theories of Despotism," *Western Political Quarterly* 43, no. 4 (1990): 741–761. I will be indicating the degree to which Montesquieu was concerned about the negative psychological and political effects of avarice, but I suggest greater ambivalence in Montesquieu's thought than is evident in Boesche's presentation.

8. Consider 12.25: "An unskillful minister always wants to tell you that you are slaves. But, if that were so, he should seek to keep it from being known."

9. This last point speaks somewhat to Montesquieu's experience. Rebecca Kingston points out that Montesquieu paid in taxes approximately the full amount of his income from his position in the Bordeaux parliament and was therefore obliged to look to wine production for the bulk of his income. Kingston, *Montesquieu and the Parlement of Bordeaux* (Geneva: Droz, 1996), 89 n.71.

10. Among those arguing for the pertinence of the natural law tradition in the interpretation of Montesquieu are C. P. Courtney (see below) and Marc Waddicor, *Montesquieu and the Philosophy of Natural Law* (The Hague: Martin Nijhoff, 1970).

11. C. P. Courtney, "Montesquieu and Natural Law," *Montesquieu's Science of Politics: Essays on "The Spirit of Laws,"* ed. David W. Carrithers, Michael A. Mosher, and Paul A. Rahe (Lanham, Md.: Rowman & Littlefield, 2001), 60.

12. I thus disagree somewhat with the great Montesquieu scholar Céline Spector's interpretation: "While man is a double being, a sentient and emotive creature, but also, by nature, an intelligent and free being (I, 1), fear reduces the human being to pure animality, governing his behavior as mechanically as the laws of movement that govern bodies." Spector, "Honor, Interest, Virtue: The Affective Foundations of the Political in *The Spirt of Laws*," in *Montesquieu and His Legacy*, ed. Rebecca E. Kingston (Albany: SUNY Press, 2009), 52. This corresponds poorly to Montesquieu's claim that "animals . . . do not have our expectations, but they do not have our fears" (1.1).

13. Thomas Pangle, *Montesquieu's Philosophy of Liberalism* (Chicago: University of Chicago Press, 1973), 37.

14. Montesquieu, *Oeuvres complètes*, 2 vols. (Paris: Gallimard, 1949, 1951), 2:1133.

15. Montesquieu mentions a fifth law, the knowledge and love of God, but we get the sense that this law is only there to defuse pious objections; he dismisses this law quickly as excessively speculative for a pre-social being, and it plays no role in his analysis of human nature.

16. In this, I disagree with the influential view of Thomas Pangle, who would have us downplay the importance of this pre-civic human nature: "Only that part of nature which led to civil society can be of relevance to civil society" (*Montesquieu's Philosophy of Liberalism,* 40).

17. Sharon Krause rightly indicates Montesquieu's ambivalence about the English; many interpreters see him as a conservative defender of the nobility in the ancien régime. It is important to recall these less laudatory passages given our tendency to focus on Montesquieu's idealized presentation of the English constitution as the most enduring elements of his thought. Krause, "The Spirit of Separate Powers in Montesquieu," *Review of Politics* 62, no. 2 (2000): 231–265. For one version of the nobility thesis, see Louis Althusser, *Montesquieu, la politique et l'histoire* (Paris: Presses Universitaires de France, 1959), chap. 6. It is a curious thing about Montesquieu that he could have been so dearly loved by the likes of Edmund Burke and yet inspire books such as that by Mark Hulliung, *Montesquieu and the Old Regime* (Berkeley: University of California Press, 1976), describing him as a forerunner of the revolution.

18. Montesquieu, "Notes sur l'Angleterre," in *Oeuvres complètes*, 1:884.

19. I have treated faction and party as synonymous here because Montesquieu predates the philosophical distinction between these two things, a distinction developed in English theory and practice over the course of the eighteenth century and expressed most clearly in the work of Edmund Burke (a great reader of Montesquieu).

20. Montesquieu, *Oeuvres complètes*, 1:372.

21. Hulliung, *Montesquieu and the Old Regime*, 213.

22. Montesquieu, *Oeuvres complètes*, 1:1449.

23. Montesquieu, "Notes sur l'Angleterre," in *Oeuvres complètes*, 1:880.

24. Kramnick, *Bolingbroke and His Circle*, 152.

25. Montesquieu, "Notes sur l'Angleterre," in *Oeuvres complètes*, 1:884.

26. Céline Spector suggests that he was confident that the English love of liberty would win out, but Kramnick indicates that late in life Montesquieu appears to have been quite concerned. See Kramnick, *Bolingbroke and His Circle*, 295 n. 45, citing Montesquieu, *Pensées et fragments inédits* (Bordeaux, 1901), 12.

27. "Notes sur l'Angleterre," in *Oeuvres complètes*, 1:878. In the *Pensées* we can read Montesquieu's later view that the English, in addition to loving money, also have esteem for merit, a point equally made in *The Spirit of the Laws* (19.27). Nonetheless, in the *Pensées* we can also read Montesquieu expressing his preference for his own country and its mores. He also declares that in France he loves—and does not fear—the government, which is moderate. The generalizations in the "Notes sur l'Angleterre" are mostly repeated in 19.27, particularly with regard to the relations between the sexes in England. This barb seems to be a view he retained of the English: "Il faut à l'Anglois un bon diner, une fille, de l'aisance; comme il n'est pas répandu, et qu'il est borné a cela, dès que sa fortune se délabre, et qu'il ne peut plus avoir cela, il se tue ou se fait voleur" (*Oeuvres complètes*, 1:877).

28. *Oeuvres complètes*, 1:881. He points out that it was passed more by accident than design.

29. Montesquieu proceeds to celebrate laws dividing inheritances equally among children in order to avoid individuals building up fortunes. Montesquieu might have gone even further and endorsed Warren Buffett's plan not to give his immense fortune to his children. (Buffett has famously quipped, "I want to give my kids enough so that they could feel that they could do anything, but not so much that they could do nothing," thereby endorsing the work ethic that Montesquieu thinks is at the heart of commercial virtue.) This insistence on equal access to inheritance mitigates the somewhat more Lockean praise of Henry VIII for having got rid of "les hôpitaux où le bas people trouvait sa subsistence," thereby increasing industry (23:29). See Paul A. Rahe, *Montesquieu and the Logic of Liberty* (New Haven, Conn.: Yale University Press, 2009). Rahe emphasizes this passage (*Logic of Liberty*, 231), but he skips lightly over the passage calling for the suppression of extreme inequality ("Montesquieu does not dwell on this option" [225]). Rahe is silent about Montesquieu's unambiguous endorsement of sizable welfare provisions in wealthy nations. This is consistent with Rahe's desire to conscript Montesquieu for the American right. See also Paul Rahe, *Soft Despotism: Democracy's Drift* (New Haven, Conn.: Yale University Press, 2009). Montesquieu is the master of ambivalence, and to isolate any strand in his many-varied thought is to risk "recast[ing] the great man's thinking along the lines of [one's] own predilections," to employ the phrase with which Rahe castigates Hulliung, Keohane, Shklar, Manin, and Spector (*Logic of Liberty*, 138).

30. On this note, Montesquieu indicates that it is both a duty (to prevent suffering) and a sensible policy (to prevent revolts) for a wealthy state to see to the needs of the poor: "Quelques aumônes que l'on fait à un homme nu, dans les rues, ne remplissent point les obligations de l'État, qui doit à tout les citoyens une subsistence assurée, la nourriture, un vêtement convenable, et un genre de vie qui ne soit point contraire à la santé" (23.29).

31. *Considérations sur les causes de la grandeur des Romains et de leur décadence* (Paris: Gallimard, 2008), chap. 3.

32. Ibid., chap. 8, p. 122.

33. Montesquieu, *Oeuvres complètes*, 1:1450.

34. Equally, he suggests that taxes ought to be lowest in despotic countries (13.10). This, of course, does not alter the fact that no property is truly secure in such countries, and the license of merchants there is no sign of healthy commerce.

35. Montesquieu derides tax farming as inherently corrupt, and prefers the English system, which is quicker and more predictable (20.13); he explains the success of the early Islamic conquests in terms of their less corrupt system of taxation (13.16).

36. This is not to say that England is a model that should be exported: Montesquieu's celebrated attack on uniformity (29.18) is an attack on purity and the excessive attachment to abstract ideals. It is equally an attack on one-size-fits-all civilizing missions. Certainly, Montesquieu would have been dismayed to see "freedom on the march."

37. Steven Levitsky and Daniel Ziblatt, *How Democracies Die* (New York: Crown, 2018), erroneously attribute to Montesquieu excessive faith in institutional design (212). (This was noted by Jacob Levy, who thought their book otherwise excellent.)

Chapter 7

1. Heinrich Heine, *Sämmtliche Werke* (Hamburg: Hoffmann und Campe, 1868), 5:186.

2. As Slavoj Žižek, *In Defense of Lost Causes* (London: Verso, 2008), 160, notes, the title of a recent Robespierre biography sums up this thesis: *Fatal Purity*. Ruth Scurr's biography, *Fatal Purity: Robespierre and the French Revolution* (London: Chatto & Windus, 2006), though evincing some sensible liberal misgivings about the Incorruptible, is extremely even-handed and quite a bit more reflective than Žižek's flamboyant gestures.

3. Jeremy Jennings, *Revolution and the Republic* (Oxford: Oxford University Press, 2011), 8–9.

4. Hegel compared Robespierre to the Prophet Muhammad for this reason. See Barrington Moore Jr., *Moral Purity and Persecution in History* (Princeton, N.J.: Princeton University Press, 2000), 103; he writes, "The behaviors that surfaced in the French Revolution were the familiar ones of monotheism." For liberal condemnation of such a project, the examples are endless, but one could do worse than consulting the list that Žižek compiles in his desire to flip that judgment on its head in his introduction to *Slavoj Žižek Presents Robespierre: Virtue and Terror* (New York: Verso, 2007).

5. In *On Revolution* (London: Penguin, 1990), Hannah Arendt argued that "the evil of Robespierre's virtue was that it did not accept any limitations" (90). She rightly noted the radical anti-Montesquieuan nature of the Terror. She went on, however, to make some dubious claims about the evils of bringing social questions into politics and even more dubious claims about the greater lawfulness of the American Revolution. The American Revolution contained massive, violent, extralegal repressions that created more refugees per capita than the French Revolution.

6. He expressed this view, among other places, in the early manuscript *The Philosophical Manifesto of the Historical School of Law*, cited by William James Booth, "The Limits of Autonomy: Karl Marx's Kant Critique," in *Kant and Political Philosophy: The Contemporary Legacy*, ed. Ronald Beiner and William James Booth (New Haven, Conn.: Yale University Press, 1993).

7. G. W. F. Hegel, *Vorlesungen über die Geschichte der Philosophie*, ed. C. L. Michelet (Berlin: Duncker und Humblot, 1840–1844), 3:501. My translation.

8. Michael Walzer, "The Problem of Dirty Hands," *Philosophy and Public Affairs* 2, no. 2 (1973): 160–180.

9. Maximilien Robespierre, *Oeuvres* (Paris: Société des études robespierristes, 2011), 10:274. Note Robespierre's celebration of Cicero's illegal actions against the Catiline conspiracy, "Sur les principes de morale politique," February 5, 1794, in *Oeuvres* 10:358. Unless otherwise indicated, translations are mine.

10. This is widely quoted. Sophie Wahnich basically follows Danton's argument in *In Defense of the Terror: Liberty or Death in the French Revolution* (New York: Verso, 2012), 59. See David Andress, ed., *The Oxford Handbook of the French Revolution.* (Oxford: Oxford University Press, 2013), 454.

11. Without entering into classic defenses of Robespierre such as that by Albert Mathiez, we might note Wahnich's *In Defense of the Terror.* Žižek gains most of his analysis from her work, periodically using the same consequentialist logic. Yet he also goes her one further and evokes the quixotic heroism of Robespierre's virtue, which doesn't worry about effects. The tension between those two positions is present in Robespierre's thought itself.

12. Robespierre, *Oeuvres*, 10:351, "Sur les principes de morale politique" (17 pluviose, an 2).

13. Ibid.

14. Ibid., 357. Note, again, the Montesquieuan overtones to this, despite its radically anti-Montesquieuan thesis.

15. See "Déclaration des droits de l'homme et du citoyen de 1789," at www.assemblee nationale.fr/connaissance/constitution.asp#declaration; for English translation, see "Declaration of the Rights of Man—1789," at http://avalon.law.yale.edu/18th_century/rightsof.asp.

16. *Bulletin des lois de la République française* (Paris: Imprimerie nationale, 1794–1931), June 1794, no. 1, p. 3.

17. Ibid., 3.

18. See Olivier Blanc, *La corruption sous la Terreur (1792–1794)* (Paris: Laffont, 1992).

19. Robespierre himself offered at one point a sophistic distinction between "moderatism" and "moderation": "moderatism . . . is to moderation what impotence is to chastity; excess . . . is to vigour what inflammation is to health." Quoted in David Andress, *The Terror* (New York: Farrar Straus & Giroux, 2005), 260. On revolutionary Anglophobia, see Sophie Wahnich and Marc Belissa. "Les crimes des Anglais: Trahir le droit," *Annales historiques de la Révolution française* 300 (1995): 233–248. That money can corrupt virtue is a universal trope, engaged by the revolution's friends and enemies. Burke, in his bloodthirsty exhortations to destroy the cancer of the revolution, complained of his own countrymen's reluctance to pay for an expensive war with France, using the very same rhetoric of wealth leading to decadence: "If our wealth commands us, we are poor indeed." Edmund Burke, *Revolutionary Writings* (Cambridge: Cambridge University Press, 2014), 260.

20. Robespierre, *Oeuvres*, 9:499 (May 10, 1793).

21. Ibid., 500.

22. Ibid., 167 (April 24, 1793).

23. The absurd story is discussed in Bronislaw Baczko, *Ending the Terror* (Cambridge: Cambridge University Press, 1994), chap. 1.

24. G. W. F. Hegel, *Elements of the Philosophy of Right*, ed. Allen Wood (Cambridge: Cambridge University Press, 1991), 39. In the *Phenomenology of Spirit*, the subsequent development is the Kantian retreat into abstract morality, which prolongs the separation between empty universals and concrete particulars, though, as we noted, under the nightcap. See *Phenomenology of Spirit*, trans. A. V. Miller (Oxford: Oxford University Press, 1977), §595 ff.

25. Dan Edelstein, *The Terror of Natural Right: Republicanism, the Cult of Nature, and the French Revolution* (Chicago: University of Chicago Press, 2009), 208. He cites Robespierre, *Oeuvres*, 4:145.

26. The reasons behind his opposition, of course, were strategic rather than philosophical. But his justification for it was to claim that the *peuple* had already spoken in its uprising, and an *appel au peuple* would actually only serve to consult aristocrats and their propagandists. Robespierre, *Oeuvres*, 9:207 (January 1, 1793). That said, on this particular issue he could have invoked Rousseau, for the question of the king's punishment is particular, not general, and thus the business of government, not the sovereign (Athenian ostracism was, in Rousseau's view, despotic).

27. Marisa Linton, "Robespierre's Political Principle," in *Robespierre*, ed. Colin Haydon and William Doyle (Cambridge: Cambridge University Press, 2006), 41.

28. Robespierre, *Oeuvres*, 10:354–355.

29. Ibid., 356.

30. Ibid., 9:496 (May 10, 1793): "L'intérêt du peuple, c'est le bien public; l'intérêt de l'homme en place, est un intérêt privé. . . . pour être bon, il faut que le magistrat s'immole lui-même au peuple."

31. Ibid., 10:359.

32. Burke, *Revolutionary Writings*, 311.

33. In his earlier pleas to abolish the death penalty, Robespierre gave a forward-looking, deterrence-based account of punishment. (See his discourse of May 30, 1791.) Robespierre's opposition to the death penalty is not necessarily in contradiction to his advocacy of terror since the one case was a discussion of legal recourse against criminal citizens, while the other was the treatment accorded to enemies of the human race, a category in which Louis XVI had belonged. (For an excellent discussion of this theory, see Edelstein, *Terror of Natural Right*, 18ff.) Robespierre was in tension with himself, however, in seeing justice toward enemies in purely retributive terms and justice toward citizens in terms of deterrence.

34. Robespierre, *Oeuvres*, 10:551 (July 26, 1794).

35. Ibid., 414 (March 31, 1794).

36. Terry Eagleton, *Holy Terror* (Oxford: Oxford University Press, 2005), 47.

37. Jonathan Israel, *Democratic Enlightenment* (Oxford: Oxford University Press, 2012), p. 744. See also chap. 26.

38. Žižek, introduction to *Robespierre: Virtue and Terror*, xxv.

39. Immanuel Kant, *Critique of Pure Reason*, trans. Paul Guyer and Allen Wood (Cambridge: Cambridge University Press, 1998), A51/B75.

40. Immanuel Kant, *Religion Within the Limits of Reason Alone*, trans. Theodore M. Greene and Hoyt H. Hudson (New York: Harper, 1960), 19n. Hereafter cited as *RWLRA*.

41. Kant, *Critique of Practical Reason*, 5:86, in *Practical Philosophy*, trans. and ed. Mary Gregor (Cambridge: Cambridge University Press, 1996). Kant's writings on practical and political philosophy will be cited with the standard Akademie edition, vol.: page, followed by the page in the Cambridge volume of *Practical Philosophy*.

42. Kant, *Groundwork of the Metaphysics of Morals*, 4:407, in *Practical Philosophy*, 61–62.

43. Kant, *Metaphysics of Morals* (hereafter *MM*), 6:307, in *Practical Philosophy*, 451–452. .

44. Kant, "Perpetual Peace," 8:366, in *Practical Philosophy*, 335.

45. See his brief reference to Platonic ideals in the *Critique of Pure Reason*, A317/B373.

46. Kant, *Anthropology from a Pragmatic Point of View*, trans. and ed. Robert B. Louden (Cambridge: Cambridge University Press, 2006), 7:259, p. 158. One rather striking difference between the two is Kant's acceptance of the distinction between active and passive citizens, a distinction that Robespierre rightly thought indefensible.

47. Kant, "Theory and Practice," 8:297, in *Practical Philosophy*, 296.

48. He calls it an "Unding" (*MM*, 6:320).

49. Kant, "Theory and Practice," 8:303 ff., in *Practical Philosophy*, 301.

50. Dan Edelstein makes this point: there is, in Robespierre's natural-right vocabulary, no Schmittian state of exception to all law; rather, there are people who are the enemies of humanity. That is, while Louis Capet is outside of civil law, natural law is in force. *Terror of Natural Right*, 150–152, 273.

51. Robespierre, *Oeuvres*, 9:121ff. (December 3, 1792).

52. Kant, *MM*, 6:320n, in *Practical Philosophy*, 464. In "Theory and Practice," however, he notes, in discussing the example of England's Glorious Revolution, that the pretense that James II had abdicated was a mere invention to render the act legally acceptable (8:303).

53. Kant, *MM*, 6:235–236, in *Practical Philosophy*, 391–392.

54. Kant, *MM*, 6:320n.

55. Kant, "Perpetual Peace," 8:372, in *Practical Philosophy*, 340.

56. Kant, "The Contest of the Faculties," 2.6, in *Political Writings*, ed. Hans Reiss, trans. H. B. Nisbet, 2nd ed. (Cambridge: Cambridge University Press, 1991), 182.

57. Ibid., 183.

58. *RWLRA*, 88. Kant employs the Latin-derived word *Korruption* as a synonym for the German *Verderbung*.

59. Kant, *Critique of Practical Reason*, 5:75, in *Practical Philosophy*, 201.

60. Kant, *MM*, 6:231, in *Practical Philosophy*, 388.

61. Kant, *MM*, 6:333, in *Practical Philosophy*, 474.

62. Mark Tunick, "Is Kant a Retributivist?" *History of Political Thought* 17, no. 1 (1996): 60–78, points out some passages that run counter to the infamous "blood guilt" passage, forcing us to nuance our account of Kant's commitment to retributivism. Kant offers a strange exception for instances in which there are so many murderers that carrying out the punishment would destroy the state. This sounds like a brief lapse, a moment of unforgivable consequentialism.

63. "Perpetual Peace," 8:378–379, in *Practical Philosophy*, 345. The German may be found in Kant, *Zum ewigen Frieden: Ein philosophischer Entwuft* (Königsberg: Friedrich Nicolovius, 1796), 92.

64. Kant, *MM*, 6:332. Kant allows for some considerations of necessity in cases when the number of criminals is so large that to punish them all would entail destroying the state. In this, he seems to back off from the logical consequence of his retributivism in the case of a mass revolt.

65. Kant, *Groundwork of the Metaphysics of Morals*, 4:435, in *Practical Philosophy*, 84.

66. Robert J. Benton, "Political Expediency and Lying: Kant vs. Benjamin Constant," *Journal of the History of Ideas* 43, no. 1 (1982): 135–144. That said, Kant was not opposed to the Directorate for which Constant's text was an apology, so one must be circumspect about attributing ideological motivations to the conflict.

67. Kant, *MM*, 6:429, in *Practical Philosophy*, 552–553.

68. Kant stipulates this point in the footnote at 8:426, "On a Supposed Right to Lie," in *Practical Philosophy*, 612.

69. Kant stipulates in the *MM*, 6:238, that lies that do not affect right (lies, say, that do not affect contracts) are breaches of duties of virtue, not of duties of right. Thus the fact that Kant's controversial essay on lying declares that lies in general undermine the source of right does not mean that the state needs to go around policing all mistruths. The claim in the essay, however, that one is legally responsible for bad consequences that arise from our lie might be thought in tension with the *MM*'s claim that it is up to the listener to decide whether or not to believe the claim made by the speaker.

70. Kant, "On a Supposed Right to Lie," 8:426, in *Practical Philosophy*, 612. Note the metaphor of the poisoned source of right "Rechtsquelle." We can see the metaphor of sickness in Kant's ethical reflection on lying to oneself (which is a breach of one's moral duty but not of right): "it is from such a rotten spot [*von einer solchen faulen Stelle*] (falsity, which seems to be rooted in human nature itself) that the ill of untruthfulness spreads into his relations with other human beings as well" (*MM*, 6:430–431, in *Practical Philosophy*, 554).

71. Kant, "Theory and Practice," part 2, 8:290–291, in *Practical Philosophy*, 291.

72. *MM*, 6:239: "Duties of virtue cannot be subjected to external lawgiving." *Practical Philosophy*, 395.

73. Ibid.

74. *RWLRA*, 87.

75. See, among other places, *MM*, 6:484, in *Practical Philosophy*, 597.

76. Kant, *Critique of Judgment*, trans. Werner S. Pluhar (Indianapolis: Hackett, 1987), par. 28.

77. Ibid. See Robert R. Clewis, *The Kantian Sublime and the Revelation of Freedom* (Cambridge: Cambridge University Press, 2009), for an examination of sublimity in Kant that accounts for its moral dimension and for the feeling of enthusiasm Kant had for the French Revolution.

78. Alasdair MacIntyre offers perhaps one of the more famous versions of this commonplace attack in *After Virtue: A Study in Moral Theory*, 2nd ed. (Notre Dame, Ind.: University of Notre Dame Press, 1984).

79. For a useful essay differentiating Adorno's treatment of Kant and Sade from that of Lacan, see Rebecca Comay, "Adorno avec Sade . . . ," *Differences* 17, no. 1 (2006): 6–19.

80. Jonathan Israel, *Democratic Enlightenment: Philosophy, Revolution, and Human Rights, 1750–1790* (Oxford: Oxford University Press, 2012), 744, incorrectly accuses Kant of self-contradiction.

81. Kant, *MM*, 6:323, in *Practical Philosophy*, 465.

82. Kant, "Perpetual Peace," 8:367, in *Practical Philosophy*, 336.

83. Kant undermines any attempt to permit conscientious disobedience. He does, however, offer, in a footnote in *RWLRA* (90–91n.), the possibility that actually evil commands could be given. Here he suggests that one would be morally obligated to disobey. But he proceeds to insist that in the event of a conflict between the state law that is not obviously immoral and one's perceived conception of divine law, one must choose the state as in fact embodying divine law, since the duty to protect the civil institution is paramount. Thus, while I do not think this passage can serve as a doctrine of civil disobedience, it does demonstrate an awareness of the problem.

84. Kant, "Perpetual Peace," 8:380, in *Practical Philosophy*, 346.

85. Kant, *MM*, 6:322, in *Practical Philosophy*, 465.

86. Kant, "Theory and Practice," 8:304, in *Practical Philosophy*, 302.

87. Robespierre, *Oeuvres*, 9:507 (May 10, 1793): "la publicité est l'appui de la vertu, la sauve-garde de la vérité, la terreur du crime, le fléau de l'intrigue."

88. "Perpetual Peace," appendix 2, 8:383, in *Practical Philosophy*, 348.

89. Kant, "What Is Enlightenment?" and "Theory and Practice," 8:35–42, 304, in *Practical Philosophy*, 17–22, 302.

90. Robespierre, *Oeuvres*, 9:503 (May 10, 1793): "ni la corruption, ni l'intrigue, ni la perfidie n'oseroient se montrer."

91. Robespierre, *Oeuvres*, 10:503 (June 24, 1794).

92. Kant speaks in "What Is Enlightenment?" (8:39) of one's freedom to write "in his capacity as a scholar." See "Perpetual Peace," 2nd supplement, 8:368–369, in *Practical Philosophy*, 337–338.

93. Kant, *Idea for a Universal History with a Cosmopolitan Purpose*, 8:27–28 in Kant, *Anthropology, History, and Education*, ed. Günter Zöller and Robert B. Louden, trans. Mary Gregor et al. (Cambridge: Cambridge University Press, 2007), 116–118.

94. The quotation is from the *Idea for a Universal History*, prop. 6, 8:23. Berlin, *The Proper Study of Mankind* (New York: Farrar, Straus & Giroux, 1998), 16, 241, 603.

95. Kant, "Idea for a Universal History," 8:23, in *Anthropology, History, and Education*, 113.

96. In his treatise on education, Kant argues that to teach children patience entails teaching them hope and courage: 9:478, in *Anthropology, History, and Education*, 466–467.

Chapter 8

1. James C. Scott compares this to the manner in which marginalized but commercially successful pariah communities sometimes employ corruption or are forced via extortion into corrupt relationships as an informal channel of protection and influence in communities where they are formally excluded; his example is Chinese traders in Thailand. Scott, *Comparative Political Corruption* (Engelwood Cliffs, N.J.: Prentice-Hall, 1972), chap. 4.

2. Of the numerous interesting contributions to this history, two examples (covering two different contexts) are the following: Edward Glaeser and Claudia Goldin, *Corruption and Reform: Lessons from America's Economic History* (Chicago: University of Chicago Press, 2006); and Harling, *The Waning of "Old Corruption."*

3. E.g., Vito Tanzi, "Corruption Around the World: Causes, Consequences, Scope, and Cures," *IMF Staff Papers* 45, no. 4 (1998): 571. Weberian bureaucracy shows up in a great many analyses of corruption and its cures. One interesting paper that attempts to disaggregate the elements of Weberian bureaucracy and assess their impact on corruption is Carl Dahlström, Victor Lapuente, and Jan Teorell, "The Merit of Meritocratization: Politics, Bureaucracy, and the Institutional Deterrents of Corruption," *Political Research Quarterly* 65, no. 3 (2012): 656–668.

4. Richard M. Weiss, "Weber on Bureaucracy: Management Consultant or Political Theorist?" *Academy of Management Review* 8, no. 2 (1983): 242–248.

5. *From Max Weber: Essays in Sociology*, trans. and ed. H. H. Gerth and C. Wright Mills (London: Routledge & Kegan Paul, 1948), 216. The most influential and accessible version of Weber's theory of bureaucracy in the Anglophone world is the selection from *Economy and*

Society presented Gerth and Mills's volume, and I will generally be referring to that text save when referring to other sections from *Economy and Society*. The bureaucracy section may be found in Weber, *Wirtschaft und Gesellschaft*, ed. Johannes Winckelmann, 5th ed. (Tübingen: Mohr, 1972), part 2, chap. 9, sec. 2 pp. 551–579. The English translation can be found in Weber, *Economy and Society: An Outline of Interpretive Sociology*, ed. Guenther Roth and Claus Wittich (Berkeley: University of California Press, 1978), chap. 11, "Bureaucracy," pp. 956–1003. Chapter numbers and subtitles differ between the dominant German and English volumes. The current gold standard is the *Gesamtausgabe*, vol. 8, *Wirtschaft, Staat und Sozialpolitik*, ed. Wolfgang Schluchter with Peter Kurth and Birgitt Morgenbrod (Tübingen: Mohr, 1998).

6. *Wirtschaft und Gesellschaft* part 1, 3.8, p. 136; part 2, 9.2, p. 558; *Economy and Society* part 1, 3.8, p. 235; *From Max Weber*, 206.

7. Weber, *Political Writings* (Cambridge: Cambridge University Press, 1994), 315.

8. Ibid., 320.

9. See his description of American judges in *Wirtschaft und Gesellschaft* part 2, 9.1, p. 545. The reforms that the Americans were beginning had a very Weberian character. Woodrow Wilson wrote, "Bureaucracy can exist only where the whole service of the state is removed from the common political life of its people, its chiefs, and its rank and file. Its motives, its objects, its policy, its standards, must be bureaucratic." Woodrow Wilson, "The Study of Public Administration," *Political Science Quarterly* 2, no. 2 (1887): 217.

10. *From Max Weber*, 88. It is a lamentation of the American right that politics has become dominated by bureaucrats; Weber accounts for this feeling, but notes its anachronism.

11. Ibid., 95.

12. *Wirtschaft und Gesellschaft* part 1, 1.2, p. 12.

13. *From Max Weber*, 95.

14. Zygmunt Bauman, *Modernity and the Holocaust* (Cambridge: Polity Press, 1989).

15. Peter Evans and James Rauch, "Bureaucracy and Growth: A Cross-National Analysis of the Effects of 'Weberian' State Structures on Economic Growth," *American Sociological Review* 64, no. 5 (1999): 748–765. Susan Rose-Ackerman gives a highly Weberian set of conditions for bureaucratic integrity in *Corruption and Government*, chap. 5.

16. *From Max Weber*, 111.

17. Quoted in Maryvonne Génaux, "Early Modern Corruption in English and French Fields of Vision," Heidenheimer and Johnston, *Political Corruption*, 115.

18. *From Max Weber*, 239.

19. Bratsis, "Construction of Corruption," 22. See also his *Everyday Life and the State*. In this deployment of Kantorowicz, Bratsis has been followed by Thomas Taro Lennerfors, "The Sublime Object of Corruption—Exploring the Relevance of a Psychoanalytical Two-Bodies Doctrine for Understanding Corruption," in *Ethics and Organizational Practice: Questioning the Moral Foundations of Management*, ed. Sara Louise Muhr, Bent M. Sørensen, and Steen Vallentin (Cheltenham: Edward Elgar, 2010). Ruth Miller, *The Erotics of Corruption: Law, Scandal, and Political Perversion* (Albany: SUNY Press, 2008), gives a lengthy discussion of the Kantorowicz thesis and its influence on Agamben. Kantorowicz's thesis is touched on in B. E. Gronbeck, "The Rhetoric of Political Corruption: Sociolinguistic, Dialectical, and Ceremonial Processes," *Quarterly Journal of Speech* 64, no. 2 (1978): 160.

20. Bratsis, "Construction of Corruption," 28.

21. Kantorowicz, *King's Two Bodies*, 9.

22. *From Max Weber*, 240.

23. Ibid., 228.

24. *From Max Weber*, 216; *Wirtschaft und Gesellschaft*, part 2, 9.2, p. 563.

25. Weber, *The Protestant Ethic and the Spirit of Capitalism*, trans. T. Parsons (New York: Norton, 2009), 96.

26. Kantorowicz, *King's Two Bodies*, 273–291, discusses the importance of this distinction and its origin in the late medieval reception of the Aristotelian doctrine of the eternity of the world, which clashed with the Platonic-Augustinian view of the temporal as corrupt.

27. J. P. Olivier de Sardan, "A Moral Economy of Corruption in Africa?" *Journal of Modern African Studies* 37, no. 1 (1999): 47–48.

28. Readers sometimes stumble over Kant's use of the word "public" (*öffentlich*) for the things one publishes on one's own time, and "private" for the duty one has as a state employee. One writer even declares this to be "subversive," though I find the argument unconvincing. John Christian Laursen, "The Subversive Kant: The Vocabulary of 'Public' and 'Publicity,'" *Political Theory* 14, no. 4 (1986): 584–603.

29. "Politics as a Vocation," in *From Max Weber*, 123.

30. "Parliament and Government in Germany under a New Political Order," in *Political Writings*, 204.

31. Indeed, they were much more responsible to industry. Weber thought that "large sections of so-called 'heavy industry' have favored bureaucratic domination rather than parliamentary government" largely because they thought it served the rationalization of the economy (*Economy and Society* part 1, 3.8, p. 284).

32. *Political Writings*, 245.

33. Ibid., 166.

34. Ibid., 167.

35. *Wirtschaft und Gesellschaft*, part 2, 9.8, 848–849.

36. Quoted in J. P. Mayer, *Max Weber and German Politics: A Study in Political Sociology* (London: Faber & Faber, 1944), 58.

37. *Political Writings*, 144.

38. That said, Weber never suggests that bureaucrats are mere automatons: "Selbständigkeit des Entschlusses, organisatorische Fähigkeit kraft eigener Ideen wird im einzelnen massenhaft, sehr oft aber auch im großen von 'Beamten' ebenso erwartet wie von 'Leitern'" (*Wirtschaft und Gesellschaft* part 2, 9.8, 836–837).

39. *From Max Weber*, 225.

40. Ibid., 226.

41. Ibid., 240.

42. *Political Writings*, 152.

43. Giorgio Agamben is incorrect to say (following Arendt) that "in the classical world . . . simple natural life is excluded from the *polis* in the strict sense, and remains confined . . . to the sphere of the *oikos*." Agamben, *Homo Sacer* (Stanford, Calif.: Stanford University Press, 1998), 2.

44. See Scott, *Comparative Political Corruption*, 15.

45. He also thought the influence of money in elections would increase if parliamentary democracy were replaced by more direct plebiscitary appointment of officials: "Although the money of vested interests plays no small part in the parties' conduct of parliamentary elections, the power of money and the leverage of the demagogic apparatuses supported by it

would assume colossal dimensions in any mass state ruled exclusively by popular elections and popular referenda" (*Political Writings*, 226).

46. This point is forcefully made by Paul du Gay, *In Praise of Bureaucracy* (London: Sage, 2000), 46.

47. Jacob van Klaveren, "The Concept of Corruption," in *Political Corruption: Readings in Comparative Analysis*, ed. Arnold Heidenheimer (New Brunswick, N.J.: Transaction, 1978), 39.

48. See, for instance, James M. Buchanan, "Politics Without Romance," in *The Theory of Public Choice—II*, ed. James M. Buchanan and Robert D. Tollison (Ann Arbor: University of Michigan Press, 1984), 13–14.

49. "Here's How to Do It," *Economist*, July 28, 2012, 24.

50. Vito Tanzi (writing for the IMF) argues that high taxation, government spending, and regulation are the sources of corruption. If one were to counter that this claim is belied by the numerous social welfare states that consistently score as the least corrupt on Transparency International's corruption perception index, Tanzi's response is that they are merely benefiting from some ill-defined cultural norms that will eventually be undermined by the inherently corrupting nature of government ("Corruption Around the World," 562); he goes on, however, to call for governance models based upon the behavior of these very states, going so far as to suggest that their bureaucracies are successful because they most approximate the Weberian ideal (587 n. 46).

51. This is, according to Peter Baehr, "The Grammar of Prudence: Arendt, Jaspers, and the Appraisal of Max Weber," in *Hannah Arendt in Jerusalem*, ed. Steven Ascheim (Berkeley: University California Press, 2001), 322, an accusation that Hannah Arendt might well have intimated in her correspondence with Jaspers.

Conclusion

1. I think—following Wolfgang Mommsen, *The Political and Social Theory of Max Weber: Collected Essays* (Chicago: University of Chicago Press, 1992), 194—that Leo Strauss overstepped the mark in accusing Weber of nihilism (*Natural Right and History* [Chicago: University of Chicago Press, 1953], 48); the purpose of Weber's value-free science is to nourish politico-ethical reflection. Nonetheless, there is a grain of truth in the accusation insofar as the moral-political philosophy necessary to buttress Weber's "value" judgments was not the object of his work, and there is a fundamental normative political philosophy that Weber's political thought leads us to expect but does not provide.

2. Condren, *Argument and Authority in Early Modern England.*

3. Ibid., 28.

4. Ibid., 347.

5. Berlin, *Proper Study of Mankind*, 269–325 ("The Originality of Machiavelli").

6. Condren, *Argument and Authority*, 348.

7. Michael Walzer's *Spheres of Justice* (New York: Basic, 2008) is an attempt to offer an account of differentiated ethical spheres, though the distinctions he makes do not pretend to universality. In the anticorruption literature, Mark Warren has offered one of the more interesting attempts of this sort, differentiating between different types of corruption that can affect different domains in a democratic regime. See Warren, "The Meaning of Corruption in Democracies," in *Routledge Handbook of Political Corruption*, ed. Paul M. Heywood (London: Routledge, 2015), 49ff.

8. For a writer advocating the type of grand theory that I am arguing is appropriate to the challenge of thinking about corruption, see Ronald Beiner, *Political Philosophy: What It Is and Why It Matters* (Cambridge: Cambridge University Press, 2014).

9. Jacob Levy has recently offered a powerful attack on what he takes to be a pervasive teleological prejudice in modern political thought that treats particular political forms (by which he does not mean regimes, but forms of political organization such as states) as the basis of healthy political life. I am entirely in agreement with his criticism of Hegelian or Whiggish historical teleologies that lead to the idealization of the modern state form (or that thinks the arc of history bends in any particular direction). I am, however, suggesting that the concept of corruption calls upon us to think of both political forms and regime types in moralized terms. Jacob T. Levy, "Contra Politanism," *European Journal of Political Theory*, first published online July 2, 2017, https://doi.org/10.1177/1474885117718371.

10. Critical disabilities studies have drawn our attention to the degree to which notions of "normality" and "disability" can reinforce certain exclusionary norms. This is an important line of reflection. But, nonetheless, even among such theorists, few but the most radical can do without some conceptual distinction between health and illness.

11. I have argued along these lines in "Political Corruption and the Concept of Dependence in Republican Thought," *Political Theory* 41, no. 4 (2013): 618–647.

12. Numerous recent works touch on the subject; one of the most successful of these is Levitsky and Ziblatt, *How Democracies Die*.

BIBLIOGRAPHY

Abensour, Miguel. *Democracy Against the State: Marx and the Machiavellian Moment*. Cambridge: Polity, 2011.

Abensour, Miguel, and Marcel Gauchet. "Présentation: Les leçons de la servitude et leur destin." In Étienne de La Boétie, *Le discours de la servitude volontaire*, vii–xxix. Paris: Payot, 1976.

Agamben, Giorgio. *Homo Sacer*. Stanford, Calif.: Stanford University Press, 1998.

Agnafors, Marcus. "Quality of Government: Toward a More Complex Definition." *American Political Science Review* 107, no. 3 (2013): 433–445.

Allen, Danielle. "Anonymous: On Silence and the Public Sphere." In *Speech and Silence in American Law*, ed. Austin Sarat. Cambridge: Cambridge University Press, 2010.

———. *Talking to Strangers*. Chicago: University of Chicago Press, 2004.

Althusser, Louis. *Machiavelli and Us*. London: Verso, 1999.

———. *Montesquieu, la politique et l'histoire*. Paris: Presses Universitaires de France, 1959.

Amyot, Jacques, trans. *Oeuvres morales de Plutarque traduites du grec par Amyot*. Vol. 3. Paris: De Cussac, 1802.

Andress, David, ed., *The Oxford Handbook of the French Revolution*. Oxford: Oxford University Press, 2013.

———. *The Terror*. New York: Farrar Straus & Giroux, 2005.

Andrew, Edward. *Imperial Republics: Revolution, War, and Territorial Expansion from the English Civil War to the French Revolution*. Toronto: University of Toronto Press, 2011.

———. *Patrons of Enlightenment*. Toronto: University of Toronto Press, 2006.

———. "The Senecan Moment: Patronage and Philosophy in the Eighteenth Century." *Journal of the History of Ideas* 65, no. 2 (2004): 277–299.

Anechiarico, Frank, and James Jacobs. *The Pursuit of Absolute Integrity: How Corruption Control Makes Government Ineffective*. Chicago: University of Chicago Press, 1996.

Arendt, Hannah. *The Human Condition*. 2nd ed. Chicago: University of Chicago Press, 1998.

———. *On Revolution*. London: Penguin, 1990.

———. *Totalitarianism*. Part 3 of *The Origins of Totalitarianism*. New York: Harvest, 1968.

Aristotle. *Nicomachean Ethics*. Trans. Terence Irwin. 2nd ed. Indianapolis: Hackett, 1999.

———. *"The Politics" and "The Constitution of Athens."* Ed. Stephen Everson. Cambridge: Cambridge University Press, 1996. Translation of *The Politics* in this edition is taken from *The Complete Works of Aristotle: The Revised Oxford Translation*, trans. Benjamin Jowett, ed. Jonathan Barnes, vols. 1 and 2, Bollingen Series 71:2 (Princeton, N.J.: Princeton University Press, 1984).

Armaingaud, Arthur. *Montaigne pamphlétaire: L'énigme du "Contr'un."* Paris: Hachette, 1910.

Augustine. *City of God Against the Pagans*. Ed. and trans. R. W. Dyson. Cambridge: Cambridge University Press, 1998.

Baczko, Bronislaw. *Ending the Terror*. Cambridge: Cambridge University Press, 1994.

Baehr, Peter. "The Grammar of Prudence: Arendt, Jaspers, and the Appraisal of Max Weber." In *Hannah Arendt in Jerusalem*, ed. Steven Ascheim, 306–324. Berkeley: University of California Press, 2001.

Bakewell, Sarah. *How to Live; or, A Life of Montaigne in One Question and Twenty Attempts at an Answer*. London: Chatto & Windus, 2010.

Baron, Hans. "Machiavelli: The Republican Citizen and the Author of 'The Prince.'" *English Historical Review* 76, no. 299 (1961): 217–253.

Bauman, Zygmunt. *Modernity and the Holocaust*. Cambridge: Polity Press, 1989.

Beiner, Ronald. *Political Philosophy: What It Is and Why It Matters*. Cambridge: Cambridge University Press, 2014.

Benner, Erica. *Machiavelli's Ethics*. Princeton, N.J.: Princeton University Press, 2009.

Benton, Robert J. "Political Expediency and Lying: Kant vs. Benjamin Constant." *Journal of the History of Ideas* 43, no. 1 (1982): 135–144.

Berlin, Isaiah. *The Proper Study of Mankind*. New York: Farrar, Straus & Giroux, 1999.

Best, Jacqueline. *The Limits of Transparency*. Ithaca, N.Y.: Cornell University Press, 2005.

Black, Jeremy. *Eighteenth-Century Britain, 1688–1783*. 2nd ed. New York: Palgrave Macmillan, 2008.

Blanc, Olivier. *La corruption sous la Terreur (1792–1794)*. Paris: Laffont, 1992.

Blattberg, Charles. *From Pluralism to Patriotic Politics: Putting Practice First*. Oxford: Oxford University Press, 2000.

Blau, Adrian. "Hobbes on Corruption." *History of Political Thought* 30, no. 4 (2009): 596–616.

Bobbio, Norberto. *Democracy and Dictatorship*. Oxford: Polity Press, 1989.

Boesche, Roger. "Fearing Monarchs and Merchants: Montesquieu's Two Theories of Despotism." *Western Political Quarterly* 43, no. 4 (1990): 741–761.

Bolingbroke, Henry St. John, Viscount. *A Collection of Political Tracts*. London: Cadell, 1788.

———. *Political Writings*. Ed. David Armitage. Cambridge: Cambridge University Press, 1997.

———. *The Works of Lord Bolingbroke*. 4 vols. Philadelphia: Carey and Hart, 1841.

Bonadeo, Alfredo. *Corruption, Conflict and Power in the Works and Times of Niccolò Machiavelli*. Berkeley: University of California Press, 1973.

Booth, William James. "The Limits of Autonomy: Karl Marx's Kant Critique." In *Kant and Political Philosophy: The Contemporary Legacy*, ed. Ronald Beiner and William James Booth, 245–275. New Haven, Conn.: Yale University Press, 1993.

Bossuet, Jacques Bénigne. *Oeuvres choisies de Bossuet*. 5 vols. Paris: Hachette, 1865.

Boswell, James. *The Life of Samuel Johnson*. Ed. Herbert Askwith. New York: Modern Library, 1950.

Bouscasse de Satin-Aignan, Xavier. "Parler sous le masque: Les difficultés de l'écoute dans le *Discours de la servitude volontaire* d'Étienne de La Boétie." In *"Parler librement": La liberté de parole au tournant du XVIe et du XVIIe siècle*, ed. Isabelle Moreau and Grégoire Holtz, 19–32. Lyon: ENS Éditions, 2005.

Bowles, Samuel. "Niccolò Machiavelli and the Origins of Mechanism Design." *Journal of Economic Issues* 48, no. 2 (2014): 267–278.

Brandeis, Louis D. *Other People's Money: And How the Bankers Use It*. 1914. Reprint, Mansfield Centre, Conn.: Martino, 2009.

Bratsis, Peter. "The Construction of Corruption, or Rules of Separation and Illusions of Purity in Bourgeois Societies." *Social Text* 21, no. 4 (2003): 9–33.

———. *Everyday Life and the State*. Boulder, Colo.: Paradigm Publishers, 2006.

Brewer, John. *The Sinews of Power*. London: Unwin Hyman, 1989.

Buchan, Bruce, and Lisa Hill. *An Intellectual History of Political Corruption*. New York: Palgrave Macmillan, 2014.

Buchanan, James M., and Robert D. Tollison, eds. *The Theory of Public Choice—II*. Ann Arbor: University of Michigan Press, 1984.

Bukovanski, Mlada. "The Hollowness of Anti-Corruption Discourse." *Review of International Political Economy* 13, no. 2 (2006): 181–209.

Burke, Edmund. *Revolutionary Writings*. Cambridge: Cambridge University Press, 2014.

Burtt, Shelley. "Ideas of Corruption in Eighteenth-Century England." In *Private and Public Corruption*, ed. William C. Heffernan and John Kleinig, 101–126. Lanham, Md.: Rowman & Littlefield, 2004.

Canfora, Davide. "Su Erasmo 'Politico': Modelli umanistici e ricezione cinquecentesca." In *Erasmo da Rotterdam e la cultura europea*, ed. Enrico Pasini and Pietro B. Rossi, 251–274. Florence: Galluzzo, 2008.

Caspari, Fritz. "Erasmus on the Social Functions of Christian Humanism." *Journal of the History of Ideas* 8, no. 1 (1947): 78–106.

Ceva, Emanuela, and Maria Paola Ferretti. "Liberal Democratic Institutions and the Damages of Political Corruption." *Les ateliers de l'éthique/The Ethics Forum* 9, no. 1 (2014): 126–145.

Chesterfield, Philip Dormer Stanhope, 4th Earl of. *Lord Chesterfield's Letters*. Ed. David Roberts. Oxford: Oxford University Press, 1992.

Christine de Pizan. *Book of the City of Ladies*. Trans. R. Brown-Grant. London: Penguin, 1999.

Cicero. *Laelius, on Friendship; and The Dream of Scipio*. Ed. and trans. J. G. F. Powell. Warminster: Aris & Phillips, 1990.

———. *On Duties*. Trans. Walter Miller. Loeb Classical Library 30. Cambridge, Mass.: Harvard University Press, 1913.

Clastres, Pierre. "Liberté, malencontre, innommable." In Étienne de La Boétie, *Le discours de la servitude volontaire*, 229–246. Paris: Payot, 1976.

Clewis, Robert R. *The Kantian Sublime and the Revelation of Freedom*. Cambridge: Cambridge University Press, 2009.

Cobbett's Parliamentary History of England. 36 vols. London: Hansard et al., 1806–1820.

Coby, Patrick. *Machiavelli's Romans*. Oxford: Lexington, 1999.

Colley, Linda. *In Defiance of Oligarchy: The Tory Party, 1714–60*. Cambridge: Cambridge University Press, 1982.

Condren, Conal. *Argument and Authority in Early Modern England*. Cambridge: Cambridge University Press, 2006.

Cooke, George Wingrove. *Memoirs of Lord Bolingbroke*. London: Richard Bentley, 1836.

Courtney, C. P. "Montesquieu and Natural Law." In *Montesquieu's Science of Politics: Essays on "The Spirit of Laws,"* ed. David W. Carrithers, Michael A. Mosher, and Paul A. Rahe, 41–68. Lanham, Md.: Rowman & Littlefield, 2001.

Dahlström, Carl, Victor Lapuente, and Jan Teorell. "The Merit of Meritocratization: Politics, Bureaucracy, and the Institutional Deterrents of Corruption." *Political Research Quarterly* 65, no. 3 (2012): 656–668.

Dallmayr, Fred. *Peace Talks: Who Will Listen?* Notre Dame, Ind.: University of Notre Dame Press, 2004.

Dejardin, Bertrand. *Terreur et corruption: Essai sur l'incivilité chez Machiavel.* Paris: L'Harmattan, 2004.

Dickinson, H. T. *Bolingbroke.* London: Constable, 1970.

———. *Walpole and the Whig Supremacy.* London: English Universities Press, 1973.

Dietz, Mary. "Trapping the Prince: Machiavelli and the Politics of Deception." *American Political Science Review* 80, no. 3 (1986): 777–799.

Dobel, J. Patrick. "The Corruption of a State." *American Political Science Review* 72, no. 3 (1978): 958–973.

Douglas, Mary. *Purity and Danger: An Analysis of Concepts of Pollution and Taboo.* London: Routledge, 1966.

Dror, Yehzkel. *The Capacity to Govern: A Report of the Club of Rome.* London: Fran Cass, 2001.

du Gay, Paul. *In Praise of Bureaucracy.* London: Sage, 2000.

Eagleton, Terry. *Holy Terror.* Oxford: Oxford University Press, 2005.

Edelstein, Dan. *The Terror of Natural Right: Republicanism, the Cult of Nature, and the French Revolution.* Chicago: University of Chicago Press, 2009.

Elshtain, Jean. *Public Man, Private Woman.* Princeton, N.J.: Princeton University Press, 1981.

Erasmus, Desiderius. *The Adages of Erasmus.* Ed. William Barker. Toronto: University of Toronto Press, 2001.

———. *Collected Works of Erasmus.* 89 vols. Toronto: University of Toronto Press, 1974–.

———. *The Education of a Christian Prince.* Ed. Lisa Jardine. Trans. Neil M. Cheshire and Michael J. Heath. With the *Panegyric for Archduke Philip of Austria*, ed. and trans. Lisa Jardine. Cambridge: Cambridge University Press, 1997.

Euben, J. Peter. "Pure Corruption." In *Private and Public Corruption*, ed. William C. Heffernan and John Kleinig, 53–80. Lanham, Md.: Rowman & Littlefield, 2004.

Evans, Peter, and James Rauch. "Bureaucracy and Growth: A Cross-National Analysis of the Effects of 'Weberian' State Structures on Economic Growth." *American Sociological Review* 64, no. 5 (1999): 748–765.

Ewald, Alexander Charles. *Robert Walpole.* London: Chapman & Hall, 1878.

Fisman, Raymond, and Miriam A. Golden. *Corruption: What Everyone Needs to Know.* Oxford: Oxford University Press, 2017.

Fontana, Biancamaria. *Montaigne's Politics: Authority and Governance in the "Essais."* Princeton, N.J.: Princeton University Press, 2008.

Friedrich, Carl J. "Political Pathology." *Political Quarterly* 37, no. 1 (1966): 70–85

Fukuyama, Francis. *Political Order and Political Decay.* New York: Farrar, Straus & Giroux, 2014.

A Full and True Account of the Strange and Miraculous Conversion of all the Tories in Great Britain: By the Preaching of Caleb D'Anvers, Prophet and Apostle to these Nations. London: J. Roberts, 1734.

Furetiere, Antoine, ed. *Dictionaire universel.* La Haye: Arnout & Reinier Leers, 1690.

Galston, William. *Liberal Purposes.* Cambridge: Cambridge University Press, 1991.

Gandhi, Mohandas K. *Hind Swaraj.* In *The Penguin Gandhi Reader*, ed. Rudrangshu Mukherjee, 3–66. London: Penguin, 1993.

Gardiner, John A. "Defining Corruption." In *Coping with Corruption in a Borderless World*, ed. Maurice Punch et al., 21–38. Boston: Kluwer, 1993. Reprinted in *Political Corruption: Concepts and Contexts*, 3rd ed., ed. Arnold J. Heidenheimer and Michael Johnston, 25–40. London: Transaction, 2002.

Génaux, Maryvonne. "Early Modern Corruption in English and French Fields of Vision." In *Political Corruption: Concepts and Contexts*, 3rd ed., ed. Arnold J. Heidenheimer and Michael Johnston, 107–122. London: Transaction, 2002.

Genovese, Michael A., and Victoria A. Farrar-Myers, eds. *Corruption and American Politics*. Amherst, N.Y.: Cambria Press, 2010.

Geuss, Raymond. *Public Goods, Private Goods*. Princeton, N.J.: Princeton University Press, 2001.

Gilbert, Allan H. *Machiavelli's "Prince" and Its Forerunners: "The Prince" as a Typical Book* de Regimine Principum. 1938. Reprint, New York: Barnes & Noble, 1968.

Gilbert, Felix. "The Humanist Concept of the Prince and *The Prince* of Machiavelli." *Journal of Modern History* 11, no. 4 (1939): 449–483.

Glaeser, Edward, and Claudia Goldin. *Corruption and Reform: Lessons from America's Economic History*. Chicago: University of Chicago Press, 2006.

Goldsmith, Oliver. *Life of Henry, Lord Bolingbroke*. London: Davies, 1770.

———. *The Miscellaneous Works of Oliver Goldsmith*. London: John Murray, 1837.

Graziano, Luigi. *Clientelismo e sistema politico: Il caso dell'Italia*. Milan: Franco Angeli, 1980.

Gronbeck, B. E. "The Rhetoric of Political Corruption: Sociolinguistic, Dialectical, and Ceremonial Processes." *Quarterly Journal of Speech* 64, no. 2 (1978): 155–172.

Gupta, Akhil. "Blurred Boundaries: The Discourse of Corruption, the Culture of Politics, and the Imagined State." *American Ethnologist* 22, no. 2 (1995): 375–402.

Hairston, Julia. "Skirting the Issue: Machiavelli's Caterina Sforza." *Renaissance Quarterly* 53, no. 3 (2000): 687–712.

Hamilton, Alexander, James Madison, and John Jay. *"The Federalist" with "Letters of 'Brutus.'"* Ed. Terence Ball. Cambridge: Cambridge University Press, 2003.

Hansen, Mogens Herman. "Was the *Polis* a State or a Stateless Society." In *Even More Studies in the Ancient Greek Polis*, ed. Thomas Heine Nielsen, 17–47. Stuttgart: Steiner, 2002.

Hardin, Richard F. "The Literary Conventions of Erasmus' *Education of a Christian Prince*: Advice and Aphorism." *Renaissance Quarterly* 35, no. 2 (1982): 151–163.

Harling, Philip. *The Waning of "Old Corruption": The Politics of Economical Reform in Britain, 1779–1846*. Oxford: Clarendon, 1996.

Hartung, William D. *Prophets of War: Lockheed Martin and the Making of the American Military-Industrial Complex*. New York: Nation Books, 2010.

Heffernan, William C., and John Kleinig, eds. *Private and Public Corruption*. Lanham, Md.: Rowman & Littlefield, 2004.

Hegel, G. W. F. *Elements of the Philosophy of Right*. Ed. Allen Wood. Cambridge: Cambridge University Press, 1991.

———. *Phenomenology of Spirit*. Trans. A. V. Miller. Oxford: Oxford University Press, 1977.

———. *Vorlesungen über die Geschichte der Philosophie*. Ed. C. L. Michelet. 3 vols. Berlin: Duncker und Humblot, 1840–1844.

Heidenheimer, Arnold J., and Michael Johnston, eds. *Political Corruption: Concepts and Contexts*. 3rd ed. London: Transaction, 2002.

Heine, Heinrich. *Sämmtliche Werke*. 18 vols. Hamburg: Hoffmann und Campe, 1868.

Heywood, Paul M., ed. *The Routledge Handbook of Political Corruption*. London: Routledge, 2015.

Hill, Lisa. "Conceptions of Political Corruption in Ancient Athens and Rome." *History of Political Thought* 24, no. 44 (2013): 555–587.

Hirschman, Albert O. *The Passions and the Interests*. Princeton, N.J.: Princeton University Press, 1977.

Hobbes, Thomas. *De Cive: The English Version*. Ed. Howard Warrender. Oxford: Clarendon Press, 1983.

———. *Leviathan*. London: Penguin, 1985.

Holmberg, Sören, and Bo Rothstein, eds. *Good Government: The Relevance of Political Science*. Cheltenham: Elgar, 2012.

Holmes, Geoffrey. *Augustan England: Professions, State and Society, 1680–1730*. London: Unwin & Allen, 1982.

Holmes, Leslie. *Corruption*. Oxford: Oxford University Press, 2015.

Honig, Bonnie. *Democracy and the Foreigner*. Princeton, N.J.: Princeton University Press, 2001.

Honohan, Iseult. *Civic Republicanism*. London: Routledge, 2002.

Hopkin, Jonathan. "States, Markets and Corruption: A Review of Some Recent Literature." *Review of International Political Economy* 9, no. 3 (2002): 574–590.

Hulliung, Mark. *Montesquieu and the Old Regime*. Berkeley: University of California Press, 1976.

Hume, David. *Essays: Moral, Political, and Literary*. Ed. Eugene F. Miller. Indianapolis: Liberty Fund, 1985.

Huntington, Samuel P. "Modernization and Corruption." In *Political Corruption: Concepts and Contexts*, 3rd ed., ed. Arnold J. Heidenheimer and Michael Johnston, 253–264. London: Transaction, 2002.

Hurstfield, Joel. "Political Corruption in Modern England: The Historian's Problem." *History* 52, no. 174 (1967): 16–34.

Ibn Khaldun. *Muqaddimah*. Trans. Franz Rosenthal. Princeton, N.J.: Princeton University Press, 1967.

Isocrates. "To Nicocles." In *The Orations and Epistles of Isocrates*, 17–29. Trans. Joshua Dinsdale. London: T. Waller, 1752.

Israel, Jonathan. *Democratic Enlightenment: Philosophy, Revolution, and Human Rights, 1750–1790*. Oxford: Oxford University Press, 2012.

Jain, Arvind. "Corruption: A Review." *Journal of Economic Surveys* 15, no. 1 (2001): 71–121.

Jennings, Jeremy. *Revolution and the Republic*. Oxford: Oxford University Press, 2011.

John of Salisbury. *Policraticus*. Trans. Cary Nederman. Cambridge: Cambridge University Press, 1990.

Johnston, Michael. "The Search for Definitions: The Vitality of Politics and the Issue of Corruption." *International Social Science Journal* 48, no. 149 (1996): 321–335.

Joseph, Richard. *Democracy and Prebendal Politics in Nigeria: The Rise and Fall of the Second Republic*. Cambridge: Cambridge University Press, 1987.

Kant, Immanuel. *Anthropology from a Pragmatic Point of View*. Trans. and ed. Robert B. Louden. Cambridge: Cambridge University Press, 2006.

———. *Anthropology, History, and Education*. Ed. Günter Zöller and Robert B. Louden. Trans. Mary Gregor et al. Cambridge: Cambridge University Press, 2007.

————. *Critique of Judgment.* Trans. Werner S. Pluhar. Indianapolis: Hackett, 1987.

————. *Critique of Pure Reason.* Trans. Paul Guyer and Allen Wood. Cambridge: Cambridge University Press, 1998.

————. *Kritik der reinen Vernunft.* Stuttgart: Reclam, 1966.

————. *Political Writings.* Ed. H. S. Reiss. Trans. H. B. Nisbet. 2nd ed. Cambridge: Cambridge University Press, 1991.

————. *Practical Philosophy.* Trans. and ed. Mary Gregor. Cambridge Edition of the Works of Immanuel Kant. Cambridge: Cambridge University Press, 1996.

————. *Religion Within the Limits of Reason Alone.* Trans. Theodore M. Greene and Hoyt H. Hudson. New York: Harper, 1960.

Kantorowicz, Ernst H. *The King's Two Bodies: A Study in Mediaeval Political Theology.* Princeton, N.J.: Princeton University Press, 1997.

Keohane, Nannerl O. "The Radical Humanism of Etienne de La Boetie." *Journal of the History of Ideas* 38, no. 1 (1977): 119–130.

Kingston, Rebecca. *Montesquieu and the Parliament of Bordeaux.* Geneva: Droz, 1996.

Klitgaard, Robert. *Controlling Corruption.* Berkeley: University of California Press, 1988.

Koenig, Gaspard. *Les discrètes vertus de la corruption.* Paris: Grasset, 2009.

Kotkin, Stephen, and András Sajó, eds. *Political Corruption in Transition: A Skeptic's Handbook.* Budapest: Central European University Press, 2002.

Kramnick, Isaac. *Bolingbroke and His Circle: The Politics of Nostalgia in the Age of Walpole.* 1968. Reprint, Ithaca, N.Y.: Cornell University Press, 1992.

————. "Corruption in Eighteenth-Century English and American Political Discourse." In *Virtue, Corruption, and Self-Interest: Political Values in the Eighteenth Century,* ed. Richard K. Matthews, 55–75. Bethlehem, Pa.: Lehigh University Press, 1994.

Krause, Sharon. *Liberalism with Honor.* Cambridge, Mass.: Harvard University Press, 2002.

————. "Politics of Distinction and Disobedience: Honor and the Defense of Liberty in Montesquieu." *Polity* 31, no. 3 (1999): 469–499.

————. "The Spirit of Separate Powers in Montesquieu." *Review of Politics* 62, no. 2 (2000): 231–265.

Kurer, Oskar. "Corruption: An Alternative Approach to Its Definition and Measurement." *Political Studies* 53, no.1 (2005): 222–239.

La Boétie, Étienne [Estienne] de. *Discours de la servitude volontaire.* Ed. Simone Goyard-Fabre. Paris: Flammarion, 1983.

————. *Le discours de la servitude volontaire.* Ed. P. Léonard. With *La Boétie et la question du politique: Textes de Lamennais, P. Leroux, A. Vermorel, G. Landauer, S. Weil et de Pierre Clastres et Claude Lefort.* Paris: Payot, 1976.

————. *Mémoire sur la pacification des troubles.* Ed. Malcolm Smith. Geneva: Droz, 1983.

————. *Oeuvres complètes.* Ed. Paul Bonnefon. Geneva: Slatkine Reprints, 1967.

————. *Politics and Obedience: The Discourse of Voluntary Servitude.* Trans. Harry Kurz. Auburn, Ala.: Mises Institute, 2008.

Laursen, John Christian. "The Subversive Kant: The Vocabulary of 'Public' and 'Publicity.'" *Political Theory* 14, no. 4 (1986): 584–603.

Lefort, Claude. "Le nom d'un." In Étienne de La Boétie, *Le discours de la servitude volontaire,* 247–307. Paris: Payot, 1976.

————. *Le travail de l'oeuvre Machiavel.* Paris: Gallimard, 1986.

Lenard, Patti. *Trust, Democracy, and Multicultural Challenges.* University Park: Pennsylvania State University Press, 2012.

Lennerfors, Thomas Taro. "The Sublime Object of Corruption—Exploring the Relevance of a Psychoanalytical Two-Bodies Doctrine for Understanding Corruption." In *Ethics and Organizational Practice: Questioning the Moral Foundations of Management,* ed. Sara Louise Muhr, Bent M. Sørensen, and Steen Vallentin, 199–214. Cheltenham: Edward Elgar, 2010.

Lessig, Lawrence. *Republic, Lost.* New York: Hachette, 2011.

Levitsky, Steven, and Daniel Ziblatt. *How Democracies Die.* New York: Crown, 2018.

Levy, Jacob. "Contra Politanism." *European Journal of Political Theory.* First published online, July 2, 2017. https://doi.or/1177/1474885117718371.

Linton, Marisa. "Robespierre's Political Principle." In *Robespierre,* ed. Colin Haydon and William Doyle, 37–53. Cambridge: Cambridge University Press, 2006.

Livy. *History of Rome.* In *Livy,* trans. George Baker. 5 vols. New York: Harper & Bros., 1836.

Macedo, Stephen. *Liberal Virtues.* Oxford: Clarendon, 1990.

Machiavelli, Niccolò. *Art of War.* Trans. Christopher Lynch. Chicago: University of Chicago Press, 2003.

———. *Discourses on Livy.* Trans. Harvey C. Mansfield and Nathan Tarcov. Chicago: University of Chicago Press, 1995.

———. *Florentine Histories.* Trans. Laura F. Banfield and Harvey C. Manfield Jr. Princeton, N.J.: Princeton University Press, 1990.

———. *Opere.* Ed. Corrado Vivanti. 2 vols. Torino: Einaudi-Gallimard, 1997.

———. *The Prince.* Trans. Harvey C. Mansfield. Chicago: University of Chicago Press, 1985.

MacIntyre, Alasdair. *After Virtue: A Study in Moral Theory.* 2nd ed. Notre Dame, Ind.: University of Notre Dame Press, 1984.

Mansfield, Harvey. *Machiavelli's New Modes and Orders: A Study of the Discourses on Livy.* Ithaca, N.Y.: Cornell University Press, 1979.

———. *Machiavelli's Virtue.* Chicago: University of Chicago Press, 1966.

Martin, Daniel. *Montaigne et son cheval, ou les sept couleurs du discours de la servitude volontaire.* Tours: Nizet, 1998.

Matthews, Richard K., ed. *Virtue, Corruption, and Self-Interest: Political Values in the Eighteenth Century.* Bethlehem, Pa.: Lehigh University Press, 1994.

Mauss, Marcel. "Essai sur le don." In *Sociologie et anthropologie.* Paris: Presses Universitaires de France, 1966.

Mayer, J. P. *Max Weber and German Politics: A Study in Political Sociology.* London: Faber & Faber, 1944.

McCormick, John P. *Machiavellian Democracy.* Cambridge: Cambridge University Press, 2011.

———. "Machiavelli's Greek Tyrant as Republican Reformer." In *The Radical Machiavelli,* ed. Filippo del Lucchese, 306–336. Leiden: Brill, 2015.

———. "Tempering the *Grandi*'s Appetite to Oppress: The Dedication and Intention of Machiavelli's *Discourses.*" In *Politics and the Passions, 1500–1850,* ed. Victoria Kahn, Neil Saccamano, and Daniela Coli, 7–29. Princeton, N.J.: Princeton University Press, 2006.

Mesnard, Pierre. *L'essor de la philosophie politique au XVIe siècle.* Paris: Vrin, 1969.

Miller, Ruth. *The Erotics of Corruption: Law, Scandal, and Political Perversion.* Albany: SUNY Press, 2008.

Miller, Seumas, Peter Roberts, and Edward Spence. *Corruption and Anti-Corruption: An Applied Philosophical Approach.* Upper Saddle River, N.J.: Pearson/Prentice Hall, 2005.

Mommsen, Wolfgang. *The Political and Social Theory of Max Weber: Collected Essays.* Chicago: University of Chicago Press, 1992.

Montaigne, Michel de. *Les Essais.* Ed. Jean Balsamo, Michel Magnien, and Catherine Magnien-Simonin. Paris: Gallimard, 2007.

Montesquieu, Charles Louis de Secondat, baron de. *Considérations sur les causes de la grandeur des Romains et de leur décadence.* Paris: Gallimard, 2008.

———. *Oeuvres complètes.* Ed. Roger Caillois. 2 vols. Paris: Gallimard, 1949–1951.

———. *The Spirit of the Laws.* Trans. and ed. Anne M. Cohler, Basia C. Miller, and Harold S. Stone. Cambridge: Cambridge University Press, 1989.

Moore, Barrington, Jr. *Moral Purity and Persecution in History.* Princeton, N.J.: Princeton University Press, 2000.

Mouffe, Chantal. *The Return of the Political.* London: Verso, 2006.

Mulgan, Richard. "Aristotle on Legality and Corruption." In *Corruption: Expanding the Focus,* ed. Manuhuia Barcham, Barry Hindess, and Peter Larmour, 25–36. Canberra: ANU Press, 2013.

Mungiu-Pippidi, Alina. *The Quest for Good Governance.* Cambridge: Cambridge University Press, 2015.

Najemy, John M. "Society, Class, and State in Machiavelli's *Discourses on Livy.*" In *Cambridge Companion to Machiavelli,* ed. John M. Najemy, 96–111. Cambridge: Cambridge University Press, 2010.

Nelson, Eric. *The Greek Tradition in Republican Thought.* Cambridge: Cambridge University Press, 2004.

Noonan, John T. *Bribes.* New York: Macmillan, 1984.

Nussbaum, Martha C. *Not for Profit: Why Democracy Needs the Humanities.* Princeton, N.J.: Princeton University Press, 2010.

Nye, Joseph. "Corruption and Political Development: A Cost-Benefit Analysis." *American Political Science Review* 61, no. 2 (1967): 417–427.

Oakeshott, Michael. Review of *The Foundations of Political Thought,* by Quentin Skinner. *Historical Journal* 23, no. 2 (1980): 449–453.

Olivier de Sardan, J. P. "A Moral Economy of Corruption in Africa?" *Journal of Modern African Studies* 37, no. 1 (1999): 25–52.

Pangle, Thomas. *Montesquieu's Philosophy of Liberalism.* Chicago: University of Chicago Press, 1973.

Pearce, Edward. *The Great Man: Sir Robert Walpole; Scoundrel, Genius and Britain's First Prime Minister.* London: Random House, 2007.

Peck, Linda Levy. *Court Patronage and Corruption in Early Stuart England.* London: Routledge, 1993.

Philp, Mark. "Defining Political Corruption." *Political Studies* 45 (1997): 436–462.

———. *Political Conduct.* Cambridge, Mass.: Harvard University Press, 2007.

Philp, Mark, and Elizabeth Dávid-Barrett. "Realism About Political Corruption." *Annual Review of Political Science* 18 (2015): 387–402.

Pitkin, Hanna Fenichel. *Fortune Is a Woman: Gender and Politics in the Thought of Niccolò Machiavelli.* Chicago: University of Chicago Press, 1984.

Plato. *Republic.* Trans. G. M. A. Grube. Rev. C. D. C. Reeve. Indianapolis: Hackett, 1992.

Plumb, J. H. *Sir Robert Walpole: The Making of a Statesman.* London: Cresset, 1956.

Pocock, J. G. A. *The Machiavellian Moment.* Princeton, N.J.: Princeton University Press, 1975.

———. *Politics, Language, and Time: Essays on Political Thought and History.* Chicago: University of Chicago Press, 1989.

———. *Virtue, Commerce and History.* Cambridge: Cambridge University Press, 1986.

Polybius. *The Histories.* Trans. Robin Waterfield. Oxford: Oxford University Press, 2010.

Putnam, Robert. *Making Democracy Work: Civic Traditions in Modern Italy.* Princeton, N.J.: Princeton University Press, 1993.

Rahe, Paul. *Against Throne and Altar.* Cambridge: Cambridge University Press, 2009.

———. *Montesquieu and the Logic of Liberty.* New Haven, Conn.: Yale University Press, 2009.

———. "Situating Machiavelli." In *Renaissance Civic Humanism,* ed. James Hankins, 270–308. Cambridge: Cambridge University Press, 2000.

———. *Soft Despotism: Democracy's Drift.* New Haven, Conn.: Yale University Press, 2009.

Redlawsk, David P., and James A. McCann. "Popular Interpretations of 'Corruption' and Their Partisan Consequences." *Political Behavior* 27, no. 3 (2005): 261–283.

Regent, Nikola. "Machiavelli: Empire, *Virtù* and the Final Downfall." *History of Political Thought* 32, no. 5 (2011): 751–772.

Reinburg, Virginia. "Liturgy and the Laity in Late Medieval and Reformation France." *Sixteenth Century Journal* 23, no. 3 (1992): 526–547.

Richter, William L., and Frances Burke, eds. *Combating Corruption, Encouraging Ethics: A Practical Guide to Management Ethics.* 2nd ed. Lanham, Md.: Rowman & Littlefield, 2007.

Rickard, Peter. *The French Language in the Seventeenth Century: Contemporary Opinion in France.* Cambridge: Brewer, 1992.

Robespierre, Maximilien. *Oeuvres.* Paris: Société des études robespierristes, 2011.

Robin, Corey. "Reflections on Fear: Montesquieu in Retrieval." *American Political Science Review* 94, no. 2 (2000): 347–360.

Rose-Ackerman, Susan. *Corruption and Government: Causes, Consequences, and Reform* Cambridge: Cambridge University Press, 1999.

———. "'Grand' Corruption and the Ethics of Global Business." *Journal of Banking and Finance* 26, no. 9 (2002): 1889–1918.

———, ed. *International Handbook on the Economics of Corruption.* Cheltenham: Elgar, 2006.

Rosen, Michael. *On Voluntary Servitude: False Consciousness and the Theory of Ideology.* Cambridge: Polity Press, 1996.

Rotberg, Robert I., ed. *Corruption, Global Security, and World Order.* Washington, D.C.: Brookings Institution Press, 2009.

Rothstein, Bo. "The Three Worlds of Governance: Arguments for a Parsimonius Theory of Quality of Government." QoG Working Paper Series 2013:12, Quality of Government Institute, University of Gothenburg, Gothenburg, Sweden, August 2013.

———. "What Is the Opposite of Corruption?" *Third World Quarterly* 35, no. 5 (2014): 745–746.

Rothstein, Bo, and Jan Teorell. "What Is Quality of Government? A Theory of Impartial Government Institutions." *Governance* 21, no. 2 (2008): 165–190.

Rothstein, Bo, and Aiysha Varraich. *Making Sense of Corruption.* Cambridge: Cambridge University Press, 2017.

Rousseau, Jean-Jacques. *The Basic Political Writings*. Trans. and ed. Donald A. Cress. Indianapolis: Hackett, 1987.

Schachter, Marc D. *Voluntary Servitude and the Erotics of Friendship: From Classical Antiquity to Early Modern France*. Aldershot: Ashgate, 2008.

Schaefer, David Lewis, ed. *Freedom over Servitude: Montaigne, La Boétie, and "On Voluntary Servitude."* Westport, Conn.: Greenwood, 1998.

———. *The Political Philosophy of Montaigne*. Ithaca, N.Y.: Cornell University Press, 1990.

Scott, James C. *Comparative Political Corruption*. Engelwood Cliffs, N.J.: Prentice-Hall, 1972.

Scurr, Ruth. *Fatal Purity: Robespierre and the French Revolution*. London: Chatto & Windus, 2006.

Seneca, L. Annaeus. *Minor Dialogues Together with the Dialogue On Clemency*. Trans. Aubrey Stewart. London: George Bell & Sons, 1889.

Shellabarger, Samuel. *Lord Chesterfield and His World*. New York: Biblo & Tannen, 1971.

Shklar, Judith. "The Liberalism of Fear." In *Liberalism and the Moral Life*, ed. Nancy L. Rosenblum, 21–38. Cambridge, Mass.: Harvard University Press, 1989.

———. *Ordinary Vices*. Cambridge, Mass.: Harvard University Press, 1984.

Shumer, S. M. "Machiavelli: Republican Politics and Its Corruption." *Political Theory* 7, no. 1 (1979): 5–34.

Skinner, Quentin. *The Foundations of Modern Political Thought*. Vol. 1, *The Renaissance*. Cambridge: Cambridge University Press, 1978.

———. "The State." In *Political Innovation and Conceptual Change*, ed. Terence Ball, James Farr, and Russell L. Hanson, 90–131. Cambridge: Cambridge University Press, 1989.

Smith, Malcolm. *Montaigne and Religious Freedom: The Dawn of Pluralism*. Geneva: Droz, 1991.

Sparling, Robert. "The Concept of Corruption in J. G. A. Pocock's *The Machiavellian Moment*." *History of European Ideas* 43, no. 2 (2016): 156–170.

———. "Impartiality and the Definition of Corruption." *Political Studies* 66, no. 2 (2018): 376–391.

———. "Political Corruption and the Concept of Dependence in Republican Thought." *Political Theory* 41, no. 4 (2013): 618–647.

Spector, Céline. "Honor, Interest, Virtue: The Affective Foundations of the Political in *The Spirit of Laws*." In *Montesquieu and His Legacy*, ed. Rebecca E. Kingston, 49–80. Albany: SUNY Press, 2009.

Stacey, Peter. *Roman Monarchy and the Renaissance Prince*. Cambridge: Cambridge University Press, 2007.

Staines, David. "Havelok the Dane: A Thirteenth-Century Handbook for Princes." *Speculum* 51, no. 4 (1976): 602–623.

Stansell, Gary. "The Gift in Ancient Israel." *Semeia* 87 (1999): 65–90.

Starobinski, Jean. *Jean-Jacques Rousseau: La transparence et l'obstacle*. Paris: Gallimard, 1957.

Stayer, James. *The German Peasants' War and Anabaptist Community of Goods*. Montreal: McGill-Queens, 1991.

Strauss, Leo. *Natural Right and History*. Chicago: University of Chicago Press, 1953.

———. *Thoughts on Machiavelli*. Chicago: University of Chicago Press, 1958.

———. *What Is Political Philosophy? And Other Studies*. Chicago: University of Chicago Press, 1959. Sullivan, Vickie. *Machiavelli, Hobbes, and the Formation of a Liberal Republicanism in England*. Cambridge: Cambridge University Press, 2004.

Tanzi, Vito. "Corruption Around the World: Causes, Consequences, Scope, and Cures." *IMF Staff Papers* 45, no. 4 (1998): 559–595.

Teachout, Zephyr. *Corruption in America: From Benjamin Franklin's Snuff Box to Citizens United.* Cambridge, Mass.: Harvard University Press, 2014.

Terris, Danel. *Ethics at Work: Creating Virtue at an American Corporation.* Waltham, Mass.: Brandeis University Press, 2005.

Thompson, Dennis. *Ethics in Congress: From Individual to Institutional Corruption.* Washington, D.C.: Brookings Institution, 1995.

Thompson, Lindsay J. *The Moral Compass: Leadership for a Free World.* Charlotte, N.C.: Information Age Publishing, 2009.

Thomson, Peter, and Glendyr Sacks, eds. *The Cambridge Companion to Brecht.* Cambridge: Cambridge University Press, 2006.

Tracy, James. *Erasmus of the Low Countries.* Berkeley: University of California Press, 1996.

Trevor-Roper, H. R. "The General Crisis of the 17th Century." *Past & Present* 16 (November 1959): 31–64.

Uslaner, Eric. *Corruption, Inequality, and the Rule of Law.* Cambridge: Cambridge University Press, 2008.

———. *The Moral Foundations of Trust.* Cambridge: Cambridge University Press, 2002.

Van Klaveren, Jacob. "The Concept of Corruption." In *Political Corruption: Readings in Comparative Analysis,* ed. Arnold Heidenheimer, 38–40. New Brunswick, N.J.: Transaction, 1978.

Vatter, Miguel. *Between Form and Event.* Kluwer: Dortrecht, 2000.

Viroli, Maurizio. *The Liberty of Servants: Berlusconi's Italy.* Princeton, N.J.: Princeton University Press, 2012.

———. *Machiavelli.* Oxford: Oxford University Press, 1998.

———. *Machiavelli's God.* Princeton, N.J.: Princeton University Press, 2010.

Voegelin, Eric. *The Collected Works of Eric Voegelin.* Vol. 23, *History of Political Ideas (Volume V): Religion and the Rise of Modernity.* Ed. James L. Wiser. Columbia: University of Missouri Press, 1998.

Voltaire, François-Marie Arouet. *L'ABC.* London: Robert Freeman, 1762.

Waddicor, Marc. *Montesquieu and the Philosophy of Natural Law.* The Hague: Martin Nijhoff, 1970.

Wahnich, Sophie. *In Defense of the Terror: Liberty or Death in the French Revolution.* New York: Verso, 2012.

Wahnich, Sophie, and Marc Belissa. "Les crimes des Anglais: Trahir le droit." *Annales historiques de la Révolution française* 300 (1995): 233–248.

Walpole, Horace. *A Catalogue of the Royal and Noble Authors of England, Scotland and Ireland.* London: John Scott, 1806.

———. *Walpoliana.* London: Burnett et al., 1800.

Walzer, Michael. "Civility and Civic Virtue in Contemporary America." *Social Research* 41, no. 4 (1974): 593–611.

———. "Liberalism and the Art of Separation." *Political Theory* 12, no. 3 (1984): 315–330.

———. "The Problem of Dirty Hands." *Philosophy and Public Affairs* 2, no. 2 (1973): 160–180.

———. *Spheres of Justice.* New York: Basic, 2008.

Warren, Mark. "The Meaning of Corruption in Democracies." In *Routledge Handbook of Political Corruption,* ed. Paul M. Heywood, 42–55. London: Routledge, 2015.

———. "Political Corruption as Duplicitous Exclusion." *PS: Political Science & Politics* 39, no. 4 (2006): 803–807.

———. "What Does Corruption Mean in a Democracy?" *American Journal of Political Science* 48, no. 2 (2004): 328–343.

Weber, Max. *Economy and Society*. Ed. Guenther Roth and Claus Wittich. Berkeley: University of California Press, 1978.

———. *From Max Weber: Essays in Sociology*. Trans. and ed. H. H. Gerth and C. Wright Mills. London: Routledge & Kegan Paul, 1948.

———. *Max Weber Gesamtausgabe*. Vol. 8, *Wirtschaft, Staat und Sozialpolitik*. Ed. Wolfgang Schluchter with Peter Kurth and Birgitt Morgenbrod. Tübingen: Mohr, 1998.

———. *Political Writings*. Cambridge: Cambridge University Press, 1994.

———. *The Protestant Ethic and the Spirit of Capitalism*. Trans. T. Parsons. New York: Norton, 2009.

———. *Wirtschaft und Gesellschaft*. Ed. Johannes Winckelmann. 5th ed. Tübingen: Mohr, 1972.

Weiss, Richard M. "Weber on Bureaucracy: Management Consultant or Political Theorist?" *Academy of Management Review* 8, no. 2 (1983): 242–248.

Wilson, Woodrow. "The Study of Public Administration." *Political Science Quarterly* 2, no. 2 (1887): 197–222.

Winton, Calhoun. *John Gay and the London Theatre*. Lexington: University Press of Kentucky, 1993.

Wolin, Sheldon. *Politics and Vision*. Boston: Little, Brown, 1960.

Wootton, David. "Friendship Portrayed: A New Account of *Utopia*." *History Workshop Journal* 45 (1998): 28–47.

World Bank. *Anticorruption in Transition: A Contribution to the Policy Debate*. Washington, D.C.: World Bank, 2000.

Xenophon. *The Education of Cyrus*. Trans. Henry Graham Dakyns. London: Dent, 1914.

———. *Oeconomicus*. Trans. Sarah B. Pomeroy. Oxford: Clarendon, 1994.

Yoran, Hanan. *Between Utopia and Dystopia: Erasmus, Thomas More, and the Humanist Republic of Letters*. Lanham, Md.: Lexington Books, 2010.

Zagorin, Perez. *Francis Bacon*. Princeton, N.J.: Princeton University Press, 1998.

Žižek, Slavoj. *In Defense of Lost Causes*. London: Verso, 2008.

———. Introduction to *Slavoj Žižek Presents Robespierre: Virtue and Terror*. New York: Verso, 2007.

INDEX

ACKNOWLEDGMENTS

I wish to extend warmest thanks to a number of people with whom I have had the pleasure of discussing various aspects of this project over the past several years: Edward Andrew, Ronnie Beiner, Emanuela Ceva, Jérémie Duhamel, Luc Foisneau, John-Erik Hansson, Rebecca Kingston, Simon Kow, Nicholas Mithen, Véronique Munoz-Dardé, David Raynor, Paul Saurette, Veith Selk, and Céline Spector. Various chapters were commented upon at conference panels: thanks to Sarah Burns, Neven Leddy, and Ingrid Makus. I am grateful to the GRIPP/RGCS colleagues at McGill, where I first began working on this project: Arash Abizadeh, Catherine Lu, Victor Muñiz-Fraticelli, Andrew Rehfeld, William Roberts, Hasana Sharp, Christa Scholtz, Timothy Waligore, Daniel Weinstock, Yves Winter, and, in particular, Jacob Levy. J'aimerais remercier tous mes anciens collègues au département de science politique de l'Université de Montréal, et en particulier Augustin Simard et Charles Blattberg. Je souhaite également remercier les collègues du Centre de recherche en éthique (anciennement le CRÉUM) où j'ai écrit quelques chapitres de ce livre: Frédéric Dejean, Peter Dietsch, Valéry Giroux, Louis-Philippe Hodgson, Christian Nadeau, Pierre-Yves Néron, Antoine Panaïoti, Christine Tappolet, et en particulier Marc-Antoine Dilhac avec qui j'ai eu des échanges très fructueux au sujet de la corruption. Merci à la coorganisatrice du Réseau de recherche en pensée politique d'Ottawa, Patti Lenard, ainsi qu'à tous mes collègues à l'École d'études politiques de l'Université d'Ottawa. Grazie ad Anna Scigliano senza la quale non sarei stato in grado di leggere Machiavelli in italiano. Many thanks also to Esmée and Rose Sparling. I would like to thank Damon Linker at the University of Pennsylvania Press for his support of this project and two anonymous reviewers for the press who read the manuscript very attentively and made extremely helpful suggestions for improvement. I would also like to thank Jennifer Shenk for excellent copyediting, and Mohamad Ghossein for his work on the index.

Most of all, I would like to thank Sophie Bourgault, without whose conversation and careful criticism I would be lost.

Chapter 4 was originally published (in a slightly different form) as "Sunlight Is the Best Disinfectant? Étienne de la Boétie on Corruption and Transparency," *European Journal of Political Theory* 12, no. 4 (2013): 483–509. Large parts of Chapter 6 first appeared as "Montesquieu on Corruption and the Limits of Purity," in *On Civic Republicanism: Ancient Lessons for Global Politics*, ed. Geoffrey C. Kellow and Neven Leddy (Toronto: University of Toronto Press, 2016).

I am grateful to the Social Sciences and Humanities Research Council of Canada, whose postdoctoral fellowship first allowed me to begin this project, and to the Centre de recherche en éthique, where it began to take shape.